MW00961366

Letting Go

Letting Go

A Memoir

William A. Gruber, M.D.

iUniverse, Inc.
New York Lincoln Shanghai

Letting Go
A Memoir

iUniverse, Inc.

For information address:
iUniverse, Inc.
2021 Pine Lake Road, Suite 100
Lincoln, NE 68512
www.iuniverse.com

ISBN: 0-595-29207-0

Printed in the United States of America

To Zita

And to all those who listened and heard

Contents

Prologue

In 1975, Mark Smetko's life changed profoundly—twice.

In 1965 he did college-kid grunt work on trains in the Clyde freight yard in Chicago. In 1972 he got a job in the Corwith yard on Chicago's south side, gradually working his way up until he could use a switch engine to move freight cars around and make up those trains. In January 1975, Mark proudly announced to his lifelong friend, Karl Sundstrom, that he was leaving for Kansas City to go to railroad school. After three months there, Mark would become an engineer, qualified at last to drive trains across the open countryside—or as he called it, "highballing 'em."

"Deep in his soul," Karl said, "Mark always wanted to be in railroading. It was his childhood dream come true."

It was bitter cold that winter. Mark complained to Karl of increasing pain in his hands. "I held his hands and they were hot," Karl recalled. "His knuckles were swollen." The year he became an engineer, Mark was diagnosed with rheumatoid arthritis.

In 1975, a thousand miles away in Boston, I was also beginning a life transformation. At the same age as Mark, I already had completed four years of medical school, a year of internship, and three years in the army. By December 1975, I was six months into a three-and-a-half year residency in orthopaedic surgery.

The avowed purpose of the training was to create total dedication to the needs of surgical patients with bone and joint problems. In the first six months I worked fourteen hours a day; on the days I was on call it was often twenty. After a call night, my next evening at home was often a dim effort to relate to my family through the stupor of exhaustion.

Work was our coping mechanism. Residents achieved stature by knowing the answers and outworking everyone else. One professor, who had no home life at all, worked from 7 a.m. until midnight and then woke up the resident on call to make rounds with him. His objective was to train us to relegate every other aspect of our lives to second place, just as he did. By December of 1975 I wore deepening fatigue with the indifference I gave to rumpled scrub suits.

Over the next three years, that residency created a new identity. I became an orthopaedic surgeon. With the skills I acquired I could solve the problems caused by musculoskeletal diseases such as rheumatoid arthritis. There was, however, a price for this skill. Other parts of my life were pushed into a distant background.

Sixteen years later I met Mark.

Introduction

One voice says,

"I am suffering.
It is coming from a problem out there.
I need to seek a solution for it."

That is a journey of the mind,
Towards comprehension and control.
The result of that search is called progress,
And that makes life easier.

A very different voice says,

"I am suffering.
It is coming from needfulness in here.
For it I will seek acceptance of what is."

That is a journey of the heart,
Towards compassion and openness.
The result of that journey is called detachment,
And that makes life deeper.

In 1991 Mark and I began a journey, a journey that took us from the first way of living to the second. It was not a journey either of us chose, but it took us there nevertheless. This is the story of how we helped each other along the way.

PART I
Patient

Solvable Problems

In the spring of 1991 I seldom heard the voice inside, whispering to slow down and be more aware. I didn't take the time to listen to it. I didn't have the time. I had a full orthopaedic practice and there were always patients that needed to be seen.

One busy office day Linda Roselle, my clinical assistant, took a call from the front desk. As I came out from one of the exam rooms, she said, "Dr. Carlin has a patient in his office he wants you to see."

Dr. Jeff Carlin, a rheumatologist whose office was down the hall, managed musculoskeletal diseases medically. A call like that usually meant one of his patients needed surgery.

"Emergency?" I asked.

"No, but as soon as you can."

The voice whispered, *It's always "As soon as you can."*

I hated cramming new patients into an already full schedule, so I started each week with half of Friday afternoon left open. It provided a slot for patients like this, and if there were no patients, who knows? I might get a head start on the weekend. "What's Friday afternoon look like?"

Linda had already checked the appointment book that ruled my life. "There are still openings," she said.

"What's the problem?" I was mentally estimating how much time this was going to take.

"They said it's a rheumatoid patient with bilateral knee pain."

"Okay, put him in there." There would be no head start to this weekend. "Ask if there are recent films," I added. "If there aren't, we'll need to get four views of both knees before I see him." With an efficiency born from years of working with me, Linda already knew that.

Fridays were the finish line of a full week. My practice schedule put me in the office all day Tuesdays, in the OR all day Thursdays, split the other three days half-and-half, and on one of those nights assigned me to ER call. Around that schedule I fit the responsibilities of running a practice, the duties of participating in a hospital staff, research in a gait lab, and reading that kept me current.

That Friday afternoon a quick scan of Dr. Carlin's office notes armed me with a preliminary impression of the specific reason for this referral. It looked like a challenge. I knocked on the exam room door, entered and introduced myself to a thin, middle-aged man waiting for me in an exam gown across the room. "Mr. Smetko?" I asked. "Hi! I'm Dr. Gruber. How can I help you?" It was an open-ended question that let patients tell me whatever they wanted.

He arose from his chair with a bit of stiffness, shook my hand, and after carefully sitting back down, began. "Doctor, it's my knees. They're getting really bad. I can't keep going on my job. Dr. Carlin thinks…maybe you can help me."

I sat down and said, "Tell me about it." Then I leaned back and listened as Mark Smetko's story began to unfold.

His knees were inflamed by rheumatoid arthritis, an autoimmune disorder in which joints literally self-destruct. Years ago, for unknown reasons, antibodies that normally protected him from microbial invaders, together with white blood cells known as T-helper lymphocytes, mistakenly identified one of his body's own proteins as a foreign enemy and began their attack. Their first target was the synovium—a thin, almost transparent membrane that lines each joint like wallpaper and normally secretes fluid that lubricates the joint. No longer able to distinguish friend from foe, the microscopic mercenaries of Mark's immune system had invaded and inflamed the synovium until it became red, thick, and painful, and wept joint fluid that produced a swollen appearance called an effusion.

For ten years his doctors had tried to stop Mark's pain with medications such as ibuprofen, which inhibited the inflammatory response in the synovium. Gradually his disease, a particularly virulent version, no longer responded to these first-line anti-inflammatories. To control persistent pain, in 1988 Dr. Carlin began prescribing more aggressive drugs for him that controlled inflammation by shutting down the immune system itself. These medications lessened Mark's pain, but they couldn't stop the destruction of his joints. By the time I obtained x-ray films in our office, both knees were worn down to bone rubbing on bone.

While Mark described the pain in his joints and the frustrations in his life, I began observing what my training had taught me to see. Although he appeared energetic, his body bore the obvious signs of his long-standing disease. As he talked with his hands, I noted their slightly bent fingers and knobby joints. Both wrists bore faint surgical scars. When his right shoulder moved, it produced an audible grating and a brief grimace. Prednisone had sapped bulk from his once wiry build. Fluid-filled knees poked out from his exam gown. His feet, less tortured by the disease than his hands, were just beginning to twist and splay into characteristic bunion deformities. As he hesitantly walked toward the table to begin the examination, his moves were deliberate and careful. I was watching the unsteady gait of a much older man.

His story, my observations, and the films began to form a diagnostic impression, always the first step in solving a clinical problem.

April 12, 1991

SMETKO, MARK J,

The patient is a 46-year-old white male with progressive pain in both knees from advanced rheumatoid arthritis.

His symptoms first appeared in 1975. He now has severe involvement of multiple joints. He is currently on Prednisone, Methotrexate and Naprosyn. He has already had several cortisone injections into both knees. Despite these measures, over the last fifteen months his knee pain has steadily worsened. He ranks the right knee as 80% as bad as the left.

He has severe involvement of both wrists. He underwent arthroplasty of his left wrist in December of 1989 and tendon transfers on the right wrist in February of 1989. He has moderate involvement of both shoulders and mild involvement of both feet. His hips and spine are almost free of disease.

He has noted increasing instability. "My knees give out on me." He can now walk less than fifty feet comfortably and has difficulty in going up and down stairs. "Just moving around is getting difficult." His muscle atrophy now makes it difficult to get up from falls. He has not used crutches or a cane.

He has no prior injuries to his knees. Last September his train was jolted while switching freight cars. He was knocked unconscious, but can't recall injury to either knee at that time.

He has been a railroad engineer for fifteen years. In the mid-eighties he had to switch from long-distance trains to freight yard work because of joint limitations and fatigue. His current job is predominantly sedentary, but his knees limit access into and out of the locomotive cab. He is now struggling to stay on the job.

He has no other medical problems. He lives alone in a one-level house. Recreationally, he enjoys hiking, but has been unable to do this for at least four years. "I try to ride an Exercycle, but the arthritis flare-ups are making it difficult."

<u>Diagnostic Impression:</u>

Rheumatoid arthritis, now down to bone-on-bone in both knees, with cyst formation, ligamentous instability and marked muscle atrophy, in a relatively young individual whose hips and ankles are only minimally involved.

The dry, precise terms dictated into my clinical notes focused on the problem rather than the person. Later I would know the man much better, but for now Mark had an orthopaedic problem that he wanted solved, and my job was to solve it.

After forming this impression, a surgeon's next task is to determine if there are appropriate indications for surgery. Has the patient tried all non-operative treatments? What did Mark want to do post-operatively that he couldn't do now? Were his expectations realistic? Was there a choice among different surgical alternatives? What would happen if he waited longer?

Mark's answers to these questions led me to my conclusions. As I sat down across from him to begin discussing them, his eyes, untouched by the disease that wracked the rest of his body, watched me attentively, perhaps taking in more than his ears did.

If he wanted to walk free of pain, he needed both knees replaced. There were no reasonable alternatives. He was already beyond the point where a simple arthroscopic clean-out of his knees would help him. Because both knees were worn out, replacing just one would solve only half of his pain and none of his functional limitations; the remaining knee would keep him hobbled. He had an aggressive disease. If he waited much longer, he would lose his job.

His only choice was whether to have both knees replaced in one operation or to have each replacement done individually, eight weeks apart. Doing both together was a bigger operation than doing one at a time, but patients liked the idea that once their surgery was over, they didn't face coming back for a second one. Often as important, both new knees could be rehabilitated together. It cut the total convalescent time in half. That was important to Mark. He wanted to get on with his life.

Mark came in knowing that he needed something done, but he needed time with me to traverse the chasm from understanding his problem to accepting my solution for it. The open Friday afternoon schedule allowed him whatever time he needed. The visit lasted almost an hour. When we were finished, I suggested that he could take more time if he needed it. "Think it over. If more questions come up, call me next week. If not, call and let us know your decision." We shook hands, he left, and I went out to the desk and the paperwork that always waited at the end of the day.

A doctor seldom knows what patients take away from their first encounter. I listened, examined, asked questions, gave my impressions, made a recommendation and tried to explain to Mark why I thought my recommendations were best for him. He, in turn, had to feel right about having me do a major operation on his knees. He called several days later to tell me he wanted both of them replaced simultaneously. I often marveled at the remarkable trust that allowed a patient to do that.

On the morning of June 6, my hands dripping wet from a ten-minute scrub, I pushed open the swinging OR door with my back and stepped into the bright lights of Operating Room #6 at Northwest Hospital. The scrub nurse handed me a sterile towel. As I dried, the circulating nurse snapped a hood with a clear plastic face shield over an adjustable frame on my head, completely enclosing it and muffling my voice and the voices of those around me.

Surgical masks kept surgeon's germs from reaching patients. After our awareness of AIDS increased in the mid-eighties, orthopaedists used these hot but all-enclosing shields, referred to as space suits, during joint replacement surgery to keep patients' germs from reaching them. In addition to the face shield, the scrub nurse held out two pairs of gloves for me. A protective layer three times thicker than surgeons normally wear stretched over each of my protesting fingertips, which sometimes responded by going numb. Some orthopaedists added another layer of armor: fingerless gloves made of Kevlar mesh. Needles poked. Saws slipped. Everyone knew the consequences.

The snap of the face shield changed my perspective, as if I were entering another world—a world made comfortably familiar by countless repetitions. Trays, filled with the parts I would soon use, crowded the back tables. The anesthesiologist had already drifted Mark into a dreamless sleep. Our group's physician-assistant, John Gullage, was completing the draping. Soon all that was visible of Mark's humanity were the knobs of two knees, protruding upward into the focused beams of the operating room lights.

I approached my side of the operating table, the center of that world. The scrub nurse busied herself by arranging the opening instruments on the Mayo stand. John stood across from me, testing the cautery and suction. I had heard Mark's history, examined his joints, and earned his trust. Now I confronted a level of intimacy few other people reach. I was about to surgically invade his knees.

I paused for a moment, my hands clasped in front of me. It was my way of tuning out everything else in the room and concentrating instead on one thin line, drawn with a skin marker, that ran down the center of Mark Smetko's right knee.

I turned to the anesthesiologist. "All set?"

"Yep."

"Skin knife, please."

The knife, slicing slowly through the skin, left behind it a widening wake of red.

So began the intense cadence of elective surgery. In it, every need is known, every step planned, every request anticipated. The skin, the bursa, the capsule, the joint…each layer was opened with predictable expectations. There were no pauses, no surprises—only a steady march through often-traveled territory.

After deepening the incision to open the joint, I flexed the knee, bringing into full view two knuckles ravaged by arthritis. Years of disease and weight bearing loads had split off fragments of weakened cartilage, as if a hammer had beaten them loose. Instead of the smooth, glistening cartilage one might see on the end of a chicken bone, the joint surfaces here were ground down, as if by a coarse rasp, to bare, protesting bone. Debris clouded the joint fluid. Angry red-purple synovium crept across nearby ligaments, relentlessly eroding anything in its path. Looking up, I saw John silently shake his head in disbelief. It always amazed us that people could even walk on knees like this, much less continue to do their jobs.

The saw blade, oscillating with a metallic screech through the slits of carefully positioned cutting guides, transformed the distorted joint surfaces into standardized shapes. Next, trial implants optimized size, motion and stability. Methacrylate cement bonded the final, polished steel components to the lower end of the femur and the upper end of the tibia and fixed a small polyethylene button to the undersurface of the patella.[1] A pin locked a polyethylene insert onto the tibial component, providing a low-friction surface.

"Drill…" "Reamer…" "Oscillating saw…" Ridding the knee of rheumatoid wreckage was not light work, and these were not light instruments. Fitted onto a heavy power handle, they could shape the ends of bone that normally has twice the strength of oak. Mark's bone, reduced by his disease to the frailty of balsa,

---

1. The femur is the thighbone. The two knuckles on the end are the femoral condyles. The tibia is the shinbone. The patella is the kneecap.

permitted no slips or misses. The whining saw left a fine spatter of red across the plastic shield in front of my eyes.

The overhead surgical lights became bright reflections on the mirror-polished surfaces of the new steel knuckles. Then, as I straightened the knee, the outer tissues slid together and the shiny metal disappeared into its envelope of flesh. John began closing, while I began a similar procedure on the second side. In a little over three hours we were finished.

While John put on the dressings, the anesthesiologist gently brought Mark's mind from merciful oblivion back into the everyday world. As I peeled off my gloves and unsnapped the now-spotted plastic shield from my face, I returned to that world as well. My legs, having stood still too long, announced their dull fatigue. Tightness in my upper back crept into my awareness. My focus re-expanded to the rest of the room. "Thanks, everyone," I said with a small smile. "That went well."

In the recovery room I wrote orders and dictated the op-note. As soon as Mark stabilized, I bent over him, my hand resting on his shoulder. His face turned upward, searching for a face, listening for a voice. Through the fog of his awakening I told him, "It went well, Mark. Everything went well. I'll fill in the details later. For now, we found what we expected to find and did what we expected to do. There were no surprises." I knew the words would register only dimly, but his eyes smiled back, and that was what mattered.

The surgical waiting room was filled with people who masked the anxiety of waiting with the boredom of used magazines and daytime TV. At the door I inquired, "The Smetko family?" A small, thin, white-haired woman looked up at me and smiled. She introduced herself and then eagerly asked, "How did Mark do?" I noticed that she inquired not about the surgery, but about her son.

"He tolerated it very well. He's in the recovery room and doing fine," I replied. Later, up on the orthopaedic floor, I became better acquainted with Zita Smetko.

Seventy-six years old at the time, she lived with her husband Steve in Wenatchee, in central Washington. Despite her age, she frequently made the one hundred and forty mile trip across the Cascade Mountains to be in Mark's room when I made rounds. Her attentive gaze followed everything that was happening to her son. Her presence, noticeable but not intrusive, conveyed a quiet concern that connected her to him in an important, but as yet undefined way.

Mark's surgical incisions healed without complication. By the fourth post-operative day he had achieved seventy-five degrees of knee motion, was regaining his thigh muscle strength and could already walk twenty feet in physical therapy.

The next day he transferred to the rehab wing, where he rapidly regained endurance. By the second post-operative week he could function independently and was discharged.

On July 24 I saw him for his six-week visit. My office notes described remarkable progress:

> He has virtually no pain in his knees. He can walk up to a quarter mile. He is able to go up and down fifteen stairs, foot-over-foot, without hesitation. He is doing his exercises regularly and can do up to twenty repetitions of straight-leg-raises with four pounds. He has 130° of flexion on the right, 117° on the left.
>
> He would like to go back to work. He states, "I'm dying of boredom."

I released him for light duty. Within six weeks, he returned to his normal work. I saw him again on October 23:

> The patient is now 4½ months from bilateral total knee arthroplasty and appears fully recovered. He can walk as far as he wishes, and estimates this to be several miles. He reports no discomfort at all in either knee. He does up to twenty minutes on a stationary bike four times a week and tolerates it well. His other joints are now the limiting factor in his activities. He is back on his job full-time.

In June 1992, I saw him for long-term follow-up:

> The patient is now one year from the time of his simultaneous bilateral total knee replacements. He has no pain whatsoever in his knees. He routinely walks up to several miles. He works full-time at his previous job.
>
> He remains on Methotrexate, Naprosyn and Prednisone to control the rheumatoid arthritis in his other joints.
>
> On physical examination, his knees have excellent alignment, with no instability or effusion. He has full extension and almost 130° of flexion bilaterally. He shows good return of leg strength against two-finger resistance. His walking pattern is smooth, without limp or unsteadiness. He steps up and down without hesitation.

Orthopaedic surgery solves many disabling problems. Fractures heal. Replaced joints work smoothly. Pain is often relieved and function restored. This capacity to solve problems cleanly and the satisfaction that goes with it were important reasons why I went into orthopaedics. I liked to hear someone say, "It doesn't hurt now when I walk!"

At that point in my career, almost half of my surgical cases involved joint replacement. Over the years this surgery had been refined into a predictable procedure that restored function and provided consistent and lasting relief of pain. By 1991, studies of total knee replacements at ten-year follow-up routinely reported good to excellent results in ninety to ninety-five percent of cases.

The procedure not only revolutionized the care of patients with worn-out joints, it was gratifying to perform. I could tell people who had often suffered for years that knee surgery could restore their enjoyment of everyday activities. When he first saw me, Mark Smetko had relentless knee pain. He struggled to walk fifty feet. He could barely work, and despite aggressive medical treatment, he was getting worse. After only one procedure, four days in the hospital, two weeks in the rehab center and eight weeks of outpatient strengthening, he was completely free of knee pain and was ready to go back to his job. After four months he could walk as far as he wanted to and was working his normal schedule as a railroad engineer. He was overjoyed when he told me, "Hey, Doc! I'm working again, and it doesn't hurt!"

Getting Mark back to railroading was the best outcome I could ever have given him.

Intractable Problems

From 1991 to 1996, Mark continued his job as an engineer for the Burlington Northern Railroad, working the graveyard shift at the Balmer freight yard at Interbay, near downtown Seattle, and the Stacy yard south of the city. Every night he climbed laboriously up into his switch engine and began moving freight cars around to make up the trains that would pull out the next morning.

Even though Mark's replacement surgery in 1991 solved the pain in his knees, his rheumatoid disease continued to wreck his remaining joints. Inflamed synovium invaded adjacent ligaments until they weakened and stretched. Nearby bone became softened and cystic until it collapsed and deformed. Exercise became painful and his muscles became weak. The resulting instability caused him to fall. Falls produced more injury, pain, and disuse, and these in turn led to more weakness, imbalance and then more falls. The process—called dysmobility—becomes a vicious cycle that relentlessly feeds on itself. Within its grip, Mark was losing both his ability to walk and his independence. Clean solutions became harder to achieve. His problems were becoming intractable.

One day I asked Dr. Carlin about the difficulty of treating Mark medically. He replied, "There is a genetic component to rheumatoid disease that is still not clearly understood. There are four or five genetic markers that are currently being defined. When all the markers are present, when all the genes line up in a row, so to speak, it really increases the virulence of this disease."

"How do you look at Mark's situation?"

"I think he has all the markers. On a zero-to-ten scale of virulence, Mark's disease is a ten. He simply isn't responding anymore to first or second-line drugs. We have to use larger and larger doses of advanced meds to control his flare-ups. Sooner or later that's going to have consequences. But without aggressive treatment his joints will self-destruct and collapse. I'm also concerned that without that kind of treatment his antibodies will start attacking his other tissues."

By 1996 Dr. Carlin's predictions were coming true. Both of Mark's ankles were collapsing. Their instability worsened his propensity to fall, and every fall in turn jeopardized adjacent joints. He had twice abraded both knees and nearly gotten the replacements infected. He knew that the next time he might not be so lucky.

That April Jeff referred him back to me. "Can you fix his ankles?"

Characteristically, it was not pain that brought Mark back to see me. "Pain's not the reason, Doc. I live with pain all the time. The problem is that I can't work. I can't get in and out of a locomotive without nearly falling over. I can't even walk along the side of the tracks!" Along with the pain in his story, I heard discouragement, anxiety, even a burdened desperation. "I need to get my ankles fixed," he said, "so I can go back to running trains."

As Mark spoke, I observed how much he had aged since I had last seen him. He seemed smaller—not so much in size, but as if some vital vigor was being leeched away. His dark brown hair was starting to show flecks of gray. By now Prednisone had thinned his skin as much as it had his muscles. His knees looked quiet, but both ankles were swollen and deformed. Inflamed synovium had eroded the ligaments that normally stabilized them. As I watched him walk, Mark's feet angled outward with each step. Instead of walking on a level foot, he wobbled painfully on each heel's inner edge. As his arms eased his body back into the chair, his shoulders and wrists grated audibly.

The ankle—a joint between the tibia and the bone below it, called the talus—allows the foot to move up and down, such as when Mark climbed up and down the steps to his locomotive cab. Beneath the ankle, the talus is connected to the foot through three other joints—called the sub-talar joints—which allow the foot to move from side-to-side, as when he walked along banked gravel beside the tracks.

Weight bearing x-ray films showed the distortion and destruction of these joints so clearly that I used the films to illustrate to Mark what I could do. Unlike his knees, this time there was no quick fix. Joint replacements weren't a possibility. Surgeons had tried for years to solve this problem with total ankle replacements, but in active patients with rheumatoid disease, the bone was inevitably too soft and the ligaments too weak. The implants routinely loosened and dislodged, and the situation became unsalvageable. Published results were awful.

I had to tell him, instead, that the only reliable choice was to fuse the destroyed joints. I would have to open each joint, clean out the destroyed cartilage and debris, rasp the remaining surfaces down to raw bone with high-speed burrs, and then tightly pack crumbly bits of bone graft into the resulting spaces. Then I would have to insert steel screws to hold the bones rigidly in place and apply a cast post-operatively to continue immobilization until the fusion became solid.

When both the ankle and the three sub-talar joints are fused, the procedure is called a pan-talar arthrodesis. If I did such a procedure on both of Mark's feet, I would have to do each of those steps on eight separate joints. It would be a long and complex operation.

The advantage to the procedure is that once a fusion is solid there is no pain, no instability and, unlike implants, no risk of ever loosening. A solid fusion will last a lifetime. With a rocker-bottom shoe, Mark's gait, even with both ankles fused, would be nearly normal on level ground. The disadvantage is that there would never be motion where the joints once were. A fused ankle is rigid. Walking on uneven terrain is difficult, sometimes impossible.

Unfortunately, the operation itself does not actually fuse the joints. The surgery only sets the stage for a process of cell growth that is similar to fracture healing. New bone cells have to grow across the prior joint space in order to unite one bone to the other. The success of the surgery is entirely dependent on this cell growth, a process that begins within a week, but may take months to complete. It was a process impaired both by Mark's disease and by the medications he took to suppress it.

After describing the procedure, I had to discuss its convalescence as well. "Mark, one important question for you is timing. We can do one side, wait three months and then do the other side. That makes convalescence at least six months. Or we can do both sides at one sitting. Like your knees, that would make this a big operation, but it could cut your convalescent time in half." Saving time was every bit as important to him now.

"But this time there's more to it than saving convalescent time. If I only do one side, you might be able to continue to walk at least short distances by using your other foot and a walker. I can't predict how far you could go, though. A walker will put a big load on your wrists and shoulders. They may not tolerate that. If they don't, you'll have to get around in a wheelchair.

"If I do both ankles at once you won't be able to bear any weight on either leg. You'll definitely be in a wheelchair all the time until the joints fuse. That could really tie you down. But if we do both at once, the overall time you spend in a wheelchair is likely to be a lot less."

As I explained away Mark's hope for a quick solution, I saw enthusiasm fade from his eyes. Being bound to a wheelchair clearly bothered him. He thought for a moment and then shrugged, "Well, I'm going to visit a friend in Colorado. He has a wheelchair and his wife is a nurse. I'll practice using his wheelchair and figure out if I can use one in my house. Then I'll decide."

I wasn't finished with the risks. "I'm also concerned about your skin and your bones. Both of them are getting pretty thin from the Prednisone. Your incisions might break down or get infected. There's also a chance that the bones won't fuse. Methotrexate can sometimes interfere with that. If they don't, we'd have to go back in and try to re-fuse them."

"Do I have any choices?" His voice had an edge to it.

I paused too long, trying to think of alternatives. He blurted out the desperate conclusion he had already reached. "I can't keep going the way I am! I can't walk!"

I could only nod in silent agreement.

After we finished, Linda set up an outpatient PT session for wheelchair training. Two days later Mark called her to schedule both sides at once. He said that if the wheelchair didn't work in his house he'd stay with his parents in Wenatchee.

After the last patient of that day I sagged into a chair, propped my feet up on the desk to ease their aching, and began to dictate a pile of patients' chart notes. When I came to my observations about Mark's aging appearance, I reflected that in the years since his first surgery in 1991, I had aged as well.

In 1990, after serving five years on the executive committee as a department chair, I was asked to lead the medical staff at Northwest Hospital. It was a position that held little attraction for me. I already had a full practice; I didn't want more stress in my life. I was tired of all the committee meetings that the position required. I wanted the hours back that so many commitments had already added to each day. I declined the nomination.

A year later such avoidance became impossible. Doctors and patients alike were being sucked into the transformation of America's health care system. Experts argued whether capitation would trim costs, or limit care. Would patients choose their doctors by personal choice, or by HMO decree? Was primary care more cost-efficient than care from a specialist? Should hospitals start buying private practices to create networks? Would a PHO—the fragile alliance of a hospital, its specialists and its primary care clinics—produce much-vaunted vertical integration, or just chaos? Nobody knew the answers. Expensive consultants, federal officials and budget experts all had firm beliefs, but during the next six years the problems proved intractable and the solutions were fleeting.

In 1992 Congress debated the Clinton health care version of managed competition, but nationally the plan went nowhere. In 1993, however, the Washington

State legislature passed the program into law. Under it, the state would, by 1996, begin a staged progression to universal health care, using a single-payer system and capitated reimbursement. It promised a radical departure from anything patients, doctors, or hospitals had ever known.

The choices I confronted were simple. Capitulation was not a consideration and escape was not an option. It came down to "Lead, follow, or get out of the way." In 1992 I accepted the nomination to serve, first as Chief of Staff-Elect and then, beginning in April of 1994, to serve for two years as Chief of Staff.

By 1995 the legislature had to repeal the Washington State Health Care Reform Act. The problems of reform proved far more complex than the state had anticipated. Problems imposed by the federal government, however, didn't disappear as easily. The press reported that a dentist had infected six patients with the AIDS virus during routine dental care. In response to public outcries, the federal government required hospitals nationwide to create a policy to protect patients from HIV-infected health care providers. Creating that policy for Northwest Hospital became my responsibility.

The ethic that surgeons need to inform their patients about the risk of infection during a procedure is straightforward. Translating this general principle into a specific policy about AIDS proved to be a lot thornier. An HIV-infected surgeon had to disclose the risk of exposure to the virus during an operation, but which operations were "exposure-prone"? Experts at the Center for Disease Control couldn't tell us. What were the risks of actually transmitting the HIV virus during such a procedure? The experts didn't know. What constituted "informed consent" when nobody knew the risk of transmission? They couldn't tell us that, either. Our committee also had to look at the other side of the problem. How could doctors and nurses protect themselves from infected patients who wouldn't disclose their status? If patients couldn't be forced to disclose their status, why should health care workers be forced to disclose theirs?

The committee I appointed of doctors, lay ethicists, board members, and the hospital attorney would have preferred hard data; instead, we had to work with politically loaded ambiguities. After months of meetings, the committee finally created a policy that satisfied federal requirements. None of us knew if it would work in our hospital.

What I did know was that by 1996, the world of private practice in which I had once delivered care was gone. In the preceding ten years, seven Seattle-area hospitals, including the one at which I had started practice, had been sold or closed. Forty percent of the orthopaedists in the north end of the city had retired, relocated to another hospital or left town. Northwest Hospital employed or controlled fifty percent of the medical staff. The hospital PHO had fractured collegial cohesiveness. In 1978 I had started as a solo practitioner with Linda and one other employee in order to provide care for orthopaedic patients. In response to the years of upheaval, I now practiced with four partners, forty-seven other surgeons in seven other clinics, and two hundred and thirty other employees, managers and administrators, all part of an orthopaedic corporation that was expanding throughout greater Seattle in order to provide managed care products.

As I sat that night in an empty office, dictating my solutions to Mark Smetko's ankle problems, tiredness beyond physical fatigue tugged at me. I was tired of health care reform. I was tired of basing policies on uncertainty. I was tired of battles within the medical staff. Perhaps I was feeling anger, perhaps depression, perhaps loss of something I cherished, or perhaps I was tired because something inside was becoming empty and worn out. At moments like this, the small voice I usually had no time for pushed its way into my thoughts.

Why are you doing this?

"Because there are problems out there," I thought to myself. "They won't just go away. Somebody has to solve them."

Is that the only reason?

I had no answer. I finished my dictation and went up to the hospital to make rounds.

In two weeks my two-year term as Chief of Staff would end, but I had already paid the wages of its stress. In a family picture in 1994 my hair was light brown. In a photograph taken recently for the hospital it was half gray. Like many doctors, I could see aging in my patients, but I was remarkably oblivious to what was happening to me.

On May 7 I performed bilateral pantalar arthrodeses on Mark's ankles. I had recruited a partner, Bob Clawson, so we could use two teams, but even with that arrangement the surgery took six and a half hours. In the immediate postoperative period, Mark was sick with fevers. His wrists and shoulders protested when he tried to use an overhead trapeze to transfer from his bed to a chair. As soon as he was medically stable and could sit up, he had to go to the Transitional Care Center to acquire wheelchair skills. Two weeks after surgery he could use the wheelchair adequately and his wounds were healed. I put him in short-leg casts, ordered visiting home care and discharged him.

By mid-July the sub-talar joints looked solid on the office x-ray films, but the ankle joints didn't. Hoping to help the ankles fuse, we applied new casts, taught him gentle weight bearing techniques, and as a last resort attached devices to each cast that used focused ultrasound to help his cells form new bone.

In mid-August, after another month of being stuck in a wheelchair and sweltering in his casts, Mark came back to the clinic. The films showed no change. His ankle joints were not fusing. His third-party carrier declined to pay for the ultrasound attachments. "New devices are not covered." Repeated requests got us nowhere. I asked the manufacturer if they could help. They said they'd check on it and get back to me.

I saw him four weeks later. Our efforts had failed.

> September 20, 1996:
>
> Mark's sub-talar joints are solid, but his films show confirmed non-unions at both ankles that are too painful to tolerate weight bearing. Further cast immobilization is unlikely to produce fusions. I reviewed a possible revision procedure with him. He is aware that there are no non-operative alternatives. The sales rep from Exogen will allow continued use of the ultrasound devices for his ankles post-operatively free of charge.
>
> He attempted to function in his own house, but couldn't do so in his wheelchair. He lives alone and frequently required a visiting nurse. The insurance company won't cover this. As a result he has had to convalesce with his parents in Wenatchee.
>
> He is having increasing difficulty doing so. His mother has to borrow a truck to bring his wheelchair with him for appointments. She is 81 and has health problems of her own. It has been unusually hot there this summer, adding to his overall joint discomfort. In addition to pain at the non-unions and difficulty in getting around, he has become clinically depressed. He is apparently at risk for losing his house.

Mark wanted me to fix his ankles so he could go back to work. I took pains to explain the orthopaedic issues; I didn't know about the symbolic ones. The railroad was more than just a job to him. Driving trains symbolized escape from the everyday world and an unfettered freedom to go where he wanted. Being stuck in a wheelchair with his parents in Wenatchee was the opposite of that freedom. He couldn't walk in his casts because of the pain. He couldn't work. He couldn't pay for his house in Seattle. He was completely dependent on his parents. Convalescence soon became captivity. As the months wore on, a gray cloud of depression closed in around him.

Blanketed by that emotional shroud, in early October he underwent bilateral revision surgery. In five hours John Gullage and I removed the prior hardware in both ankles, placed intramedulary rods up through his heels into his tibias, and packed in more bone graft. The surgery went smoothly.

The post-operative course did not. Dr. Carlin watched his own predictions come true. Mark's medical complications became ominous indicators of his advancing disease.

He had chest pain. An EKG was non-specific and the lung scan was negative for clots, but an echocardiogram showed early loss of ventricular function and his chest x-ray showed free fluid, called a pleural effusion. The cardiologist diagnosed early congestive heart failure. Lasix cleared the effusion, but not the questions. Why was a man this age in congestive heart failure?

He had persistent fevers, but no evidence of infection. His chronic anemia, related to his rheumatoid disease, worsened until he needed a transfusion.

He had increasing heartburn. Since Mark had a history of prior bleeding, the gastroenterologist advised endoscopy. Examination through the fiber-optic tube revealed severe inflammation and chronic erosions in the lower esophagus. A biopsy came back positive for "Barrett's esophagitis." That diagnosis was even more worrisome.

For years the anti-inflammatory medications Mark took for his pain had irritated the lining of his stomach and lower esophagus, weakening the valve between the two. Without the valve, stomach acid refluxed up into his esophagus, eroding and ulcerating its unprotected lining. Barrett's esophagitis meant that the chronically irritated lining cells were undergoing an ominous transformation. They were scarring down the esophagus and slowly obstructing Mark's swallowing. Even worse, just as chronic sunburn can lead to skin cancer, these cells could eventually turn malignant.

Fortunately, Mark's stomach symptoms responded to treatment. His depression improved with Prozac. His therapist modified his wheelchair to meet his needs. His team of medical consultants pronounced him stable. After arranging for his medical follow-up, I discharged him back to Wenatchee.

When I saw him in the office a month later, his progress suggested that we were back on track. Mark had no pain in either ankle when standing. He could walk in place with only mild discomfort. The x-ray films suggested early fusion. I suggested that perhaps he could cautiously get back on his feet.

He did. By mid-December, eight weeks after his surgery, he could walk two hundred yards using a wheeled walker, bearing full weight, with no pain. X-ray films showed both ankles solidly fused. I removed his casts and placed him in short leg braces.

By February 1997 he was able to walk two hundred yards in rocker-bottom shoes with no pain and no instability. He used a cane only for balance. His gait was nearly normal. He moved back to Seattle and to his own house. It was the best possible anti-depressant. The surgery had worked. He was elated. I stopped his Prozac.

It was premature. Despite his orthopaedic progress, Mark's medical condition continued to spiral downward. Worried about a persistent lesion on the front of the left shin, that same month Dr. Carlin performed a skin biopsy. The report was ominously positive:

> "Sections from the skin biopsy of the left shin show a marked and acute vasculitis. The capillaries, venules and arterioles of the superficial dermis all show numerous acute inflammatory cells, fibrin and nuclear dust. This is entirely consistent with immune complex deposition.
>
> Diagnosis: Severe acute leukocytoclastic vasculitis"

The scaling skin lesion on Mark's shin was only the surface sign of a pervasive process. His autoimmune disease, for twenty years confined to his joints, was now attacking his blood vessels. Plagues of antibodies were attaching themselves to proteins in the vessel walls, provoking inflammation that produced clotting and then obstruction of the vessels. The resulting loss of blood flow, called ischemia, could gradually wither any vital organ.

The biopsy report altered Mark's prognosis completely. It was as if a cancer, localized for many years, had finally spread everywhere. The cause of Mark's congestive heart failure became suddenly clear. Without aggressive treatment, the rest of his body would eventually follow the fate of his joints.

Dr. Carlin said, "Vasculitis is rare, but when it appears it is an ominous sign. Before this biopsy, on a zero-to-ten scale, the virulence of Mark's disease was a ten. After the diagnosis of vasculitis, it was a fifteen."

He started Mark on Cyclosporine, a potent immunosuppressive agent. The skin lesion improved, but like a smoldering warning, it didn't go away. Within a month Mark had to have forty milliliters of fluid removed from his right shoulder. The lab report was negative for infection. Three weeks later, without any new injury, he came in with an effusion and low-grade ache in his left knee. I removed a hundred milliliters of cloudy fluid from it. That fluid showed no infection either, but the knee kept swelling. On the radar screen of risk, joint effusions were starting to show up with alarming frequency.

None of these problems deterred Mark from what was important to him. When he saw me in mid-March, he proudly announced that he had found a thirty-day program of light duty he could do. "Doc, the railroad is willing to take me back. What do you think?"

Zita begged him not to do it. She thought he should apply for disability instead. She later told me, "He wouldn't hear of that. He wanted to get back on his locomotives."

I saw Mark for final follow-up of his surgery on May 16, 1997. During the visit he told me he could walk a quarter mile with no discomfort in either foot or ankle, could walk across loose gravel, and no longer needed a cane at all. He wanted to go back to regular duty.

One night in early June, at the beginning of the graveyard shift at the Balmer freight yard, Mark walked cautiously along the tracks, testing the stability of his fused ankles on the gravel around the rails. He had picked up his work orders and his crew from the trainmaster at the yard office, and now he approached a green and black GP-30 locomotive that sat idling on Track 19. He did his customary walk-around inspection and then perhaps grimaced as he gripped the handrails and hauled himself up four steel steps to the catwalk that led to the cab.

Settled into his chair on the cab's right-hand side, Mark scanned the gauges, checking air pressure in the brake lines and output from the diesel engine. He leaned his head out the cab window. The rails ahead of him glinted green and red from nearby signal lamps. The switchman on the catwalk in front of the cab gave him an "all-clear" with a lantern. Satisfied, Mark eased the reverser into forward. Two-thousand two-hundred and fifty horsepower began sending amperage to the traction motors between the wheels.

I imagine he smiled to himself as he sounded the warning horn, as if to announce that at last he was on the move again. He slowly released the air brakes and clicked the throttle lever forward one notch. The rumbling response of the diesel was so deep he probably felt it rather than heard it. The locomotive began to move, and the freight cars behind it followed like obedient children.

This time it had taken him thirteen months, fusions of four joints in each ankle, extensive bilateral revisions, and multiple medical consultations, but Mark was back to running his trains. A trainmaster who had worked at the Balmer yard for twenty years said, "Mark Smetko was an absolute inspiration. I've never met anyone else so positive."

The Golden Killer

For four years the specter of infection slipped in and out of the shadows of Mark's disease.

In 1993 I received a report that while he was visiting his parents in . Wenatchee, he suddenly became very sick. An infection abruptly appeared in his left shoulder that required treatment with arthroscopic drainage and then six weeks of antibiotics. Although the infection didn't spread to his knee implants and Mark seemed to recover fully, the report's implications disturbed me. Without any apparent source, bacteria had simply appeared, first in his bloodstream and then in his shoulder, a condition called spontaneous septicemia.

A year later Mark had severe pain and swelling in the same shoulder. In 1995 he had another flare up, another in '96, and two in 1997. After he was started on Cyclosporine his knees began producing similar swellings. Since the septicemia, every one of these episodes had to be evaluated immediately. He would call, Linda would work him into the day's schedule, and under local anesthetic I would have to stick the joint with a large needle to draw out the cloudy fluid. Every time, laboratory stains of the fluid showed worrisome white cells, but the culture reports were always negative for bacteria. Every time, Mark responded to local treatment with irrigation or injections. We knew the ubiquitous villain that had caused his first septicemia, but after 1993 we couldn't lure it out of the shadows where it lurked. Its name was fearsome in the annals of medicine.

Lab technicians looking down the barrel of a microscope readily recognize a pale blue, grape-like cluster of bacteria. It is *Staphylococcus aureus*, a virulent invader whose name *aureus* comes from the Latin word for golden, because a colony of it growing on red culture medium produces a small golden halo. A bacteriology professor of mine in medical school coined a different description. He called it "the golden killer."

Even though it appears to be a primitive life form, *Staph aureus* can marshal complex defenses against our most aggressive medical attacks.

Its first defense is to form an abscess. The staphylococcus kills off white blood cells in such a way that the dead cells accumulate into a thick fluid. What we call pus is actually the debris of fallen cellular soldiers. Within the pocket of pus there is no blood supply. Since antibiotics arrive by way of the bloodstream, they can't reach bacteria that are inside the abscess cavity. No matter how high the drug dosage, *Staphylococcus* has effectively walled itself off, safe within the soup it has created. The only solution to an abscess has been used since antiquity. The cavity has to be surgically opened, washed out, and drained.

S. aureus's second defensive tactic evolved more recently. The bacterium can acquire mutant genes that make it resistant to antibiotics. Shortly after penicillin was discovered, doctors found that some strains of *S. aureus* were resistant to it. After extensive use of penicillin, only the resistant strains remained, especially in hospitals. Drug companies developed a new generation of antibiotics to kill those strains, but resistant mutants reappeared. The mutants survived, proliferated, and the cycle began again. Five generations of antibiotics later, this duel is far from over. Strains of *S. aureus* have recently appeared that are resistant to all known antibiotics.

Even against sensitive bacteria, antibiotics alone are not a complete answer. The body relies for its health on an intricate immune system of white cells and antibodies to fight off bacterial invasion. Mark's autoimmune disease and the Prednisone he needed to suppress its attacks had badly weakened his host defenses. His white cells no longer worked well. For him, enemies were at the gates, but only feeble soldiers came out to fight them. Spontaneous septicemia told me that indeed, Mark could no longer even hold the enemy outside the gates.

The third defensive tactic of *S. aureus* is the one orthopaedists fear the most. *Staphylococcus* produces a protein film called a glycocalyx that tenaciously coats the plastic and metal surfaces of joint replacements, sealing in the bacteria and preventing them from being attacked by white cells, subdued by antibiotics, or washed away by irrigating fluids.

Staph aureus has a fourth impregnable defense. It is able to go dormant, and when dormant it is metabolically inert. It won't grow in cultures and is impervious to antibiotics. It can't be caught, and it can't be killed. It just sits there, like a seed in the winter, waiting for its chance to reawaken. Once Mark's shoulder was infected, completely eradicating the invader became difficult, even with extensive antibiotics. Dormant *S. aureus* osteomyelitis can reappear twenty years after a surgeon supposedly suppressed the first infection. For Mark, with his host defenses relentlessly deteriorating and large metal targets in both of his knees, it wouldn't take that long.

After my term of office as Chief of Staff was over, I declined any further administrative positions and the stress that went with them. I wanted to simplify my life, but it proved hard to do. I couldn't seem to detach from the duties I had created. Sick patients needed to be seen. Years of research on fall prevention needed to be published. Consolidating our growing orthopaedic group into an effective corporation needed more committee time. Something always seemed to snare me.

I concluded that to get free, I had to step outside the practice completely for a while. I wanted to go away long enough to not worry about problems I couldn't solve. In August 1997 my wife Beverly and I escaped to the Canadian Gulf Islands for three weeks of complete relaxation. It was only the second time in twenty years that I had allowed myself to be away from my patients that long.

While I was gone, on August 28 Mark came into the office. Four days previously he had tripped over the railroad tracks and landed on his right knee. He felt immediate pain, but despite subsequent swelling he could walk reasonably well, so he continued to work. In my absence, our clinic's physician-assistant saw him when he finally came in.

He had extensive bruising extending down the right thigh, across the knee and into the shin area. His right knee was diffusely swollen, but there was no break in the skin. He could walk without pain or a limp. X-ray examination showed no evidence of fracture or loosening of the implants. The findings suggested a large contusion, but no deep injury. The PA recommended crutches, elevation, light duty, and follow-up with me in three weeks. After a few days Mark set aside his crutches and went back to switching freight cars.

On Thursday, September 11, he tried to step down from a locomotive but stumbled on the last step and fell forward, this time landing on the gravel with both knees. He inspected them carefully. There was no abrasion, indeed, no break in the skin of any kind. Reassured, he walked around a bit, concluded that he had not injured anything, and stayed at work.

This time, however, the enemy entered. Soon his right knee became painful and his right shoulder began to swell. He began to feel feverish and sick. By Friday he couldn't go to work. He hated the thought of yet another Emergency Room visit, but by Saturday he couldn't even get out of bed. When he called Zita that evening, she told her son firmly that if he didn't go to the hospital on his own, she was coming to Seattle to take him there.

Zita and Mark arrived at the Northwest Hospital emergency room on Sunday afternoon. Although Mark was by then seriously sick, it wasn't initially clear whether this was a flare-up of his rheumatoid disease, an injury from his fall, or something else. Aspiration of his right knee in the Emergency Room confirmed that it was something else. The knee was full of pus.

After writing admitting orders, Dr. Carlin told Zita how serious the situation might get. She told him I was due back in the office the following day. Later that night he called me at home and asked me to see Mark as soon as possible the next morning.

Monday morning it took me only a quick examination to determine that Mark was critically ill. Bacteria were in his bloodstream again. No break in the skin meant another spontaneous septicemia. Given his lack of host defenses, where there was one infected joint there would be others. His left knee and his right shoulder felt hot. I aspirated them at the bedside and found putrid fluid in both. I didn't need to wait for lab reports to guess the diagnosis. All three joints grew *Staphylococcus aureus*.

The golden killer was back.

Waiting for me to come out of Mark's room, Zita had the drained look of any mother fearful for her son. I motioned toward the waiting room. As we sat, she unburdened her worries.

"He had fallen three more times since he was in your office. He was with us last weekend, and both his knees looked badly swollen. I pleaded with him to see the doctor in Wenatchee but he said 'I have an appointment with Dr. Gruber next Monday. He is on vacation until then, and I don't want to see any other doctor.' So he drove back to Seattle!

"I called him every day. At first, he said everything was fine. Friday he said a friend was taking care of him and that I didn't need to come. He was so stubborn! Saturday evening when he couldn't get out of bed, he finally asked me to come over, just to help him get to your office on Monday. He had no idea how sick he was!

"The first flight out of Wenatchee was at five-thirty on Sunday morning. When I finally got to his house, I found him all alone. His friend had brought him a milk jug for a urinal and a hamburger for food. Other than that, there was nothing. I called the ambulance right away. You know the rest."

From Zita's story, I guessed that Mark's knees had probably been infected for at least a week. Antibiotics alone wouldn't have a chance. He needed immediate surgical drainage.

Dr. Bill Ehni was a specialist in complex infectious diseases. He saw Mark next, and then talked to me. He said, "I told Mark that if everything in the joint is coated with bacteria, we won't clear the infection unless all of the implants are taken out. He told me he understood that, but he'd rather you left them in. What do you think?"

I shook my head. Raging sepsis overruled Dr. Ehni's reasons. "He's too sick to take them out now. That's at least a three-hour case. He'll never tolerate the anesthesia. He'll crash. All we can do today is wash out both knees through an arthroscope under a spinal, put drain lines in, and get out. If I can, I'll wash out his shoulder. I know that isn't the best choice, but right now it's the only one there is."

He looked at me, and in a characteristic understatement said, "You know, this is going to be a real problem."

Multiple infected joint replacements in an immunosuppressed patient are indeed an orthopaedic nightmare, but the immediate danger was even worse. For days the bacterial hoards had been releasing toxins that poisoned Mark's blood vessels until their walls began to leak. As fluid seeped out from capillaries into the tissues, his blood volume fell until there was little left to pump. His fever and his heart rate went up. His breathing became labored. His blood pressure became unstable and his kidneys started shutting down. Caught in a fight for his life, Mark was descending rapidly into a condition known as septic shock. It is one of the leading causes of death in U.S. intensive care units.

Highly trained people moved quickly to insert Mark's surgery into an already-full OR schedule. One was both a trusted colleague and close friend, Dr. Lee Barnes. On that Monday he was the anesthesiologist assigned to the open room, the operating room kept available for just such a situation.

Dr. Barnes examined Mark in the anesthesia prep area near the OR and then came out to talk with me. He had a subdued look on his face and a way of saying a lot without using many words.

"What are you planning to do here, Bill?"

"What will he tolerate?"

Lee shook his head. "Not much."

I went over the plan. Lee asked, "Is John going to help you?"

"Yes. Why?"

"I suggest doing both knees at once, if you can."

"He's that sick?"

"Yes."

The team wheeled Mark into the operating room.

Arthroscopic instruments need only two small incisions. As soon as I made them, a hundred milliliters of thick, foul-smelling liquid poured out of each knee. A half cup of pus is a horrific bacterial load. While I arthroscoped and washed the right knee, John rinsed six liters of saline under pressure through the left. Then, while I arthroscoped the left knee, he started putting large-bore suction-irrigation lines into the right.

The steady eep-eep-eep sound from the heart monitor began to speed up. Mark's heart was trying to maintain a failing blood pressure by beating faster. With a side-glance I saw Lee putting in another large IV line. Within ten minutes another full liter of fluid went in. It wasn't enough.

"Bill, you better hurry up down there. This guy is getting very unstable."

With a series of deft moves, Lee placed a tube in Mark's airway and hooked him up to a respirator. The circulating nurse called the OR control station. "We need more people down here, now." Everyone in the room heard the grim urgency in her voice. I motioned to the scrub nurse. "Millie, bandage the right knee. John, prep his shoulder and see what you can get out with a needle. I'll get the drain lines into this knee and close it. We need to get this finished."

Reinforcements joined the battle. Lee turned to them. "I need more lactated Ringers and I need a Neosynephrine drip made up. I've already done a Neo push, and he isn't responding." A few minutes later, from the other side of the surgical drapes I heard his voice get tense.

"Bill, I'm having trouble getting a blood pressure. We may be losing him."

Mark's life was being measured in minutes. Without a detectable blood pressure his lungs could no longer oxygenate his blood. The red river of life within him started to stagnate and darken. The numbers on the oxygen saturation monitor began clicking downward, its alarm warning of the danger. As cells throughout his body became starved for the oxygen that sustained them, their delicate molecular machinery began to fail. Mark's heart and brain began shutting down. The agonal phase approached. He was dying on the table.

The swarming resuscitation team fought back. Faced with a man's mortality, every person in the room struggled to suppress adrenaline-loaded anxiety and instead focused on the steps they were rigorously trained to perform. As actions became automatic a strange depersonalization took place. Voices seemed farther away. There were no thoughts, no feelings, as if we were separating ourselves from the soul of the man at the center of our efforts. It was not a trance. Focus and effort were at their absolute peak, and yet we felt serenely insulated from the fear of failure that was nonetheless ever-present. It is a state mercifully obliterated from our memory when the effort is over.

Two more liters of lactated Ringers began bolstering Mark's intravascular volume. More steroids stabilized his small-vessel leakage. The racing rate on the heart monitor steadied, then grudgingly started to improve. The numbers on the blood pressure monitor, with excruciating slowness, began to tick upward: 40/0...60/20...80/40.... It looked like he might make it. After more immeasurable minutes, both his heart rate and his blood pressure stabilized. Instead of going to the recovery room, the team took him straight to intensive care.

An intensivist, Dr. Brent Pistorese, one of the clinical warriors who care for the critically ill and whose world night and day is the intensive care unit, joined us there. He picked up where Lee left off. His consultation note summarized a still-desperate situation:

9/15/97

Problem list:

1. Severe rheumatoid arthritis, steroid dependent

2. Distant history, shoulder septic arthritis

3. *Staphylococcus* sepsis

4. Bilateral infected knee prostheses

5. Infected right shoulder

6. Severe hypotension

7. Ventilatory failure

Examination: A poorly responsive male. Blood pressure is 78 systolic on low-dose dopamine and lactated Ringer's at 500 cc/hr. Resting pulse is 124 in sinus tachycardia. His oxygen saturations are difficult to obtain. He has poor color. He can move all four limbs, but not spontaneously. He is not alert at this time.

Impression: *Staphylococcus* sepsis with multiple septic joints and septic shock requiring recent surgical drainage. Risks are for avascular tubular necrosis of his kidneys, adult respiratory distress syndrome, endocarditis and possible disseminated intravascular coagulopathy. Other possible complications of septicemia may develop, including brain abscess, liver function abnormalities, pancreatitis and multiple organ system failure.

His concise words characterized the urgent pace with which his breed worked, but the note had no story of a person in it. Completely problem-oriented, it instead mirrored the same depersonalization of the resuscitation I had just witnessed.

As I finished my own dictation, Jeff Carlin told me the family was waiting. The minute it took to walk to the waiting room was all I had to disengage from implacable problem solving and re-enter the world where people mattered most.

Zita was waiting. Both Jeff and I spoke to her about what had happened and what we were facing. It was hard to find the words that tell a mother that her son might not make it. Sometimes there can be too much information.

She sat stunned and alone, her emotions trapped between worry, wishing, and hopelessness. All the comfort I couldn't convey to Mark I now wanted to give to her. I gently put my hand on her shoulder.

She asked numbly, "What should I do?"

"Are there other family members?"

"Yes, Mark has three brothers."

"Do they live nearby?"

"No. Carl, the oldest, is in California. John lives near Chicago, and Paul is in New York."

"It probably would be a good idea to call and ask them to come." Zita's eyes questioned me. I added, "It would be best to come soon." The word "soon" answered her question.

We went with her to visit Mark. She stood at his side, speechlessly blinking away tears that were trying to form. A priest touched Mark's forehead with the oil of the last rites. Jeff helped her make the calls to the other brothers. Later I saw her sitting silently beside her son, forlornly fingering her rosary.

An ICU room is not a peaceful place. When patients are unresponsive and on a respirator, when they could go either way at any moment, a feeling of precarious fate is always present. The rhythmic hiss of the respirator, the busy monitors of morbidity and the movements of nurses checking on each change all crowd out a mother's message. Nevertheless, as she sat quietly at Mark's bedside and watched her son, Zita's message was unmistakably there.

It was not a message made of words. It was a message from the heart. Nurses in the ICU know it happens often. "The nurses let me wash his face and that was a blessing for me. I touched him. His face was warm and he was alive. I could feel his pulse and he was breathing, even though it was through a machine. My thoughts were chaotic. I kept repeating in my mind that he had a good heart and his body was strong. I told him to keep on fighting. I don't know if he could hear me, but the nurses said he could, so I kept on talking to him."

Early the next day, Carl and John joined Zita in Mark's room. Together they stayed until 4 a.m., when the nurses gently suggested that everyone go home and get some rest. By the time they returned at 6 a.m., Zita was running on grit alone.

One evening several days later, I joined John and Carl in the ICU visitor's room. Our lives were connected by a shared concern for a man down the hall who was struggling to emerge from the fog of nearly dying. As I answered their questions, I searched for the right balance between candor and hope. It was not hard to read the response in their faces. John was visibly upset.

He said, "When I saw Mark in a deep coma and inflated from the water that was being pumped into him, I couldn't believe that this was my brother." John had gone for a walk to try to unwind, but it hadn't worked. "I tried to walk outside, but I soon found myself wandering in the cemetery across from the hospital, looking at the names of people long deceased. I thought about Mark and whether he would be joining them."

Within several days, massive doses of antibiotics cleared the bacteria from Mark's bloodstream. One by one his organ systems recovered from the onslaught of the toxins. His fever improved. His heart showed no evidence of infected valves. His pulmonary function improved to the point where Dr. Pistorese weaned him from the ventilator. After several aspirations at the bedside, his shoulder quieted down. His knees, however, remained hot.

During the first surgery we had placed suction-irrigation tubes in both knees. From then on, antibiotic irrigant flowed in through tubes on one side of each knee and was suctioned out through tubes on the other side. The objective was to irrigate the joint continuously so bacteria couldn't re-accumulate. Nine days after the first surgery, the tubes finally filled with debris and clotted. They had to be replaced. I scheduled Mark's second surgery for the next day.

Even though he was improving daily, Mark was still too sick for a major operation. The most he could tolerate was to have his knees arthroscopically washed out again and new drain lines inserted. When I opened the prior incisions, faintly cloudy fluid came out of both knees. Through the arthroscope, his right patellar tendon looked abnormal.

In the urgency of his first surgery, I hadn't look at the tendon closely. This time, after washing out clots and debris, I saw portions of tendon that looked disrupted. The inflamed tissues bled easily, preventing a clear view, but an ultrasound after surgery confirmed my suspicion. It showed a large gap where the right patellar tendon should have been. The next day I had to tell Mark that the tendon was completely torn, probably from the time he tripped over the tracks.

It wasn't enough just to give Mark that piece of information. He needed to know its meaning. He was always asking, "What does that mean, Doc?" The gap meant that without repair the tendon wouldn't heal, and if it didn't heal, his knee wouldn't function. Repair couldn't be done arthroscopically; it had to be done as an open procedure—and soon if the tendon was to have any chance of healing. Regardless of what happened to his infection, a torn tendon meant he would need another operation.

Mark tolerated stressful news a lot better if he understood what was happening to him, but I could no longer keep him informed with just a few remarks. The decisions weren't simple and the solutions weren't ideal. I struggled to describe the alternatives in an evenhanded way.

The most difficult choices were about his implants. Mark's cultures from the second surgery were negative, and a white blood cell-labeled bone scan showed no evidence of deep infection around the implants. Those were very encouraging findings. Nevertheless, both the orthopaedic literature and my own experience told me that completely eradicating infection while the implants were in place was unlikely at best.

The alternative, removing all the implants in both knees, was not an easy choice either. That kind of case would be big surgery. I remembered Mark's stormy recovery after the second ankle surgery. This time, in addition to his rheumatoid disease he had debilitation after sepsis, two bilateral surgeries behind him and two weeks confined to bed. Above all, I wanted to minimize the risks of more medical complications.

Mark wanted me to keep the implants in because he knew that if they came out, he wouldn't be able to walk. He would lose his job, and with it he might lose his health insurance. He would probably lose his house. His worst fear was that he might even lose his legs. Zita described his deepening depression.

"Mark didn't want to mingle with anyone. He wanted his door shut so he couldn't hear any talking from other rooms. He would just lay in his bed, staring at the ceiling. He felt that nothing would help him return to work, or even to continue to live by himself in Seattle. How can one know the thoughts of a sick man who had a difficult time all through his life with school, his relationship with his father, and now with such severe illness and no job prospects? I think he was in complete despair and probably wished he could die."

Mark couldn't talk openly to me about his inner fears, but as I listened I began to realize that he was confronting a loss greater than his livelihood, or even his independence. He was confronting the loss of something deep inside, a part of his identity. When he was driving trains, he could be free. If he couldn't do that, he'd lose not only a feeling of freedom, but also an identity with it, as if he would no longer know what freedom was.

One day I said, "Zita, he's on medication for his depression, but I have a different idea. When we talk about trains Mark always brightens up. Does he have any pictures of trains around his house? I don't care if you put pictures of trains all over the wall. Just bring in anything you can. I think it'll do him good."

Zita brought in a large print of a painting by Howard Fogg, a train artist Mark liked. The print showed four Great Northern diesel locomotives, like the kind Mark used to run, hauling a long line of freight cars up and over a western mountain pass. We set it on a shelf across from Mark's bed, directly in his line of sight. He stared at it as we talked, as if he could somehow draw upon the strength of the enormous engines in that picture. If someone had asked me at the time if such a thing was possible, I wouldn't have even understood the question.

Within a week, re-accumulation of cloudy fluid in both of Mark's knees forced me to act. I had sorted through the available choices with him; now I told him my recommendation. I would schedule an open, complete clean-out of both knees and a repair of the right patellar tendon. If the main metal implants looked okay, I would leave them in place and just exchange the plastic inserts. If I saw any evidence at all of loosening or deep infection, however, everything would have to come out. He agreed to the plan.

I was troubled by doubts. Mark was immunosuppressed. The probability of getting away with leaving the implants in was precariously poor, and I knew it. But this plan burned no bridges. If I left the implants in and they loosened later, I could take them out when he was stronger. If I took them all out now, there'd be no going back. He could get horribly sick. Something told me he couldn't handle that right now.

There were no clean solutions to this anymore. I could only do what had the least risk. For more than two thousand years doctors have tried to practice the principle "First, do no harm." With Mark's knees, that was getting harder and harder to do. The time for solvable problems and satisfying solutions was far behind us. The choices ahead involved anxious uncertainty, dismal alternatives, and the possibility of terrible outcomes. Surgeons don't deal well with those kinds of choices.

I suppressed my doubts. On October 2, I took Mark to surgery for the third time.

Immediately after opening the right knee I found that the eroded patellar tendon was completely torn from the lower edge of the patella. Reconstructing it required suturing the tendon fragments back to the bone and then reinforcing the repair with heavy wire, which was threaded through a drill hole in the tibia, passed up over the top of the patella, and then twisted down tightly.

The synovium, rabidly inflamed from Mark's rheumatoid disease, was now doubly so after his infection. It piled over the metal and plastic in angry, purplish mounds and bled at the slightest touch. Samples of it sent for immediate microscopic examination showed no invasion by staph, but to preclude any possibility of leaving bacteria behind I performed a complete synovectomy, meticulously removing every bit of synovium from each fold and recess of the joint.

After the tendon repair and synovectomy, popping the polyethylene tray off the tibial insert began the critical process of determining if the metal implants were loose or the bone infected. Using magnifying loupes, I saw no bone erosion along any metal edge. Levering on the implants with an instrument produced no micromotion between them and the bone, and compressing them expressed no fluid. Based on all of the findings and the negative bone scan, I decided to leave the implants in. After thorough irrigation I snapped a new polyethylene tray into place and inserted its locking pin. During the wound closure we inserted new suction-irrigation tubes. A hinged brace over the dressing protected the tendon repair.

When I opened the left knee, its implants looked the same. Except for the tendon repair, I carried out a similar procedure on that side. Even without removal of the metal implants, the operation took two and a half hours on the right and two hours on the left.

Mark's immediate post-operative course was precarious. He needed to be in the ICU for a day and a half, but he escaped major complications. His fever eventually subsided. His white blood count returned to normal. His incisions healed normally. Within a week, he began to walk. As he found he could walk without pain, his pall of depression began to lift. A small smile crept into his voice and a little bit of light came back into his eyes.

After three bilateral operations and three weeks in the hospital, much of it in the ICU, Mark was transferred to the transitional care unit in mid-October for physical therapy. By early November he was transferred to rehab to see if he could regain independent function. As his walking distance steadily improved, he became encouraged. It looked like the gamble had paid off.

Despite his surgical progress, however, resentment and hurt clouded Mark's hopes. During his six-week purgatory of disaster, depression, and pain, his father never once came the hundred and forty miles from Wenatchee to visit him.

A Deeper Connection

Doctors usually make hospital rounds on their patients in the morning, but I started my workday with medical staff committee meetings. I could never get up early enough to make rounds before a 7:30 meeting, so I made my rounds at night. After the scheduled part of my day, I came from the office or the OR to the orthopaedic floor and started in.

Rounds consisted of reviewing the day's x-rays or test results, examining each patient briefly, talking with them or the nurses about the plan for the next day, and then writing a progress note. I usually had four or five inpatients. If I had no additional consultations to see, I usually made it home by 7:30 p.m.

Making rounds in the evening meant I didn't have to rush in order to get to surgery or the office on time. I liked the option of spending extra time with patients who had a difficult problem. In September 1997 Mark's problems were so complex that simply explaining them took extra time.

Eventually I saw him last. That way I didn't have anything else waiting for me, and I could spend as much time with him as he needed. He was a man anxious about each day's symptoms, depressed by more bad news, and nearly broken by a total-body battering. The extra time allowed him to begin describing to me the choices he confronted, the conflicts they caused, and the complexity of his coping.

By mid-October, as Mark stabilized, my rounds with him began to change. Our conversations drifted from my descriptions of his orthopaedic progress to his descriptions about what mattered to him. They became very unusual conversations. It was odd that they took place at all. I was a man drained after a day's work who looked forward to finishing up, going home to dinner, and relaxing in a recliner. Instead, I began to look forward to seeing him. As we gradually opened to one another, a different and deeper connection began to bridge our worlds. As I did less talking and more listening, I started to focus less on a patient with a problem, and to see instead a remarkable human being.

During a doctor's visit, most patients talk about their symptoms. Mark had an amazing ability to live outside of his. He often spoke as if his physical sufferings were oddly irrelevant. This was a man who had nearly died, had been fighting for his life for three weeks, had already undergone three bilateral surgeries, had twelve active medical problems, was medicated, debilitated, depressed and immobilized, and yet who often talked to me as if we were chatting over a beer in a bar. It was an extraordinary experience.

His brother John described this quality: "Mark and I talked often on the phone. He had a remarkable attitude. He seemed very down at times, but he didn't complain. I was angry at his condition. He seemed to accept the cross he was made to bear. Amazingly, he could joke about his experiences at Northwest Hospital. He told me a lot about the Russian cemetery across from the hospital. He knew it well. He had once walked in there. It was amazing what my brother knew."

In twenty years of practice, I had seen this ability to live outside life's burdens only a few times. It was not just deflection. When Mark spoke this way there was a transcendent quality to him. His eyes and voice acquired an animation that invigorated these conversations. Sometimes he would be animated with humor, sometimes with excitement or even apprehension, but when he was like this he was clearly focused on a world beyond the day's details.

He never described having a near-death experience to me. He had no bright awakening the September day he nearly died. Nevertheless, that passage held deep if undefined meaning for him, a meaning he didn't want to let slip away. I think it was this quality of a deeper meaning that kept me sitting in his room long beyond the time when I should have gone home.

He would struggle to describe what mattered most, and then suddenly switch to what seemed like mundane topics. It was as if he was trying to tell me something about himself that was terribly important, but couldn't find the right words, so instead he told me about his life on the railroads, or about Mozart. As the weeks wore on I began to appreciate that this was not just tangential thinking; in fact, he wasn't switching subjects at all. Even though they seemed to be different on the surface, at a deeper level all of the subjects were interwoven. Gradually I realized that he was actually continuing, through different metaphors, an intricate description of his inner life.

Mark had loved railroads all his life.

"Doc, did you ever see a steam locomotive go by?"

I smiled. "Yeah, I have. When I was about four, we'd take my dad down to the train station. To this day I can see the engine next to the platform—a big black locomotive as huge as a house, hissing steam and impatient to leave. Dad let us put a penny on the tracks. Then the whistle would blow my ears off and he'd get on board. A minute later the main drive wheels began to turn. They were bigger than I was. The car couplings clanked tight, and then the whole monstrosity started to move. Sometimes I could see my dad waving goodbye from a window. Afterward, we'd go find the penny. It was mashed as thin as a piece of paper. I'd never seen anything that powerful in my life."

Mark leaned forward with a wry half-smile and looked at me closely, as if we shared a private world. A warm light in his hazel-brown eyes belied the intensity of the intelligence behind them. He knew he was talking to a kindred spirit.

"Same here. On Friday evenings around dusk my dad would walk with us down to Windsor Avenue. There was a mainline track of the Chicago, Burlington and Quincy there, and we'd watch for the freight train from the Cicero yards. You could hear the steam locomotive coming through a viaduct in the distance, picking up speed until at last it thundered right past us. Then we'd go get ice cream."

"Where did you live then?"

"We lived in Berwyn, near Chicago. That's where I grew up. Trains were a part of everyday life. We took the El everywhere. I loved it. I used to fight to get into the front seat. Every afternoon at 3:15, rain or shine, I'd bolt out the door of our house to watch the Empire Builder go by."

I dimly remembered that name. "That was a special passenger train, wasn't it?"

"Yeah. It was Great Northern's best train from Chicago to Seattle. They named it after James J. Hill, the big railroad tycoon who put together the Great Northern Railroad. His nickname was "the empire builder." The Great Northern became the Burlington Northern and then the Burlington Northern Santa Fe, but through all the mergers they kept the name, "The Empire Builder." It has Amtrak diesels now, but early on, it was pulled by 2-8-4 steam locomotives. You know what a 2-8-4 is, Doc?"

Tentatively I replied, "I think so." My oldest brother once had a model railroad with Lionel locomotives. I dredged up what little I remembered about their wheel designations. The first number described the little wheels in front, the middle was the number of main driving wheels, and the last number designated the small wheels under the cab. "I remember reading about 4-6-4 Hudsons and then Mikados and Mallets."

"Yeah. Those were 2-8-2's and 2-6-6-2's. They were big. Not as big as some, though. The biggest were the Union Pacific's mountain freight haulers. They called 'em "Big Boys"—4-8-8-4's—and the engine alone weighed almost four hundred tons. They could pull fourteen-thousand-ton coal trains.

"They were too expensive to maintain, though. When the Big Boys were running wide open they ate up twenty tons of coal an hour. That's what did them in. They were powerful as hell, but they were no match for a diesel's efficiency. Most steam engines got replaced by the mid-fifties. Now just a few relics keep running—for memory's sake."

I wondered if my explanations to him about orthopaedic procedures sounded as arcane as his explanations about locomotives did to me.

He went on, excitement building in his voice. "Every summer, when I was a kid, I went on the Empire Builder out to Wenatchee to visit my aunt. By then it was a diesel streamliner with a dome car. My brother Johnny and I sat up in the dome car and watched the prairie roll by. We loved the clickity-clack of the wheels on the tracks. We never slept. Even at night we'd keep peering out at lights in the distance, wondering who lived out there and what their lives were like. The trip took forty-five hours. Back then, that was fast."

I was amazed. I knew trains as leftover Lionels. Mark knew trains because he lived them.

"I loved the steam locomotives, though. There was just something about them. A lot of people feel that way. When I was just a boy, my friend Karl and I would go down to the freight yards on Ogden Avenue to watch the steam engines come into the roundhouse. I couldn't get enough of the place. We'd watch the yardmen move rail cars around and the men would talk to us and I'd ask them questions. I couldn't talk about it much at home, though. My dad never listened."

Mark talked as much about his boyhood dreams as he did about his job as an engineer. Gradually I realized that they were one and the same.

"Mark, did you ever dream of just running off and riding the rails?"

"Dream about it? Hey, we did it! In college I started working summers at the Clyde freight yard. It was heavy, dirty work, but I loved it. I saw how to get into freight cars and talked to guys who rode the rails. Between my junior and senior year in college, Johnny and I decided to do it. We hopped a freight and rode out to Wenatchee in the boxcars, dodging the railroad police. Do you know how cold it gets in those things, Doc? My parents had a real fit. It scared the hell out of my mother. It was worth it, though. It was fun and freedom, all rolled into one. We loved every minute of it." Mark told the story as if he was Huck Finn heading out to the frontier. His eyes danced when he talked about freedom and adventure. His words gave a hint of something important hidden inside him.

"Is that when you decided to become an engineer?"

"Nah. That took me a while. After college I got drafted. That was 1969. When I got out I got a job doing social work in Chicago, but after a few years I hated it. I felt trapped in the system. You know how it just closes in around you, Doc? One day I just quit. I couldn't stand it anymore. I came home, told my parents I wanted to run trains, and that was it. That's what I'd always wanted to do. I never looked back."

I thought about all of the people who stayed trapped in empty jobs. His move wasn't just a job change. It was an epiphany.

"I started at the Santa Fe yards on the south side of Chicago, but eventually I wanted more than just yard work, so I went to engineer training school in Kansas City in 1975. I did pretty well, too. I had the second highest score in the country on the final exam. I've been running trains ever since."

"How did you wind up out here?"

"After my dad retired my folks moved out to Wenatchee to be near my aunt. I got tired of Chicago. I'd broken off with a girl and was kind of drifting. I kicked around for a while on short lines near Denver, but I didn't like it there, so I came on out to Wenatchee. After a while my mom helped me get a job with the Burlington Northern."

"Did you ever think of settling down?"

Mark paused for a minute. A flicker of sadness slowed his story. "No.... I dated a girl for a while in Seattle and we were.... Well, it didn't work out. I just wanted to keep traveling." I heard the pause. There was sadness in it, a loss he couldn't talk about.

"What kind of trains did you drive?"

"I loved handling big freight haulers. My favorite lead was a GM SD-45 diesel. I'd need three or four helper units behind it to get up the grades. Most of my routes were here in Washington. I drove a passenger train a few times as a relief engineer, but it wasn't regular. If I went down to Oregon or up to Canada, my hours would get really crazy. After my legs started giving me trouble I couldn't handle freight haulers anymore. Since '85 I've been working in the switching yards down at Interbay, making up trains. It isn't as much fun, but the hours are regular and it keeps me doin' what I love."

"What's it like?"

"Running trains?"

"Yeah. I mean...really barreling along with all that machinery under you."

"Highballing? It's easy, Doc...if you know how to think five miles ahead."

That was Mark. For him trains were more than a fascination, or even an obsession. They were instead an expression of something inside him.

There was more to Mark's life than trains, though. As our conversations went on he showed a depth and breadth of interests that belied his image of being just a diesel jockey.

His mother was a violin teacher. His father filled their house with concert music from records or the radio. As a boy he had studied violin; as an adult he loved concerts and operas. Unable to escape from his hospital room, Mark would put on a Mozart CD and escape instead into the musical beauty of eighteenth-century Vienna. When I came by on rounds I'd often find him with his headphones on and his eyes closed, smiling to himself. He would look up, put his finger to his lips, and gesture me into a chair. My rounds would have to wait a bit, until he paused the magic of the music inside him.

We also shared a fascination with the Civil War and ancient Rome. He could talk equally easily about Lee's Army of Northern Virginia or Caesar's legionnaires. He enjoyed astronomy and could discuss quantum physics and the concept of time. After his brush with death, he said he wanted to explore what time was really about. He liked Stephen Hawking's *A Brief History of Time*, and identified with how Hawking, physically crippled by his disease, could still explore the cosmos with his mind. And if Mark started in on politics, I'd never make it home for dinner.

In early November the carefree conversations came to an end. Mark began having small but worrisome spikes on his temperature curve. His legs ached more, he walked less in PT, and his knees reaccumulated fluid. On November 12, I ordered a bone scan. The report confirmed the worst possibility: bilateral osteomyelitis. That evening I had to talk to Mark about it.

"What does osteomyelitis mean, Doc?"

"It means that despite being on maximum IV antibiotics for the last six weeks, you've still got active infection under the metal implants and it is starting to invade the bones in both of your knees."

"What does that mean?" Anxiety crept into his voice.

"It means we have to take all the implants out. This time there's no choice."

"But what does that really mean?" The anxiety turned to fear.

"It means we're going to do our damndest to try and save your legs." The edge in my voice hit him in the gut.

"What do you have to do?"

I explained the necessary procedure, but by then Mark wasn't listening. After I finished he looked straight at me for a frozen moment. When he finally spoke, his voice had a smoldering sound in it.

"I'll tell you what it really means, Doc…" He was looking five miles down the tracks and saw what was coming. "It means…I'll never drive trains again!"

The four walls of his hospital room started closing in around him, as if the room itself could crush him out of existence. For the last month he had been able to endure incredible physical suffering and still find a smile. Now a pitiless disease was closing in, threatening to snuff out of him a life he loved. In his eyes there was a silent scream of claustrophobia. He stayed still for another moment, and then exploded in desperation, "I've got to get out of here!"

The words were agonal. I was watching him die again, but this was dying of a different kind. This time his disease was ripping out part of his soul, and there was nothing I could do that would ever make it whole again. A dream that had given him life was disintegrating in front of me, and I had no solution that would save it. For the first time in our relationship, the path of solving problems, the path I had used so successfully for so many years, was not enough to help his suffering. I could only nod my head, sit silently next to him, and hold his hand while he cried.

He needed time, and I needed time. He needed time to improve his strength and lessen his risks for surgical complications. He also needed time to cope with a life change that was drowning him. He could grasp what was happening, but it was all happening too quickly, sweeping him along like a man caught in a raging river. He was struggling desperately to regain control, to find something he could hang onto before he was swept under. He was already on antidepressants. I offered to add crisis therapy. He wanted none of that. The desire that boiled into his voice was to run. "I need to get out of here!" Escape was the only coping tool he knew.

He had been running all of his life. He was desperate now, not only because he couldn't drive trains, but also because he couldn't run. One by one, the means he had used to flee from his suffering were being stripped from him. He couldn't work, he couldn't walk, and now he faced the loss of the legs that had always let him leave. He was caught in the cross-hairs of a condition he could no longer escape.

He had nowhere to go. He could barely do basic activities of daily living. He couldn't stay in his own house. It was a cottage that couldn't accommodate a wheelchair, much less the care he needed. He hated staying with his parents.

Unable to avoid the loss of his implants he could only lie alone, curled up in his bed, and attempt to cope with the scraps that were left of his life. Like an injured bird unable to fly and flopping around on the ground, he was terrified and helpless. All he could do was pull the sheet over his head and try to hide.

The only nurturer he had ever known sat for days at his bedside. To Zita, he screamed his despair: "I'm a man in my fifties, and I have to be dependent like a little kid!" He was aghast at the image of losing his legs. "What will become of me then? I'll wind up in some God-forsaken nursing home for the rest of my life!"

Zita tried to reassure him that she would always be there for him, no matter what, that they had pulled together through all of his previous crises, and that no one was going to desert him now. She told me, "This was probably the lowest point in his life."

Mark agreed that he needed time to get stronger and to sort things out. I suggested that we book his surgery in the first week of December. As he nodded his silent consent, his eyes became pools of empty loneliness.

While Mark faced his nemesis, I faced mine. I needed time to plan a procedure that would eliminate persistent *Staphylococcus aureus* osteomyelitis in both of his knees. The bacteria had burrowed into the bones. Three surgical clean-outs and six weeks of potent IV antibiotics hadn't budged them. Immobility had weakened Mark's bones. Immunosuppression had weakened his white cells. Now the invader was entrenched. This operation would be our last chance to kill it.

If removing the old implants failed to end the infection I would never be able to put in new ones, and without implants Mark knew he would never walk again. Even worse, if this procedure failed and the infected bones kept seeding his bloodstream with staph, Mark knew that either I would have to amputate both of his legs above the knee or he would eventually die the septic death he had so narrowly escaped in September.

I hated the thought of amputation. I saw the surgery in my mind, a vision of quickly severing muscles and nerves, clamping arteries, cauterizing veins and sawing across the mid-shaft of both femurs until the bones snapped in two. It was a mutilating procedure that would leave Mark forever staring at stumps and me with the memory of dropping two bloody legs into a black plastic bag. I needed time to plan a surgery that would prevent the horror of that vision from ever happening.

Over the years principles for salvaging infected implants had evolved, but no one had definitive answers. Neither the orthopaedic literature that I searched nor other surgeons whom I asked had sure-fire solutions for saving bilateral staph-infected knees in immunosuppressed patients. I would have to think my own way through this.

When I removed the infected components there would be a one-inch gap where the joint used to be. The first problem was to find something to fill the gap; otherwise, the leg would be floppy. The cement that orthopaedists use to attach joint implants to bone is called polymethylmethacrylate. Making a spacer out of it in the OR to fill the gap would solve the first problem.

Inert cement spacers can't fight the multiple defenses of *Staph aureus* any better than inert metal implants can. The second problem was to make the spacers into weapons that could. Normally, we add a liquid monomer to methacrylate powder to begin a polymerization reaction that creates the solid cement. If, before adding the liquid, I added a broad-spectrum antibiotic to the powder, the resulting spacer would give off, by a process called elution, a very high local level of antibiotic for many months, killing any living bacteria and preventing dormant forms from reactivating. Tobramycin was the best antibiotic we had that would mix with the methacrylate.

The third problem was that a spacer made as a single block of cement prevented knee motion. The spacers would have to stay in place until all traces of infection were gone. With Mark's weak white cells, that might mean months. Ligaments immobilized that long tend to tighten down. If both knees became stuck out straight, even with new implants Mark might not recover much motion, and if that happened he wouldn't regain much function. With two stiff knees, it would be hard for him to use stairs, get out of a car, or even get off the toilet.

To preserve some chance of future function I had to find something better than one solid spacer. I learned that a leading implant manufacturer had just started making hollow plastic molds that matched Mark's implants. I could pour liquid cement into the molds, allow the cement to harden, cut away the mold and thereby reproduce, in antibiotic-impregnated methacrylate, the complex shapes of his metal implants. The sales rep told me he could have the molds shipped whenever I needed them. Over the next week I assembled a plan that was going to work. It had to work. There would be no rehearsal, and no second chance.

On December 5 Mark went from the rehab floor back to surgery.

First in one knee and then the other, we extracted all of the implants and chipped out all of the old cement. All foreign material had to be removed, even the reinforcing wire from the right patellar tendon. The infected bone I searched for in October was now plainly apparent. Dead bone or infected film had to be meticulously curetted out of every cyst and recess. A pressure irrigator drove antibiotic solution deep into the ivory latticework. Then John and I, working in tandem, added 1.2 grams of powdered Tobramycin into each of four batches of powdered methacrylate, mixed them with the monomer and poured the lethal liquid into the femoral and tibial molds. In fifteen minutes, the polymerization reaction was over. The antibiotic spacers were ready.

Unlike the mirror-polished steel of the implants I removed, the cement spacers, held to the softened bone only by the constraining ligaments around them, looked rough and temporary. Nevertheless, as they disappeared under the soft tissue closure, they promised stability, mobility, and a local level of antibiotic that I hoped was deadly enough to do its job. The operation in both knees took the two of us four and a half hours.

Mark's immediate post-op course was debilitating for days. His blood pressure was unstable enough to require the ICU. His anemia plus his blood loss required three more units of blood, but once again he slowly climbed out of the well of weakness. Within a week he could transfer from his bed into a reclining wheelchair. After ten days he went back to the rehab section.

There he remained depressed and alone, unable to interact with other patients. He cared about them, sometimes expressing compassion for their situations, but he couldn't communicate with them. A simple conversation in the dining room became an ordeal. When we talked, his conversations seemed far away, as if I were talking with a different person than the one who had told me fascinating train stories. Even after so many surgeries, Mark's only pressing question was "When do you think you can put in the new knees?" The timing determined how long he would be incapacitated. His incapacitation determined how long he would have to live with his parents.

He wanted desperately to keep his own house in Seattle. It was a refuge whose walls kept the world away and a shelter that gave him the solitude he craved. He knew that if he lost his job and went on disability he would lose both his house and his last vestige of independence. One day two officials from the railroad came to his hospital room with disability forms for him to fill out.

Even though Mark kept pressing me about the timing of his new implants, this time I had no reassuring estimate for him. I couldn't give him a clear picture of what would happen next, because I didn't have one. This case had gotten so complex that I couldn't guess how long his knees would take to heal, or even if they would ever heal at all. A predictable outcome was a consoling comfort that I could no longer give, either to Mark or to myself.

My uncertainty amplified Mark's depression. I guessed that his deepening despair was due to his loss of mobility and independence. No adult wants to return to his parents' house and the dependency of childhood. I guessed wrong. I had no idea how wounded Mark's childhood had been. There was no room for him in the house in Wenatchee physically or psychologically. He had no privacy or personal space there; instead, he always seemed to encroach on the recriminations of his father. Despite our long talks, this was a demon he could not discuss with me. Zita described the person that shadowed Mark's life:

"You never met Steve. He was the same way. When he was sick, he wanted to be left alone. He could wall himself off completely. When Mark was first admitted, a friend offered to drive Steve to Seattle right away. He refused to come. You would have had to know Steve, I guess, to understand that. He was concerned about his sons, but he was often so distant. He didn't know how to be a father."

In late November, when Steve finally visited, he was shocked to see his son so depressed and debilitated. After their visit, Steve and Zita went to Mark's house. There, Steve was even more shocked to see how his son had lived his life.

The house was a decrepit cottage. Overgrown grass, peeling paint, and weeds growing in driveway cracks testified more to chronic indifference than medical disability. The living room table was piled high with work schedules, newspapers, and old railroad magazines. Books were half-read and CD's unopened. The carpet looked as if it had never been vacuumed. The refrigerator held only a few basics and some moldy leftovers. Mark rarely ate there. He had only one set of usually-dirty sheets and often just slept on the couch. It wasn't a home; it was a mirror of the chaos of his chronic depression. The railroad had been the organizing element in his life. Now that was gone, and this was all that remained.

Steve sat in Mark's chair in the dingy living room. Zita noticed him crying quietly. "I asked him to tell me what was wrong. He said, 'I'm thinking of the lonely life Mark led.' There really was nothing for me to say."

On December 15 Mark was discharged from Northwest Hospital and transferred by ambulance to Central Washington Hospital in Wenatchee. He had been at Northwest for three months. It would be two more months before he would be discharged from the Wenatchee hospital to his parents' house. He never returned to live in Seattle. In January Zita put his house up for sale.

One Solution

The latest literature suggested that two months of IV antibiotics, together with the Tobramycin that seeped from the spacers, should kill off any remaining staphylococcus. Proving that it did so was another matter.

In January 1998 Mark's debilitation, winter weather and a risky drive across the mountains made follow-up in Seattle too difficult for him, so I asked Dr. Richard Tucker, an Infectious Disease specialist in Wenatchee, to help assess Mark's response to treatment. On January 20 I consulted with Dr. Tucker by phone. His findings six weeks after surgery were encouraging. There was no pain, swelling or warmth in either of Mark's knees. Conventional lab tests showed no evidence of infection.

His rheumatoid disease, however, was worse. He required Prednisone and Plaquinil to control the pain in his shoulders and wrists. Because these drugs suppressed inflammation, they made it harder to detect any infection in his knees. Dr. Tucker agreed that a special bone scan, using radioactively tagged white blood cells, might help define the situation. The scan subsequently showed only mild abnormalities, felt to be post-op changes rather than a focus of infection. The findings were evidence in the right direction, but not proof.

In mid-February we stopped Mark's IV antibiotics. His only defense now was a dwindling level of local Tobramycin. Dr. Tucker would watch him closely for two months. If there were no evidence of infection after two months without antibiotics, then it would be reasonable to consider new knee implants. If infection did reappear, that meant the antibiotics had only suppressed the infection, not eradicated it. Under those conditions, new implants would be out of the question. Mark would have to keep the spacers, continue the antibiotics, and resign himself to a wheelchair existence indefinitely.

Week after week, Mark's knees remained quiet. The plan appeared to be working.

If he was making progress against one problem, however, other problems kept beating him down. Mark's rheumatoid disease continued to worsen. His doctors had to push his doses of Cyclosporine, Methotrexate and Plaquinil to the maximum to control flare-ups of pain in his shoulders and wrists. These were last-resort medicines. Beyond them, there were no other medical means to control his disease.

His insurance company added to his problems. After his IV antibiotic treatments were over, the company would no longer pay for the rehab facility. "The patient will have to go to a skilled nursing facility." Depressed by the very thought, Mark increased his physical therapy, even though propelling his wheelchair worsened his wrist pain. By late February he could function well enough to go instead to his parents' house.

His osteoporosis was becoming severe. Disease, disuse and steroids were relentlessly weakening his bones. Joint surfaces that would have to support new implants were reaching a density less than Styrofoam. If he could resume some activity it would help his bones, help his depression, and give the antibiotic in the spacers more time. He was enthusiastic about a nearby swimming program. Linda faxed the PT orders over to Wenatchee.

His depression was a continuous problem. Since September, a man who once prided himself on being independent and in control had been shuffled from doctor to doctor, hospital to hospital, and city to city. Like a chess pawn passively being moved from square to square, he had a sense of the game going forward but no sense of belonging anywhere. He lost his job and with it his identity, his freedom and his dream. He lost his house and with it his sense of place in the world. His possessions were stored away and with them went the comfort of his personal space. Worst of all was his growing awareness that his body was at the whim of a disease that was slowly but implacably worsening. On the horizon of his life Mark saw only drift, discouragement, and emptiness.

His family tried to provide the sheltering stability that was otherwise missing from his days. Carl and John came to have Christmas dinner with him in his hospital room. Paul and Diana brought their new baby from New York in January. Zita brought constant comfort and support; more than once I doubted that Mark would have made it without her.

The caring concern of people reaching out to help him began to breach his isolating walls. His brothers came from across the continent to visit him. Nurses came from Central Hospital to show Zita how to care for him. A therapist came to exercise his joints and take him swimming. One friend loaned her pickup so Mark could take his wheelchair with him to his doctors' appointments. Another kept him supplied with books. A third brought over visitors who talked trains. A Japanese friend took him to see a large model train layout. The little locomotives chugging around the miniature track let Mark dream again. Later he told me that some day…some day…he was going to build a model train layout of his own. All around him, people were drawn to his determination not to let his dream die.

With that same determination, Mark began to walk again. Each day he struggled past his pain and depression just to put one foot in front of the other. I told him I wasn't sure temporary spacers would tolerate full weight bearing. He tried it anyway. I wasn't sure his psyche could overcome such battering. Again, he proved me wrong. He was surrounded by caring support, but he was fueled by an inner grit—a resiliency that never left him. Again and again, his disease beat him down. We would see him lying there, the life nearly crushed out of him, looking for a time as if he were defeated. Then, slowly, he'd get up. He might be angry, afraid, helpless or depressed, but he got up. And after he got up, he'd smile, as if to say, "Well, what are we waiting for?" Everyone around him would pause and blink, as if Lazarus had just shown up, and say, "Well, yeah…what *are* we waiting for?" And with that he would start going again. Whatever power the locomotives symbolized was still in him. He was no longer just an orthopaedic patient suffering through complex surgeries. He was a person with incredible endurance who taught others about it by his example.

Zita told me, "Mark had an amazing resilience, something he had developed as a child out of sheer necessity. It was always a part of him from the beginning to the end. He accepted the fact that he wouldn't work anymore, but he believed he'd keep his legs. He began to dream again. He wanted to visit his brothers and friends and eventually go to Hawaii."

In mid-April, the two months of observation without antibiotics were up. The cement spacers had functioned far longer than intended. Soon time would deplete their Tobramycin. The methacrylate, never designed to carry the load of full weight bearing, would eventually crack and break apart. I had to face the decision of whether or not to put in new implants.

Dr. Tucker reported that the rheumatoid flare-ups were finally under control. Mark was swimming regularly. His temperature was normal. His knees were comfortable with full weight bearing and showed no reaccumulation of fluid. Cultures taken two months after stopping the antibiotics showed no growth. An MRI was negative for further bone erosion. Dr. Tucker cautiously endorsed surgery. I hadn't seen Mark for five months. It was time for a face-to-face meeting.

On May 13 Zita brought him over from Wenatchee. I scheduled this visit as the last appointment of the day to give us as much time as we needed to cover a complex and risky operation. When I walked into the exam room and Mark beamed, I realized how much I had missed seeing him. Even with his knee spacers and his shoulder pain, he struggled to get up from his wheelchair to greet me. I walked over and bent down to give him a hug. I meant it when I said, "It's good to see you again."

He looked well, seemed upbeat, and had even gained a bit of weight. "I feel great," he said. "It's my mom's cooking. I don't have to rely on the stuff I used to fix for myself." The patellar tendon repair functioned well. He was able to do basic transfers in and out of his wheelchair. Films of both knees showed healthy new bone forming around the spacers. After I finished my examination, he faced me expectantly.

I began by summarizing the findings so far. For five months he had done better than we had any right to expect. We had ruled out as much as we could. No test could determine for certain that the bacteria were completely gone. We would have to take the next step without any guarantees. It was an all-or-nothing gamble. There were no other options. When I finished he just nodded and said, "Go on."

"Mark, I think it's important to go over what reimplantation surgery is going to involve for you." There were so many aspects to it that I got out a felt-tipped pen and began writing my points on the exam table paper to give him something he could tear off and take home with him in case anything was unclear.

His first joint replacements had left Mark with high expectations. As gently as I could, I had to lower them. Compared to primary knee replacements, surgical complications were more common during revisions, and functional outcomes were not nearly as good. Sitting in a wheelchair for five months had sapped his strength and impaired his balance. Using a walker after surgery would be difficult because of his shoulder and wrist pain. He could see in the mirror what prolonged Prednisone had done to his muscles and skin. He couldn't see how it weakened his bones. With tissues as tired as his, a lot could go wrong. It was hard for me to reassure him about how much function he might have afterward, because I wasn't certain if he would regain any at all.

Unlike Mark's primary replacements, his revisions would be so complex that I couldn't do them simultaneously. This time he faced two large operations and two separate convalescences. He would finally get going after the first operation and then have to come back and start all over. Two operations doubled the risk of medical complications and the duration of his convalescence. Finally, both of the revisions had to work. If one was successful but the other became infected he would have gone through everything for nothing.

Mark knew that we were about to take a committed step, and that once we did so there would be no turning back. I asked him if he had any questions or if he needed more time to make a decision. He paused for a moment, shook his head and simply said, "No…go ahead and set it up." We scheduled the right knee in June to allow him time to donate his own blood, and then the left knee six weeks later.

Sometimes not knowing about surgical risks feels safer to patients. They can't fear what they don't know. For Mark, there was no such place to hide. He couldn't close his eyes to the events of the last nine months. He not only knew about possible complications; by now he had lived through many of them. He didn't have to have this surgery; he wasn't septic like he was before. He would take the gamble because he wanted to walk again. Despite all that he had endured, he chose to go forward. As I listened to his answer, I was not at all sure that I would have had the courage to make the same decision.

On Friday afternoon, June 12, I spent my lunch hour in the office with the implant manufacturer's technical rep. Mark's surgery was scheduled for the following Monday. The rep needed to know what to have available. Spread out over our long conference table were four large cases filled with custom components and revision instruments. Using clear plastic templates placed over the x-ray films, we planned every size of every part that might be needed.

That evening, after seeing patients and finishing dictation, I went back to my private office and studied Mark's films on the light box above my desk. Step by step, I thought through a procedure that promised to be far more complex than Mark's first surgeries.

A primary knee replacement is like building a conventional house on a solid foundation. Standard parts fit neatly together; positioning them is a practiced procedure and the foundation is strong, fresh bone. By comparison, a revision replacement is like building a complicated house on an eroded foundation after tearing down the building that used to be there. After erosive infection, multiple surgeries, and five months with only the spacers in place, the joint architecture of both knees was severely distorted. Custom components would have to be assembled piece by piece; positioning them would be by trial and error, and their foundation would be weakened, osteoporotic bone that could fracture at any moment. Small metal wedges called augments would have to be individually positioned to make up for bone that was missing. Because each knee had a different deformity, each required a different set of implants. I couldn't tell if the right patellar tendon had fully healed. Because neither ligaments nor tendons show on x-rays, there was also no way to know pre-operatively whether Mark's ligaments would stabilize custom assemblies without being too tight, too loose, or even tearing apart.

Mark's two reimplantations would be one-of-a-kind cases at the outer limit of orthopaedic technology. Planning them was a side of surgery that others seldom saw. *Staph aureus* had stealthy defenses. Against them I would use surgical skill and experience, but the battle would begin with pre-operative planning. Analytical problem solving was my first weapon in a war I didn't want to lose.

Monday afternoon, as we scrubbed in together, I described my plan to John Gullage. He had been with the clinic for eight years, assisted all five partners all week long, and had seen many different ways to solve surgical dilemmas. I valued his input. He listened thoughtfully, directed my thinking with a few short questions, and then we finished scrubbing and entered the operating room.

This time I needed no skin marker to make a line on Mark's right knee. The thickened scar of multiple prior procedures was line enough. Tough tissue parted grudgingly behind the knife, leaving only a gap of white. Such a diminished blood supply meant wound healing would be unpredictable.

Matted scar left no natural tissue planes to guide my way into the joint. The prior tear of the patellar tendon, obscured by adhesions, looked healed when I flexed the knee. I fashioned a flap to reinforce it when we closed.

At long last the inside of the joint looked clean. There was no angry synovium and only a few drops of clear fluid. The tibial and femoral spacers popped out easily, worn veterans that had done their job. Bone beneath them looked healthy and hard.

Positioning the trial implants was tedious. The tibial side only needed a simple stem extension, but the femoral side was badly distorted. Working through custom cutting guides, the oscillating saw reshaped each condyle a millimeter at a time to reestablish correct rotational and front-to-back orientation for the femoral implant. Next, we began fitting into place each component of the trial implants. The parts not only had to fit, they had to work together smoothly. Every time I added a thicker augmentation wedge, I had to reassemble all of the other components to test the tightness of the ligaments in flexion and extension. In a primary case, positioning the components takes fifteen minutes. This time it took an hour to test multiple trials until they fit perfectly.

Removal of the old plastic button under the patella had left only a thin wafer of residual bone. Putting in a new button would risk fracturing the wafer when the knee bent. Thick, clean gristle covered the site. It was a reasonable substitute for cartilage. I chose to leave the patella alone.

While John assembled the final components, I pressure irrigated the bone ends with two liters of antibiotic solution. All of the evidence indicated that the

Tobramycin had been effective. I mixed two grams of it into each batch of methacrylate to finish the job. After the final implants were firmly cemented, the knee had good stability and seventy degrees of motion. John looked across at me and nodded. Every move had gone according to plan. Layer by layer, we began to close the wound.

Mark's post-operative recovery was remarkably smooth. He didn't need the ICU. He had no post-operative medical complications. I'd make rounds, look at his knee, and as if he could grab me with his words he'd say, "Hey look, Doc! Look what I can do with it. Watch this." He'd move his knee a bit, watch me closely and then with half a laugh ask, "What do you think, Doc? Think it's gonna work?"

I thought that if grit alone could do it, the answer would be "You're damn right it'll work."

After a brief stay at rehab, in early July Mark went back to Wenatchee. His surgical swelling continued to subside. Within two weeks he had no effusion, no fever, and very little pain. On July 20 he underwent another three-hour anesthesia for a similar revision on his left knee. When he woke up, he began the last lap of his long struggle to keep his legs.

Again, he had no complications. All of the intra-operative cultures came out negative. The joints were clean. The staph was gone. By August 1 he had gained eighty degrees of flexion, had good quadriceps control, and could walk fifty feet with a walker. A week later he was up to five hundred feet before he had to rest, bearing full weight on both legs. Best of all, even after walking he had no pain in either knee. The Tylenol he asked for was usually for his hands and shoulders.

On August 7 he transferred from Northwest Hospital to the rehab service in Wenatchee. His question about whether the surgeries would work stayed with me. Eight weeks after his second operation he chugged into my exam room with his walker, grinning broadly, and said, "Doc, I think it worked!"

I asked him how far he could walk. Most patients at this point would be pleased with a hundred yards. His enthusiasm beamed across the room in reply.

"Oh, if I use my walker and take my time, maybe a quarter mile."

I looked at him and blinked. "Um…what do your knees feel like after that?"

"No pain at all in either knee! The right knee starts to feel a little wobbly when my muscles get tired and it may swell a little if I walk a lot, but the only things that really bother me are my hands and shoulders. Other than those, I feel great!"

His orthopaedic examination was far better than I had expected. He had regained a hundred and thirty degrees of motion in both knees and his right patellar tendon was regaining function. There was only trace effusion in the right knee, and none in the left. Best of all, there was no evidence of infection on his exam, his lab tests, or his follow-up x-ray films.

"What should I do next?" he asked.

I wrote orders to his therapist in Wenatchee for him to increase his weight-loaded leg lifts slowly and to progress from his walker to crutches.

I speculated aloud, "Mark, normally I'd suggest a neoprene sleeve with drop-lock hinges to stabilize your right knee, but I suspect that you might have a hard time getting it on and off with your hands the way they are."

He replied, "Tell you what. You write me a prescription. I'll get whatever you write for in Wenatchee and see if I can make it work.

"Okay. What about your exercise program?"

"We have an Air-dyne exerciser at home. I like it," he almost boasted. "I can pedal with my knees and exercise my shoulders at the same time without a lot of effort."

"Good. Use that and continue the swimming if you can. What else is going on?"

"Well…" For the first time, a note of discouragement shaded his voice. "I'll probably be seeing you from Wenatchee for a while. I…sold my house in Seattle."

I knew it was a difficult move. "That was a big step," I said, looking at him closely.

He let out a sigh. "Yeah, it was. But…it was the only thing I could do." He was trying to put the best possible face on this. "I just don't see myself being able to be on my own for a while. I'm really happy with how these operations turned out but…being alone is what got me into all of this in the first place. So for now…I guess I'm going to have to stay with my folks for a while." Only a little of his story seeped out. It was clear he wasn't comfortable about it. I paused, but he didn't go any further.

"Well, okay. You've done a great job since the surgeries. If everything stays stable we can arrange for Dr. Tucker to follow you over there. See him in a month, and if everything is fine, ask his office to fax me his notes to keep me up to date. If something changes or if you have any questions, call me at any time."

"Okay, Doc. I'll set it up. And…thanks for everything. It's great to be able to walk again."

I was able to follow his progress in Wenatchee by phone. In late October he called to say he had no pain at all and, using only a cane, could walk as far as he wished. He used his neoprene brace regularly, had no instability, and reported no further falls. When I spoke with him in late November he was hoping he might be able to start traveling. He said, "I've been cooped up way too long." Over the phone, I could hear a smile in his voice. It meant a lot to both of us. I told him that I wouldn't need to see him in Seattle for at least six months.

The smile in his voice didn't last that long.

The Suffering Inside

A month later, just before Christmas of 1998, Mark had his next brush with death. Alone in the bathroom, he tried to get up from the toilet and collapsed. Zita heard him yelling for her. "Mom! Come quick! I need help!" She found him lying on the floor in a spreading puddle of blood. He was hemorrhaging massively from somewhere in his bowel.

Zita grabbed the phone. Long minutes later, medics had him in an ambulance heading to the hospital. Despite doctors and nurses working at a desperate pace, by the time he reached the ICU he was deteriorating into unconsciousness from hemorrhagic shock. His blood pressure dwindled downward toward the undetectable, until he stood once again at the brink of the abyss. He needed twenty-seven units of blood before his vital signs stabilized and the surgeons could begin to search for the source of his bleeding.

Late into the night Zita waited helplessly outside the ICU in fear and uncertainty, this time stunned by the image of her son bleeding on the bathroom floor. Mark's nurse gently suggested that the doctors wouldn't operate until they had found where the bleeding was coming from, and that perhaps she should go home and get some rest.

The surgeons were sitting on a deadly set of choices. Because Mark's bowel was full of blood, the tests couldn't pinpoint the part that was bleeding, but because he kept bleeding, the team couldn't wait much longer to find the source. At 2 a.m. they called John in Chicago to get permission to operate. Afterward Mark explained to John that he had begged them not to disturb Zita. "I didn't want them to call Mom because I didn't want her to be worried." Mark dismissed his precarious situation. "I'm just lying here, cleaning out the Wenatchee blood bank." John described the conversation differently: "He was unbelievably courageous and strong of spirit." At 5 a.m. Zita learned from John that the surgeons could delay no longer. She got to the hospital just in time to see her son being wheeled into the OR.

The anti-inflammatory medicines that Mark had used for years to control his pain irritated and then eroded the lining of his bowel; eventually underlying blood vessels broke open and bled. Mark hemorrhaged from multiple perforations of his jejunum, a portion of his small intestine. The surgeons had to remove a foot and a half of it.

John and his wife arrived from Chicago after the operation was over. They faced a sight that was becoming too familiar. Mark was lying unresponsive in an ICU room on a respirator. His mother was sitting silently next to his bed, waiting and hoping.

Shock is a shattering experience. The body loses more than blood. Energy is exhausted, reserves are depleted, and recovery remains precarious for days. What is left of a patient looks limp and flat, an empty balloon after the air has rushed out. The surgery stopped Mark's bleeding, but for five days in the ICU he had little sign of vitality. Ointment crusted his dulled eyes, his words were labored, and his bowel rebelled at resuming its duties. After a week he tolerated transfer to the general surgery floor. There he began again the plodding process of recovery, with a body that was growing weary of the effort.

For some people, multiple brushes with death can turn debilitation into dread. Medical science no longer provides comfort or security. The bedrock of reality—one's continued physical existence—is no longer certain. Each day becomes doubtful; each night becomes a reminder of the void. This was the second time that Mark had stared beyond the dark doorway, and he knew that it could happen again at any time. He could count on nothing he had known. Everything in the material world—his job, his possessions, his identity, his health—had been taken from him. What remained for him here? What had he seen on the other side?

It was a measure of the man that instead of descending deeper into despair, Mark somehow grew stronger from these experiences. With each crisis he seemed more certain of what was important and what was not. John described the strength that was growing inside. "Mark fought his way through again. He had fully accepted his fate, but he was not going to stop fighting. And yet, even while fighting for his life he was noticeably stoical this time. His faith was even stronger."

Zita said, "I believe that his loss of independence and the fact that he could not live alone caused a deep change in him. He became transformed by his illness. Even though he had bad moments, he developed a deep faith, a belief that God would see him through, even if it meant death. He believed in another level of existence after his time was finished here on earth. He was not afraid anymore. He had faced death too often."

By early January, even though he was still weak from the stress of shock and surgery, Mark had recovered enough to return to his parents' house. Once there, he would need what little strength he had regained. Another mortal shadow waited for him. His father's health was deteriorating.

Mark never spoke to me about his father. He left many hints, but during the years of his orthopaedic care I never thought it appropriate to push beyond his reluctance. Steve was a story that flowed like a dark river through Mark's life—a story of abuse, a story of hurt and fear that he kept hidden deep within. Zita said, "In his fights against depression, Mark never let anyone know that in his inner soul he had so much torment."

Steve Smetko was born in Chicago in 1910 to a sixteen-year-old Croatian girl who was coerced by interfering relatives into marrying the father, a distant cousin. She soon left her husband and took Steve back to Croatia. For the first five years of his life the boy had no father. When Steve and his mother eventually returned to Chicago, he had a dependent bond with her, but couldn't relate at all to his dad, and eventually had little to do with him. His mother directed all of her life's bitterness toward his father, and her constant criticisms left a lasting impression. When Steve was twenty, his parents divorced.

Early in Zita's marriage her new husband was warm and caring, but soon after their first son, Carl, was born, Steve changed. He could relate to each new baby for a while, but as the infants grew into childhood he became increasingly distant. Zita said, "Steve related to his sons with silence while they were growing up. He just didn't know how to talk to them about their schoolwork, their friends, or their personal concerns."

He began to vent unabashed anger at small boys who couldn't escape. He became critical, condescending, and contemptuous, wounding his sons indiscriminately. In time, he became physically abusive as well. Zita described the terror. "His anger was capricious. He would slap them for no reason at all, and when they failed at anything his sarcasm and scorn were devastating." Carl recalled that at about age six, "Steve slapped Mark so hard it knocked him down and made a red welt on his face." A nephew said, "Nobody ever confronted Steve. He cursed at all of us." One of Mark's boyhood friends was more succinct. "Steve," he said, "was a tough son of a bitch."

Zita was appalled. Once Steve's abusive pattern was clear she wanted nothing more to do with him. Their early intimacy dissolved, but she didn't leave. A devout Catholic, she simply said, "It was different back then." She felt she was the only protector the boys had, so she stood her ground. Despite her diminutive size, she defended them like a mother bear, sometimes by making excuses, sometimes by physically standing between them and their father.

Carl, John and Paul gradually acquired enough emotional armor to protect themselves, but not Mark. Paul described the growing tragedy: "The rest of us learned how to deal with our dad, but Mark couldn't. He was the blotter." The little child began to distance himself from others so that they wouldn't hurt him. The rejected young boy could no longer trust and became fearful of strangers. The withdrawn grade-schooler, forced by his teachers to stand and recite in class, began to stutter nervously. The defensive adolescent, stricken with test anxiety, believed he was dumb. The young man who loved music, nervous about making public mistakes, put down his violin. Paul summed it up: "Year after year, he just stood there and took it."

Carl recalled, "Steve seemed to zero in on Mark more than the rest of us." John had similar observations. "Steve established in Mark's mind that the world was a terrible and threatening place. Mark gradually learned that he could never measure up, and that no matter what he did he could never gain his father's approval."

Father and son became locked in a relationship of need and rejection, fear and silence, of buried hurts and a bottomless well of walled-off pain. The other sons eventually found ways to reassure themselves of their worth, but nothing Mark did ever gained him the recognition he craved from his distant dad. The disparaging voice of his father became internalized. Eventually, Mark believed that in some incomprehensible way, he was fundamentally unlovable.

Paul said, "Mark learned early on that the only thing he could do to save himself was to run." He fled from the confinement of a stifling office career in Chicago. He fled out West on empty miles of railroad tracks. He ran until he had no home except a shabby cottage in Seattle. He kept running harder, but it was all in vain. All of the hurt and rage were buried inside.

By the time his arthritis forced him to Wenatchee with legs that wouldn't work, Mark could run no longer. The only coping tool he knew had been stripped from him. His disease dragged him back to the dependency of a childhood he hated and cooped him up with the fearful figure he had fled for so long. All of the anger buried inside him began seething toward the surface. Perhaps it was the Naprosyn that eventually burned a hole in his gut, or perhaps it was the rage.

Both men had stuffed volcanic anger inside. Steve took it out on his children; Mark lived with no one but himself. Zita said, "There were often times when Mark fought his inner battles to the point of utter despondency. Any hope that his illness would get better, or that he might once again be independent, would abandon him; rage about his fate of pain and suffering would completely overwhelm him and he would sink into the blackness of deep depression and despair."

When Mark could no longer contain it, his anger erupted in fierce outbursts. Often he projected them elsewhere, toward injustices he saw in the world, but sometimes he hurled his wrath at those around him. Zita described how seldom Mark saw the effects of these outbursts: "I sometimes wondered if he really realized how angry he became and how he lashed out with words that cut so deeply."

He had, by some insidious transmutation, taken on the traits of the father he had tried so desperately to flee. Both were badly wounded and heavily defended men who projected their rage at the world around them. When they couldn't live life on their own terms, both retreated into walled-off stoicism. Both refused to see a doctor—Mark when he was feverish with sepsis, Steve when incapacitated by pain. Neither could express his inner demons to anyone. At the time, Mark had no awareness that the anger he feared in his father had gradually become his own.

He tried to talk with his dad. He continuously craved some crumb of recognition that seemed forever withheld. Zita saw it as a dance of destruction between two people she cared for deeply. "It was painful to see Mark try in so many ways to get Steve to communicate with him, but Steve had never talked about anything to his son, and he certainly wasn't opening up to Mark now." Steve worried when Mark was ill. At some inexpressible level he cared about his sons, but he had lived his entire life unable to say so openly. "Steve simply didn't know how to show any kind of feeling for his boys."

Eventually Mark just kept his distance. He learned the hard way to stay with safe subjects such as sports or the weather. Even then, he and his father drifted into disagreements. Like two blocks of ice, they were stuck together in a frozen relationship. As Steve's health began to deteriorate, there was a sense to it all of impending disaster.

Steve had smoked Camels incessantly for most of his life. He quit around age sixty, but by then it was too late. Deep within his chest, smoke-damaged cells in the lining of his lungs were slowly metamorphosing into distorted atrocities that, as the years passed, began to multiply malevolently. Shortly before Christmas, he began to feel weak.

Mark saw his father's decline. The two blocks of ice could not stay frozen in place much longer. The situation became unbearable. In early March, Mark finally detonated. Zita described the explosion. "One day Mark went to the family room and asked Steve a question about a baseball game. He felt that this was a safe subject. Steve let him know in a curt way that he wasn't interested. Something in Mark snapped. He screamed at Steve in a violent fit of anger and called him horrible names. It was awful." Perhaps the scream was Mark's pent-up rage over years of rejection. Perhaps it was a desperate last attempt to break through an impregnable wall. Whatever it was, the ice remained frozen. Steve refused to talk to anyone. "He remained walled off to the end."

Steve was being eaten alive by more than anger. Malignant cells were on a murderous march into the lymph nodes near his aorta. By Saturday, March 20, he lay curled in bed, sapped of strength. He labored to breathe, but he refused to go to the hospital. In desperation, Zita called an ambulance. She said, "You can imagine how Mark felt when the ambulance came for his father. He went to Steve before it arrived and asked his forgiveness for yelling at him. Steve was nice about it, I think, but for months afterward Mark would tell me how anguished he felt about cursing his father."

When the ambulance arrived Steve refused to go, and the medics couldn't make him. Zita shook her head in frustration, but her husband's obstinacy didn't deter her. The next day she asked Dr. Peterson, a family friend, to come over. Taking one look at the situation, he told Steve he was calling the ambulance, and that this time there would be no arguments.

A chest x-ray taken on admission showed a large cancer in Steve's lung, encroaching on his airway and the great vessels near his heart. Diagnostic studies on Monday and Tuesday defined its extent. On Wednesday evening, at Zita's request, the family physician, Dr. O'Donnell, told Steve his fatal prognosis. In shock, Steve clutched Zita's arm "so hard I thought he was going to hurt me."

Thursday evening Zita, John and Mark gathered at Steve's bedside. According to her, Steve "looked at his boys and suddenly became deeply agitated." The dying man could no longer stifle a cry that came from deep within. Feelings of contrition he had suppressed for years suddenly came spilling out. With tears in his eyes, he told his sons that he was sorry for anything he had ever done to make their lives difficult. He realized, he said, that he had not been there for them when they needed him. Then he pleaded with them to take care of their mother. "You must never let her suffer in any way."

Who knows what happens at moments like that? Perhaps as the malignancy in Steve's chest relentlessly reached its conclusion, the malignancy in his life somehow receded. Perhaps as he saw his sons gathered around his bedside, he awakened in one brief burst of awareness to an affection he had never felt before. In that moment of his remorse and contrition, perhaps Steve was offered his last chance at redemption, and like the thief on the cross, he took it.

Friday Zita arranged hospice care at home. "That night we were all at the hospital. Steve was happy at the thought of coming home again. He spoke openly to us until it was time to leave. It was as if he had shed a huge burden and could finally tell us what really mattered to him. Later, after we left, he talked to the nurse for hours about Croatia, about our courtship, his love for me, and about his sons."

Those brief hours of openness were the only ones Steve was allowed. Suddenly, in the middle of the night, he stopped talking. The nurse turned to see a choking look on his face. He coughed twice and then a great gout of blood burst out of his mouth onto the bed. The malignant mass in his trachea had eroded into his aorta. In a brief breath of a moment, Steve was dead.

Who will ever know what happened during that final week? Perhaps a desperate cry beneath Mark's raging outburst finally got through to his father. Perhaps in return the contrition of his father's dying words brought forgiveness to them both. When the family returned to the hospital to say goodbye, Mark stood for a long moment looking down at the now-lifeless repository of so many painful memories. Then his mother and brother watched in silence as he bent over and slowly kissed his father's gray forehead. In an all-too-brief moment, father and son had at last touched each other.

With that parting kiss, Mark's compassion rose above his years of suffering. Perhaps it was only a small crack in the thick wall around his heart, but I believe that as he stood back up, something too long locked away slowly began to open outward. I believe that his simple act of kindness started him on a path away from the pain he had carried since childhood.

Steve Smetko died on March 27, 1999. Zita, eighty-four years old, widowed and worn down from her efforts, could no longer physically care for Mark by herself. Within weeks she put her house in Wenatchee up for sale and began a move with Mark to Staten Island to live with Paul, Diana and their two children.

Prior to their departure, Mark scheduled an appointment to see me. From Dr. Tucker's notes I knew that both knees were doing well. When I examined him he had no pain or limp in either knee. Only his overall fatigue limited his walking distance. He only used a cane outdoors for balance. Both knees could flex to a hundred and thirty degrees. The right knee had trace effusion, but its tendon appeared fully healed; he could arise from a sitting position with only light assistance from his hands. His x-ray films showed no evidence of bone erosions or implant loosening.

When the clinical part of his check-up was over, we sat and chatted for a bit. I knew little of the other changes in his life. He mentioned his father's death, but, in characteristic fashion, only as the reason he was moving with his mom to New York. The brevity of that explanation hinted that he was leaving much unsaid. I offered my condolences. He expressed regret that he wouldn't be seeing me back in follow-up. There was an awkward silence. We both knew there was more to say. There was simply not enough time to say it.

Eighteen months before, Mark had arrived at the door of Northwest Hospital nearly dead from staphylococcal sepsis. Since then he had persevered through four bilateral clean-outs, two reimplantation surgeries, countless medical complications and profound depression. Now he was finally free of the devastating infection and the havoc it had caused.

"Doc," he said, "I don't know how to thank you enough for everything you've done for me."

"Mark, watching you walk again is thanks enough. It's been a privilege to take care of you."

He struggled to find his words. "Well, I just wanted to give you something. I hope…maybe it's something you can remember me by. Either way, it's part of me…so I wanted to give it to you."

Inside the package he had carefully wrapped was the picture Zita had placed in his hospital room so long ago, the picture of the four Great Northern diesel locomotives hauling a heavy freight train upward through a western mountain pass. Mark was giving me his most precious possession, a picture of the power that had pulled him through.

For eight years I had solved Mark's orthopaedic problems. His new knees served him well for the rest of his life. Now there would be no further follow-ups. This was our last visit as a doctor and a patient.

PART II
Friend

My Turn

Doctors are high on the list of people who procrastinate about seeking health care. For five years, ever since I had turned fifty, I kept promising myself that I would get a thorough checkup. For the same five years, mumbling that my health was okay, I kept putting it off. Finally, in March of 1999, something inside me said, "You're going to be fifty-five in April and you still haven't done it yet, have you?" A few days later, in the hospital parking lot, I talked to an internist I had known for years, Dr. Rob Saunders, and asked about seeing him professionally. Less than a month after my last visit with Mark, Dr Saunders' office scheduled an appointment for me for May 11.

In truth, my health wasn't okay. I felt more fatigued. Fatigue is probably the easiest symptom for doctors to dismiss. During the years of training it becomes a fact of life, a subtle dullness in daily existence to which I eventually adapted. Recently, however, it had become more noticeable. I took longer to bounce back from long days of surgery or late nights on call. It wasn't terribly pronounced, but it was there, different from normal background tiredness like the annoying tick of a clock.

At my general checkup, my blood pressure was high. Even doctors get apprehensive about going to the doctor, so I measured my pressure at home for a while. In early June, after three weeks of normal readings, I called the office nurse and said, "You can tell Dr. Saunders to take high blood pressure off the problem list." She replied, "Okay, but he wants to talk to you about your lab results." In a minute, Rob got on the line.

"Bill, your cholesterol and triglycerides are high. You should start by really working on changing your diet." That wasn't hard advice to follow. I had been working on changing my diet for years, with glacial progress. My father had devoured steak and eggs, lived a stressful executive life, and by the time he was sixty needed a heart operation, so I was already a believer.

Then Rob mentioned that one of my liver enzymes was moderately elevated. That wasn't so easy to explain away.

"Bill, how much do you drink?"

"I have an occasional glass of wine with meals. A fifth of scotch lasts six months. Rob, I think you're looking under the wrong rock there."

"Well, let's start by rechecking those results. In the meantime, stop your alcohol intake until we see what's going on."

"Okay. I'm going to be out of town during the end of June, but I'll have the tests drawn before I go." I gave no further thought to the conversation.

In early July Rob called me with the results of the repeat liver tests. The enzyme called ALT was still elevated and my hepatitis-B antibody test was positive. The latter was no surprise. I had antibodies because I had been vaccinated against hepatitis-A and B six years previously, when journal articles publicized the risk of hepatitis to surgeons.

"Well, Bill, your hepatitis-C antibody test is also positive." Antibodies meant that I had been exposed to the disease. I was puzzled by that news, but not terribly concerned about it. In thirty years of medicine I had been exposed to more diseases than I cared to think about. In medical school I had a major exposure to TB. My skin test for it turned floridly positive and I had to be followed with chest x-rays for years, but I never got the disease. I reassured myself that these antibodies meant the same thing: I had been exposed to hep-C and developed antibodies to it. My assumption was true, but it wasn't the full answer.

Rob pursued the question further. On July 13 I had a blood test called HEP-C RNA PCR, a test specific for a protein on the surface of the virus. On Friday, July 23, I had just finished my afternoon clinic when Rob called me with the results. I took the call in my back office, away from patients.

"Bill…that test was positive."

"What does that mean?"

"It means you have the virus in your bloodstream."

"But what exactly does that mean?"

"Well, when taken together with your elevated liver enzymes, it means you have active hepatitis-C."

I froze to the phone. Like a shotgun round, something imploded in my gut and left a gaping emptiness. My surprise changed to panic with frightening speed. I slumped in my chair and struggled to say something intelligible.

"Rob, I'm fifty-five. I'm at the peak of my career. What's going to happen to me?"

His explanation sounded hollow and hard to comprehend. After he hung up I wanted to disappear. I numbly finished whatever needed doing and then hurried from the office, as if by fleeing from the phone I could escape from his news.

One of my favorite spots in the summer is a marina overlooking downtown Seattle and the blue waters of Elliott Bay. On clear days it has a view of Mt. Rainier, towering in the distance. I needed a place like that, a tranquil place where I could try to regain my composure. I drove straight to the marina, parked and then sat on a bench for a long time, looking out over the water to the mountain in the distance, like Mark once looked at the picture of his train.

I struggled to think through Rob's words. All my life I had coped by thinking. Years of training had taught me to keep my emotions at bay in order to think. Whenever a surgical situation became desperate, disciplined thinking got me through.

I knew about hepatitis-A and B. They were well-known viruses that caused either acute jaundice or chronic inflammation that could scar the liver into a condition called cirrhosis. By comparison, the hepatitis-C virus was a relative unknown. Until recently, even the experts could only define it by what it wasn't; for years they had called it "non-A, non-B hepatitis." The little I knew about it was grim. Most of the time there was no treatment for it. It usually scarred the liver insidiously until severe cirrhosis produced liver failure. The only hope then was a liver transplant. Most of those didn't last very long.

In the past, analytical problem solving had always given me a solution. Now those skills were worthless. I didn't have enough facts to overcome my apprehension. Fragments of knowledge tumbled in my thoughts like clothes in a dryer, but they gave me no answers. Thinking wasn't solving anything.

What I did know was that from now on my life was going to be very different. For years I had sat at the side of hospital beds, giving patients news they didn't want to hear. Now it was my turn. No matter how much I fought it, in the space of a phone call my self-image had changed from a picture of a successful surgeon to that of an ignorant patient with an incurable disease. Memories of countless hospital experiences left me no room for denial or escape. A bed, an IV, and a doctor standing over me; that's what it was going to look like. Something sickening started knotting up my gut, something I couldn't wall off as I had been trained to do. I was terrified. I sat looking out over the water and tried to blink back tears.

Walking helps me dissipate stress, so I got up from the bench and began wandering along the water's edge. In my confusion and anxiety I lost track of the time. I forgot I was supposed to meet my wife for dinner.

Bev was angry that I was late. We walked in cool silence toward the restaurant at the marina. Finally I paused, turned to her and said, "Look, I need to tell you something really important. Once I say what I have to say, things won't be the same, ever again." It was the only way I knew to begin. "I was late because I went walking, and the reason I needed to walk was because Rob Saunders called me this afternoon. He told me I have active hepatitis-C."

She looked stunned and sat down with the same "Oh no!" feeling and the same worried question, "What does that mean?" I couldn't tell her. I didn't know. We began to walk and talked late into the long summer twilight. If walking could have answered any of Bev's questions, we probably would have walked until morning. Instead, the night ended the way it began—with worried uncertainty. "I don't know what will happen to me," I kept repeating. "I just don't know."

That night was the first of many when sleep came slowly and brought no rest. My reply to Rob mocked everything I had worked so hard to achieve. All of my accomplishments suddenly felt pointless. Staring into the darkness of the middle of the night I thought, "Your life's going to turn to crap."

Rationality returned in the morning. I didn't know the answers, but we could at least start sorting through how to get them. As we sat at the breakfast table Bev asked, "What's the next step?"

"I have no idea when I got this," I replied. "I have no idea how bad it is. I'll have to have it evaluated. It has to be worked up and staged. Rob will refer me to a gastroenterologist. I'll probably need a liver biopsy."

"Where would you have that done?"

"I don't know." The choice was either Northwest Hospital or some facility where I could stay anonymous and hide the diagnosis. I couldn't think my way through the choice, but I knew how I felt. "I hate the thought of getting treatment somewhere else. I've worked at Northwest Hospital my entire career. I know these people. I credentialed half of them. They're good doctors. If I get sick or have to go to the ER, I don't want it to be at a strange place where nobody knows me."

Bev stared at her coffee cup for a minute, and then asked, "So why don't you just have the biopsy done at Northwest? Is that a problem?"

"If I get this worked up at Northwest, the diagnosis will be all over my medical record. If I ever have to go to the Emergency Room or get admitted, everyone in the hospital will know. I have an elective surgical practice. If this gets out, yes, that's going to be a problem, a big problem."

The only alternative to Northwest was University Hospital. Monday morning Bev called the hepatitis clinic there. They didn't have an opening until early October. I couldn't stand the thought of leaving everything hanging until then. I arranged to see Dr. Steve Wegley, a gastroenterologist I knew at Northwest, on August 16. That meant I would have the biopsy done by someone I knew, at a hospital where I was known.

Over the weekend we combed the Internet for more information. My prior impressions were accurate. The statistics were dismal. Hepatitis C had become four times more prevalent than infection with HIV, the AIDS virus. It was the leading cause of liver transplants in the U.S. "Deaths from hepatitis-C will eclipse deaths from AIDS within several years."

Most of the statistics had an impersonal quality to them. "Approximately 10,000 people die each year from the disease. This number is expected to triple by the year 2015." The numbers were scary, but they seemed distant and didn't touch me. Then I came across one that stopped me cold: "Ninety percent of hepatitis-C cases are transmitted by contaminated needles." IV drug usage didn't apply to me, and I had never had a blood transfusion. I had a history of surgical needle sticks. Over the years, they had added up.

Anger and resentment grabbed at my gut. I said to Bev, "I got this just doing my job. I got it from somebody I was trying to help." Maybe they knew they had it and didn't tell me. Maybe they were just like me and never even knew they had it. Either way, I got it from just doing what I was supposed to do. I had nowhere to go with the raw unfairness of that thought. I knew I needed to get past recrimination. I knew I'd never find out who infected me. For the moment, however, I couldn't silence a sense of grinding bitterness.

From the Internet I learned that there was no protection against this disease. Unlike hepatitis-A and B, the C virus had variations in its genetic makeup called genomes that prevented development of a vaccine. Even worse, there was no such thing as just being exposed to it. I was exposed to TB, but I never got the disease. Hep-C was different. Within days of penetrating the body, one hep-C virus could make a trillion copies of itself. No prophylactic medications existed to prevent such rapid replication. If people got stuck, they got the virus. If they got the virus, they got the disease.

The only available treatment was a year of an injected drug called Interferon, and a second drug, Riboviron. The cost of this combination for a year was "about $18,000." Twenty-five percent of patients had to stop it because of severe side effects, including suicidal depression. Worst of all, seventy-five percent of patients with viral genomes 1-a or 1-b, the most common types, didn't benefit at all from Interferon. My initial recollections were well founded. Treatment was a year of chemotherapy, with wretched side effects and a low probability of response, and the only salvage solution was a liver transplant.

The Internet disgorged fact after fact about the disease until I was drowning in a whirlpool of bad news, but I had no idea how much of it applied to me. I knew a friend who had suffered from hep-C for a long time. On July 27 I talked with him for an hour, trying to get a better perspective about what I was facing.

He had relatively advanced disease, so he had to be on Interferon. He was able to continue working, but his fatigue dragged him through the day's schedule. The depression that came with the Interferon added more fatigue. He described multiple liver biopsies, failed attempts at other treatments, and the gloom of watching his daughter grow up without knowing how much longer he had. From the Internet I had learned dry data. From a fellow traveler I learned the emotional cost and personal isolation of a disease nobody knew much about.

On Thursday, July 29, I did a total knee replacement on a woman who was a long-term patient and a friend. Anxious about having an operation, she had chosen for years to endure the worsening wear in her knee, until pain and unsteadiness finally forced her to schedule the surgery. I said hello to her before she went into the operating room. She looked up at me, smiled, and said she felt good about going ahead with the procedure.

Moving smoothly though the case, we began at last to close the incision. Then, in one single move, it all went wrong. A new assistant was suturing the fascial layer beneath the skin. I worked across from him, concentrating on closing the skin itself. He passed his needle down through the tissue, across the incision and out the other side. In an instant of distraction, my hand bumped against it. The point of the needle stuck me.

Needle sticks are not rare. Orthopaedists report an average of two to four glove penetrations a year. In a routine situation the surgeon discards the needle, changes his gloves, and goes on with the operation. This time, however, one person in the room knew that this was not a routine situation.

The point of the needle had not retracted back into the patient's flesh. Quietly I said, "Stop. Don't move! Give me a needle holder." With it, I grasped the point, pulled the needle from the wound, cut off its suture, and put the needle and needle holder down on a table outside the sterile field. Then I took off my glove. Even though the poke had been tiny, a small drop of blood beaded up on the tip of my left index finger. I stared at the drop for only a moment, but that was enough to freeze in my mind its frightening image.

The voice I had no time for whispered, *You can't do this.*

The scrub nurse waited next to me with a new set of gloves. I snapped out of my distraction, regloved, and finished closing the skin. Later, when I described the moment to Bev, I said, "Standing there, I almost lost it."

That night I knew I had.

It was my first night of total insomnia. For years, I had made little rooms in my mind in which I sealed away awful clinical sights so I never had to look at them again. This time I couldn't shut out what I had seen. The vision of the drop of blood wouldn't go away.

That's how it happened to you. It only took an invisible film of blood on the end of a needle to infect you…and that's all it will take to infect someone else the next time.

In my mind, I saw the patient smiling up at me before she went into the OR. *She's been a friend all these years. She trusted you. If you had contaminated her, would you have been able to tell her that she might get hep-C? Would you have been able to tell her you operated on her knowing you had it? What would you have said to her?*

If you were a patient and you found out your surgeon had hepatitis-C, would you still have him do your surgery?

If your referring doctors find out you have this, will they keep sending their patients to you?

You only have two choices. That's what it all comes down to.

One choice is to hide it all. You can still cancel your biopsy appointment. Have it done somewhere else, far from here. Get treated anonymously. It can be done. Other doctors have done it. Stuff the whole thing. Don't tell a soul. Look at all you've got. Don't throw it all away.

But every time you operate, you'll know. If a patient ever gets stuck, you'll know. And all the while, your anger and fear will just get worse. Hide it! But if you do, you'll be trapped, with no way out.

Or don't hide it. But don't kid yourself. As soon as the word gets out, it's all over. There will be no going back. You'll be finished. Everything that paid your bills will be gone. Everything that got you admiration and satisfaction and respect will be gone. Dr. Gruber will be gone. It will just be Bill, just plain Bill.

In the stillness, the small voice that nudged me would not be silenced. *Those are the only two choices you have. Everything else is details. What's it going to be? Can you run? Can you hide?*

The test for the HEP-C RNA protein coat confirmed that I had the virus, but it didn't say how many were present, so next I had a HEP-C RNA quantitative level drawn. The results were appallingly high. I had three and a half million viruses in every cc of blood. It would only take an infinitesimal amount of my serum to transmit this disease. I was as contagious as my next needle stick.

During the first week in August I continued doing my scheduled surgeries, but even during the most routine of them I couldn't concentrate. I kept looking at the points on instruments instead of at the incision. Rising anxiety smothered the satisfaction of performing good surgery. Moves that should have been effortless became forced and distracted, as if a symphony conductor had a tooth abscess.

Needles aren't the only risk in orthopaedic surgery. That Tuesday evening I was on call for the ER when a patient came in with a three-part ankle fracture that routinely required surgery. One part was a long spiral fracture. At its tip was a sharp spike.

The patient agreed to have the fracture fixed. I took him to surgery that night. The operation is a common one and followed a set routine. After I opened the fracture site I tried to get the fragments back in line by pushing on the bone. Suddenly I felt the spike go through my outer glove.

Like the needle stick, this was not rare either. Orthopaedists routinely double-glove because the risk of sharp bone fragments is always present during fracture surgery. I stepped away from the table and peeled off my outer glove. Stretching out the inner glove, I saw that it was still intact. Less than a millimeter of latex had saved the situation.

I finished the case with intense concentration, trying to suppress thoughts about what might have happened. The post-operative x-rays looked perfect. All of the fragments were exactly aligned and rigidly held with plates and screws. The patient recovered uneventfully.

I didn't. I got home late that night, exhausted by the anxiety but unable to sleep. The incessant questions came back. *This time everything was okay. What about next time? What would you have done if the spike had gone into your skin? You've gone six months without any events, and now you've had two penetrations in ten days! What's going on here?* The phrase *You can't do this* wouldn't go away.

Every Friday before office hours the five partners of Northwest Orthopaedic Clinic met with our office manager to grapple with the day-to-day problems of running the practice. The complexities of government regulations, insurance reimbursements and hospital relations often made this meeting the most stressful time of the week.

During the Friday morning meeting of August 6 I was more stressed than usual. The partners dealt with problems in the practice, but my mind wasn't with them. I focused on problems that no one else in the room even knew about. For the first time I felt the duplicity of living a double life.

I had shared call with these guys for nineteen years and had been partners with them for thirteen. We often assisted one another on difficult cases. On weekends I trusted them to operate on my patients, and they trusted me to operate on theirs. Now what? If I told them what I had, things would never be the same. Not in the office. Not in the OR. Not ever again.

One of the issues we had to sort through that morning was the arrival of a new doctor. The preceding May we had signed a contract with Dr. Bruce Thomas, an orthopaedist from San Diego, to join our group. He was scheduled to start work in just a few weeks, on September 1. This Friday we had to decide how to get him started. Everybody else in the meeting talked about Bruce as an addition. I wasn't listening. I was thinking about him as my replacement.

Without Bruce, if I suddenly stopped operating there'd be chaos in the clinic. The other partners already had full practices. They couldn't take my caseload and didn't want my call. My patients would have to go somewhere else. But if I stepped out now Bruce could just step in. He'd have a good start on a surgical practice and the other partners could continue working at their usual pace.

After the meeting I looked at the surgeries I had scheduled for the next several months. I was due to leave on August 27 for vacation. I always tapered down my elective surgery schedule before I left. I had only a few cases scheduled until then. Autumn, on the other hand, was always a busy time. My schedule in October was already filling up. This was the time to make the move. Bruce's arrival made a transition as easy as it was ever going to be. "If you wait," I thought, "doing this will only get harder."

The weekend after the meeting I weighed and balanced every possible reason to keep doing surgery or to stop. Would I need treatment? If I did, would I get sick from it? If I were treated, would the virus go away completely? If the hospital found out I had hep-C, would they let me operate? If they didn't, what would I do? If I contaminated a patient and they sued me, would my insurance company defend me? If they didn't, I could lose everything. If I didn't operate, I couldn't cover my office expenses. Would overhead insurance cover them? What about my own bills? Would disability insurance cover them? I couldn't reach a decision because I couldn't answer any of the questions. Monday morning I started making phone calls, only to find out that no one else could answer them either.

I contacted my malpractice carrier and asked if they would cover me. They replied, "We are unable to give you a determination on that at this time."

I contacted our disability insurance broker and asked about personal coverage. He replied, "I'm pretty sure you're covered for this, Bill, but I can't say for certain."

"What about overhead insurance?"

"It should cover this, but they won't tell you for certain until you file a claim and they review the facts."

"How long will that take?"

He paused as if looking at a calendar, and then said, "At least thirty days from the time they get the claim."

I e-mailed an even tougher question to Rob Saunders. He was not only my internist, he was also one of my main referring physicians:

Rob,

I recognize that you are swamped but I need to ask you an important ethical question. You are a dedicated internist who wants to do the best for your patients. For years you have been able to say to them, "Gruber is a good surgeon. He does good work and he cares about his patients. I suggest that you go see him for your elective total joint replacement."

Knowing what you now know, could you still say that? Could you still refer patients to me? You need not answer this if you wish, but it will give you an idea of what is turning over inside me.

Thanks for listening.

Bill

The next day I received his reply:

As if your medical challenges were not enough! Thanks for sharing the details of the journey you are taking as a surgeon and a partner in a practice as well.

As to your posed question, can I say yes or no, would I refer, the answer is a clear and resounding "I don't know—yet" The knee jerk is to say no, thus not putting people at risk of contracting the virus. I hope expert experience and literature will permit a rational decision acceptable to all of us.

Rob

I didn't know the answers, and nobody else could give them to me. Strangely enough, a part of me responded with indifference to the replies, as if the non-answers no longer mattered. In some odd way, even the questions no longer mattered. Down deep I already knew what I had to do, knew it from somewhere beyond all the weighing and balancing swirling in my head, knew it at a level deeper than knowledge itself.

In that place, I knew that no matter what hung in the balance, I simply couldn't lead a double life. Others might choose to do so. I knew some who did, but I couldn't. I knew inescapably that for me, choosing such a path would be profoundly destructive. I would have to wall off a part of me and deny that it existed. Perhaps I could continue my career in that condition, but only at a killing emotional cost. Like a man having an affair, I would have to live with the chronic anxiety that someday my carefully compartmentalized world might suddenly collapse. Maybe I could hang on to a surgical practice, but there would be no joy, no satisfaction, no sense of service in it. There were many answers I still didn't know, but with absolute certainty I knew that much.

It was time to come out of the closet. I picked up the calendar and started penciling in what would have to happen and when.

On August 11, we were all together at an office party. As it ended and people started to leave, I went up to Bob Clawson.

"Bob, do you have anything on your schedule tomorrow evening?"

"Not that I can think of."

"I need to talk with you about something important. Do you mind if I come over to your house for about an hour?"

It was an unusual request. Concerned, he asked, "Is something wrong?"

"Um…I'd like to cover it tomorrow. Will seven-thirty work?"

"Sure. See you then."

Once I told Bob, I could no longer hide anything from anyone. It wasn't that he couldn't keep a confidence. My anxiety went deeper than that. Telling him meant that I wanted this diagnosis to be known.

I still had twenty-four hours to reconsider my decision.

That night, staring sleeplessly at the ceiling, I saw myself splitting into two halves. One half wanted to keep analyzing every angle. It wanted to know every answer to every question and wait longer before I opened up to anyone. It wanted protection. It wanted to hide. The other half didn't want to analyze anything and it didn't need any more time. It already knew.

I saw with terrible clarity that if I chose to lead a double life I would split into those two halves. If I kept hiding I would relentlessly submerge the half that wanted to be open and honest, and eventually I would disown it completely. In time there would be no double life left, only a false one. My life would have no integrity to it, either in the sense of honesty or in the sense of wholeness.

I kept hearing the phrase, *Let's just get on with this.* They were loaded words that haunted me with a horrible memory.

John Fulton[1] was a patient I first saw in 1978, just a month after I had started practice. He was in his early fifties, a strapping Irishman with a warm laugh and a worn knee. By 1982 he needed a knee replacement. Afterward, he needed a transfusion. At that time HIV wasn't well known and blood banks weren't screening for it. In 1986 he needed his other knee done. By then we knew the risk, so I asked him to donate his own blood preoperatively. When he went to donate, the blood bank told him he was HIV positive and that it was from the unit I had ordered for him in 1982. By 1988 he was emaciated, wracked with debilitating infections, and dying of AIDS. His words as he went into hospice were, "Let's just get on with this."

John never blamed me for what had happened to him. In a remarkable act of acceptance he was able to let go of recrimination about his fate. He suffered a wretched death because at the time no one knew about virus-contaminated blood. Now it was different. From now on I would know. There was peril in ignoring the voice that spoke his words. If I continued to do surgery I would be maintaining a façade, and eventually it would be at the expense of a patient who had trusted me.

I awoke the next morning shaking with unresolved tension. *If you go over to Bob's tonight, you're going to put an end to the role of surgeon.*

"Yes," I thought. "I know that."

Bob was a close friend as well as a professional colleague. We had hiked together and talked deeply during a difficult time in his life. He and his wife Kristina were just finishing dinner when I arrived. We all chatted a bit, and then he and I went to the living room.

"What's on your mind?" he asked.

I went right to the point. "Bob…a few weeks ago my life took a sharp turn. My internist told me I have active hepatitis C." I saw him take in a breath, but he said nothing, so I told him the details of the diagnosis and the impending evalua-

---

1.   Not his real name

tion. Finally, I told him my decision. "My plan is to stop doing surgery and turn my surgical practice over to Bruce as soon as he gets started."

Bob asked, "What do you think will happen?" He was trying to piece together the implications.

"I really don't know. Up until now I've just been trying to cope with it all. I haven't had time to figure out what's next. I don't even know what's possible."

I told him my plan, as far as it went. "The whole thing seems to be sorting out into two areas. One is the disease work-up. I need a biopsy to find out how bad this is and whether I'll need treatment. Jeff Carlin treats people with Interferon. He says the side effects are like having a really bad case of the flu for a year. If I need to be on it I probably won't be able to work a regular schedule.

"The other unknown is the practice. What I'd like to do, at least for a while, is to see if I can keep practicing in the office. I have no idea if our overhead insurance will cover that, so it's impossible to say if it will work, but I want to try. Right now, it's bad enough to think about not being a surgeon. I can't handle the idea of not even being a doctor."

We sorted through questions for two hours, but without facts he couldn't come up with any better answers than I could. My entire professional future consisted of unsupported speculations. For now he could only offer empathy, so that's what he did; as I got up to leave, he gave me a hug.

Driving home, I felt remarkably lighter, as if I had just put down a heavy load. The lightness helped me to realize what had actually happened that evening. My worries were not only about my disease. The heavier burden came from the isolation of hiding and the fear of being found out. I felt lighter now, not because I knew more answers, but because I had told someone about my diagnosis and he had responded with a hug. Regardless of how this condition turned out, I had at least gotten rid of the cost of stifling it inside.

Talking to Bob set in motion an irrevocable process of openness. I didn't know what would come next, but I knew that from now on there would be no turning back. Friday over lunch, I told Sandy Ziegler, our office manager, the same news.

Saturday morning after breakfast, Bev and I went for another long walk. It was good to walk in the summer sunshine with her. After twenty-seven years of marriage, she knew where my worries were.

She asked, "If you don't operate, what do you think you'll do?"

"I don't know. I'd like to try office orthopaedics, at least for a while. That would keep me seeing patients. It isn't much, but it's better than nothing. The problem is that it will only work if overhead insurance covers my office expenses.

That's the safety net. Without it, there's no way office practice alone will produce any income. The big problem is that I won't find out if the insurance will cover me for at least two months."

She asked, "How do you feel about what might happen?"

"If I stopped?" My reply to Rob rushed forward again. *"I'm fifty-five. I'm at the peak of my career."* I had other interests, lots of them. All the years of medical staff leadership, the effort of forming a new corporation, the research ideas that were finally being published—they all paraded past me. But surgery had always defined who I was. "It's a frightening thought. All of the alternatives are really depressing. Even worse, I'm not sure if any of them will work. That just adds anxiety to the mess."

She kept peeling back the layers of resistance. "What do you think's going to happen?"

"Bev, I just stepped off a very high diving board without knowing if there's water down there. I sure as hell hope there is, because if there isn't, the next sound you're going to hear is the worst SPLAT! you can imagine. The whole damn practice will disintegrate. I could be out on the street."

On Monday, August 16, I saw Dr. Steve Wegley. The history and physical examination were straightforward. So was the conclusion. "Bill, you need a liver biopsy."

He described the procedure. It was a quick poke into my belly with a thin needle, but because of possible bleeding afterward, he wanted me observed in the day-surgery area for several hours. It didn't sound like much. Then he talked about what it meant.

If the biopsy showed advanced disease, I'd need treatment. Interferon would have bad side effects but might eventually clear the virus from my bloodstream, or at least slow down progression of the disease. If the biopsy showed only minimal changes, then treatment wouldn't be worth the side effects, but the disease would progress.

Then he gently introduced a third possibility. I might not be treatable regardless of the results. "Seventy-five percent of Americans have genome 1-a or 1-b, so that's likely to be the case for you. If so, even if we had to try it, it's unlikely that Interferon will work." I looked at him blankly. He was telling me that statistically there was no solution.

Steve's news hit harder than just telling me about no treatment. It blew away a basic process by which I had always made my way in the world. I coped by solving problems. That wasn't just my surgical orientation or even my professional career; it was me, it was how I functioned. Now that wasn't going to work. Hearing "There may not be a solution" felt like hitting a brick wall.

I rearranged Wednesday's schedule to accommodate the liver biopsy. As I did so I reflected that this was just the beginning of rearranging what had been a neatly scheduled life.

When I arrived for my biopsy and signed the consent, I saw the admitting diagnosis on my chart: "hepatitis-C." Everybody in the day-surgery unit who looked at that medical record would know what I had, and the news, in a whispered way, would eventually spread down the hallways.

The nurse prepped my belly. I had known these nurses for years, but always as a doctor directing their care of others. Now I was the patient, and they were giving me directions. I told myself, "Get used to it."

Dr. Wegley said, "Take a deep breath!" As I sucked in, he poked a long, thin biopsy needle into my liver. All I managed was a short yelp, and then it was over.

When he came back later to discharge me, Bev was sitting at my bedside. He went back over the implications of the genome for her. If the genome was 1-a or 1-b, he recommended no treatment. My prior vision of a patient in a hospital bed, hooked to an IV with a doctor giving the wife the bad news, became depressingly real. He saw us glance at each other and offered to set up a second opinion at the University. I took him up on it.

The biopsy report was favorable. "No increased fibrosis and only rare areas with lobular inflammation. The portal triads are relatively un-inflamed." Two days later I asked the pathologist who read the slides, Dr. Madeline Woodward, to go over them with me.

Through one set of the two eyepieces on the microscope I looked at densely packed cells that formed the intricate architecture of the liver. Through the other set, guiding an illuminated arrow, Madeline pointed out her findings, using the grading scale that was now the national standard for hep-C. She saw no evidence at all of fibrosis or scarring, so that was graded 0/4. She saw a few inflammatory cells infiltrating the lobules of the liver, so that was graded 0.5/4.

From the beginning of medical school, I had been fascinated with looking at tiny cells through a microscope. As a surgeon, I often went over difficult diagnostic cases with the pathologists. This discussion, however, was more than a clinical conference between colleagues. The detachment I acquired in medical school was gone. The cells on that slide were mine.

The biopsy showed early disease. My genome came back 1-b. There would be no treatment and no solution. The conclusion was straightforward: live with it.

I spent the following week spreading the news of my decision. Monday evening I talked to another partner, Allan Jackson. A friend who had just retired from orthopaedics had recently told him how strange and jarring the transition had been. "Allan," the friend said, "I'm just not Dr. Boettcher anymore."

Tuesday over lunch I told Linda Roselle, my medical assistant. We had worked side-by-side for twenty-two years. She had grown quickly from a clinical assistant into a trusted comrade whose judgment I valued. She knew what was important and what could wait until the next day. She knew where to reach me with an emergency and if I was running late, how to reschedule unhappy patients. We joked that when patients who knew us called in, they asked for her instead of for me. Each morning I smiled when I greeted her, and each spring I brought her flowers from my garden. Now our future wouldn't be the same. Along with openness came loss. I would miss her very much.

Wednesday and Thursday I talked to the other partners—Herb Clark and Tim Daly—and placed calls to members of my extended family. Everyone asked the same question, "What are you going to do?"

I only had one answer. "I don't really know yet." What I did know was that with each conversation the ripples of change were irretrievably widening.

Changing a surgical practice is like turning an ocean liner; it can't be done on a dime. Cases are booked months in advance. They are scheduled through a tightly coordinated system involving our surgical scheduler, the patient's preferences, and the hospital OR. The following Tuesday, I told our scheduler the situation and what needed to be done. Case by case, she began the process of transferring my scheduled surgeries to Bruce Thomas.

As the scheduler changed each case, the staff at the appointment desk arranged an office visit for that patient. I wanted to tell these patients in person why I couldn't do their surgery. I planned to be in the operating room with them, but not scrubbed in. If they wished I would see them on rounds afterward. Beyond that, Dr. Thomas would continue to care for them. I had to transfer their operations, but I didn't want them to feel orphaned.

The office moved every case but one—an arthroscopy that Thursday on a patient who couldn't reschedule. Arthroscopy uses minimal incisions. I felt there would be no risk. John Gullage was scheduled to assist me. Wednesday afternoon I left a message in the operating room, asking him to see me in the office after he finished. When he arrived I told him my diagnosis, the plan and the significance of the next day's case. The word had spread faster than I thought. He already knew.

The following day, August 26, little more than a month after I took Rob's phone call, I came to the OR as a surgeon for the last time. At the sink outside the operating room, John and I talked as we scrubbed in.

Scrubbing in is a ritual that hasn't changed in years. A friend took a picture of me scrubbing in medical school thirty years ago, and what I was doing now didn't look any different. As I worked the brush back and forth over my forearms and hands, I reflected on all the cases I had done since that picture had been taken. John had helped me with many of the difficult ones, including all of Mark's surgeries. I thought about the teamwork and trust we had built together.

This is what you're really losing. It isn't the challenge or the satisfaction. It isn't the role of the white coat or the green scrubs or the income. What you're losing is connectedness. This is how you connected with people. Linda in the office...the team here in the operating room...the staff nurses on the hospital floors...they'll all be gone. And John will be the first.

We finished scrubbing and entered the room. The team quietly moved through their well-practiced routine, unaware of my loneliness. I slipped into my gown and gloves. John finished the draping. The anesthesiologist nodded. Everything was ready. I felt for the landmarks that located the incision and with the usual request, began the case.

"Skin knife, please."

The discipline of routine made the surgery go smoothly, but as we finished, my concentration began to crumble. While John put on the dressing, I peeled off my gown and sat down to write orders, a task I did every day, but this time nothing came out. "After all these years," I thought, "there should have been at least a little ceremony. There should have been something." But there wasn't. No trumpets, no drums. This was it. I tried to fight back tears.

"John, write the orders, will you? I need to go."

"Sure."

With that, I left the room, walked down the empty corridor to the locker room and changed out of my scrubs.

At the University of Washington, Dr. Robert Carithers was Chief of Hepatology, the specialty that deals with liver disease, and was nationally recognized for his research in hepatitis-C. The next afternoon Beverly and I met him at his office, and after brief introductory remarks I started asking him questions that contained a month of uncertainties.

"Given my findings, what do you think about treatment?"

"I wouldn't recommend it."

"Are there reasons other than the disadvantages of Interferon?"

His reply reflected his years of experience. "About 40 percent of people with hepatitis-C have a problem with progressive cirrhosis. If you don't get cirrhosis, you don't have a problem. The best predictor of whether patients will go on to cirrhosis or not is the amount of fibrosis present on their biopsy. Currently you have no fibrosis on your biopsy."

"If I have no treatment, what is the likelihood that this will get worse?"

"We don't know for certain, but it's probably low. If your biopsy is benign because you just got infected, the condition may progress, but we can determine that by watching your liver function tests. On the other hand, if you've been infected for years and still have this benign a biopsy, then you will probably stay stable."

"How do we find that out?"

"That's the critical question. We know from your biopsy that the current effect of the virus on your liver is minimal. What we need to find out is whether it's going to stay that way. I recommend liver function tests every three months, a repeat quantitative viral count every year and probably a repeat liver biopsy in three to five years. That will answer that question. If you stay asymptomatic, if the liver enzyme levels stay normal, and if there is little progression of your biopsy, you may never need treatment. If there is progression, you can jump into treatment at any time, and it's unlikely that you will have burned any bridges in the interim. It's also likely during the interim that treatment will improve significantly for your genotype."

I liked how he was sorting through this. I asked, "Are there going to be better treatments for genotype 1-b in the future?"

"A lot of federal and pharmaceutical money is being focused on genotypes 1-a and b because they are the most prevalent and also where our worst results are. Enormous strides are being made. Ten years ago we knew almost nothing about this virus. Five years ago we could only get ten percent remission. Now we can get twenty percent remission for genotype 1 and fifty percent remission for genotypes 2 and 3. We expect a continued rate of improvement."

Cautiously I asked, "What is the likelihood of sexual transmission in a monogamous relationship?" It was an antiseptic question about an intimate worry. Information on the Internet suggested the possibility of sexual transmission. Could I give this virus to Bev? One of the few bright spots in the last six weeks had been when her blood test for hep-C turned out negative, but we needed to know what might happen in the future.

He looked at me, paused, and then looked at Beverly. "Essentially none. Continue to do what you've always done." He saw us glance at each other.

"In the older literature hepatitis-C was thought to be transmitted by indiscriminate sexual contact. We subsequently found that sex was not the issue. Most of the partners got it by doing drugs together. IV drug use now accounts for ninety percent of transmissions.

"What about alcohol? Is an occasional glass of wine with a meal okay?"

"Don't drink." He was very emphatic. "Of all the variables that influence the progression of this disease, drinking is the one you can control. Even social drinking shortens the time to cirrhosis by half. So my advice is, don't drink."

I asked, "What is my expected longevity without treatment?"

The question was coolly impersonal, as if by using detached clinical language I could dodge a question about my fate. At first he gave me a factual reply. "At your age, with your profile, you have normal longevity and will probably die of unrelated causes. In other words, you will probably die *with* your disease, not from it."

I was not the first scared surgeon this man had counseled. He saw through my defensive distancing. Setting aside his dry probabilities of death, he turned instead to what remained of the rest of my life. He spoke directly to me, not doctor to doctor or even doctor to patient, but as one human being to another. He said, "I don't want you to think of yourself as a sick man. I want you to think of yourself as a well man who has a virus."

His compassion reached out to me. It was a powerful antidote to the image I had formed of myself and the empty prognosis of "Just live with it." My simple thank-you couldn't express my gratitude. He had given me back my life.

My next question was about a different kind of life expectancy. Dr. Carithers was not only a dedicated clinician, he was a man who had built a successful career. I wanted his advice about what would happen to mine. I asked, "If I have an ongoing viremia, would you comment about continuing a surgical practice?"

"This is a different question than the ones about treatment." He paused for a moment, as if choosing his words carefully. "Scientifically, the likelihood of transmission to patients from healthcare workers in general is very small, but for certain specialties it's real. Cardiac surgeons and orthopaedic surgeons have the highest probability of transmitting the virus. There is a published report of a cardiac surgeon with hepatitis-C who infected numerous patients during surgery."

Up to this point he had given me scientific data, information that he knew cold. But this question crossed a line, and he knew it. He sat back for a moment, and then continued. "Politically however, the issue is much different than just what the facts say. In the past, if your diagnosis became known, you would be fired. Now what happens is that, if your diagnosis is known, your referral sources disappear. Orthpaedics is a highly competitive field. If people out there have a choice, this will decide it."

"Yes," I thought, "this will decide it."

The visit was drawing to a close. I had only one question left. I described the isolation of my experience and asked, "Is there a physician support group around here?"

"Not that I know of. Are you interested in starting one?"

"I haven't thought about it. But if you know people who need someone to talk to, let me know. I'd like to be available." My response was the first flicker in what would be a long attempt at healing.

That Friday, August 27, three hours after my appointment with Dr. Carithers, the partners met again. Since the ignorance and anxiety of late July I had learned a lot about hepatitis-C in general, and my disease in particular. After four chaotic weeks a clear plan for the medical part of my problem was now in place.

Figuring out the professional part was not as easy. Labor Day was a week away. I was scheduled to be on call for the three-day weekend, and the other partners intended to be gone. That was a problem. If I didn't do surgery, I couldn't cover the ER, so on short notice we had to hammer out new coverage. We agreed that I would talk to Bruce Thomas about the new situation as soon as he arrived. He and I would make rounds together that weekend on the group's in-patients. That would help him get oriented. I would be available to back him up in the ER all weekend. One of the other partners would be available if an ER patient needed surgery. Compared to what would have happened without Bruce, the plan for the weekend held the hope of a smooth transfer of ER call and emergency surgery.

Beyond that, I still didn't have enough financial facts to plan an alternative to surgical practice. All I could do was focus on the present, the gritty process of transition, so that's what I did. The first priority was to counsel previously scheduled patients. The second was to get Bruce settled in.

On Friday, September 3, I met with the first of the rescheduled patients, Diane Albert, to let her know that I would not be doing her surgery. I had known Diane for years and had operated successfully on her in the past. Now I was dismantling both a confidence I had created and the expectations that she had nurtured. Finding the right words would eventually become easier, but this encounter was as awkward as a teenage breakup. She didn't know Bruce. She and all the subsequent patients had to take my word for him. Remarkably enough, they all did. None of the surgeries went elsewhere.

That Saturday morning, a few days after he arrived, I met with Bruce in the office conference room. I described my diagnosis and my decision to stop operating. I discussed how the office would fit my cases into his schedule and that I would be available when he did them. I covered the dates and details of how and when it would all happen. He expressed his condolences. Then we went up to the hospital to begin rounds together.

Over the Labor Day weekend I wrote a long letter to my extended family. At first I focused on the details of my condition and my decision to discontinue surgery. I found it far harder to describe my isolation and anxiety. As I wrote, however, I gradually recognized the fear that underpinned them both.

> Being a surgeon has provided me with respect, authority, satisfaction and financial security. Recently I have begun to realize what losing that role will mean. It is more than facing a frightening diagnosis or the odds of treatment. It is like a woman facing a mastectomy. It is the fear of losing one's identity and the security it provides in the world. It is this loss that lurks in the emptiness of the night and the apprehension of the past four weeks.

A summer of chaos, ignorance, and uncertainty was over. I had chosen my path. The months ahead promised uncharted change. I needed to rest and prepare for it. The following week, I left the office for a long-awaited vacation.

Autumn

After August 1999 I was no longer a surgeon. After my vacation in September, I began to dismantle the daily details that defined that role. Piece by piece I discarded the patterns of a busy surgical practice, like a man switching off lights in room after room of a house he would soon turn over to someone else.

I confronted piles of surgical journals that chronically obliterated my desktop and threw them all out. Catalogues of instruments crashed into the trashcan after them. I took down the calendar of my call schedule and threw it out. At the hospital I finished dictating a chronic stack of discharge summaries and then walked out of the record room for the last time. I would have no more medical records because I would have no more inpatients.

The structure to life that a tightly scheduled workweek once provided began to loosen and disappear. I canceled my operating days; from now on, I would be in the office all the time. With no inpatients, I made no rounds after office hours. Soon I had no early-morning committee meetings, and eventually I had no need to go to the hospital at all. Instead, I drifted toward a workday I had never known before: nine-to-five.

I turned in my pager. Handing it to Sandy meant more than just returning a small piece of equipment. The act severed a psychological tether, an invisible leash I had worn for years. I had been part of a call schedule ever since medical school, and when I was on call I was always answerable to my pager. When it was on, professional duty relegated every other aspect of my life to second place; its intruding beep claimed priority over anything else I might be doing. The end of my ER and weekend rotation meant the end of that routine, a pace around which I had previously planned the rest of my days. When I clicked the button to "off" and set the pager on Sandy's desk, I felt the change inside me.

Within a week Bruce began operating on people who had been my patients. On September 23 Diane Albert got her new knee. For the next two weeks I sat in the OR without scrubbing in as another surgeon asked for a scalpel to start the case. Being a passive observer left me disconnected and unsatisfied. These were long-term patients whose problems I had once solved with surgery. Now I had no helpful role for them. There would be no grateful thanks, no more "Doctor, I can walk again," comments. By the time Bruce had performed all of my rescheduled cases, I didn't want to be in the operating room any more.

During the same two weeks I struggled to write a letter to my referring physicians. I wanted to inform them that I was tapering down and transferring the surgical part of my practice to Bruce. I didn't mention why I was doing so; that still felt too painful to reveal. Instead, I wrote that I intended to remain in office practice, and then described several non-operative areas in orthopaedics where I could still provide expertise.

It was a dismal effort. For years I had earned referrals from these doctors by giving their patients successful surgical outcomes. The respect produced by those results connected me to the medical community. This letter would end that connection. Once the word was out, I would no longer belong.

I told Jeff Carlin in person. He had referred many arthritic patients like Mark, but he was also a close friend. I could be more open with him than I could be with others. His gaze fell sadly at my news. After we talked, I went back to the clinic and started sending out letters to everyone else.

The office staff was curious to see me sitting there alone, stuffing envelopes. They had no way of knowing that this was not a chore I could delegate; it was part of a process I had to perform myself, a process I had begun with John during my last procedure, a process of disconnecting. The computer printed the body of the letters, but I hand-wrote each greeting. "Dear Kathy..." "Dear Ken..." "Dear Jack..." "Dear Joel..." I signed and sealed a hundred and thirty-five letters that day, thinking of each doctor as I did so. When I mailed them, I ended twenty-one years of professional relationships.

The letters went out a week before a reception that the hospital trustees hosted every year for the medical staff. I spent that evening introducing Bruce to as many colleagues as I could. Because everyone had received the letter by then, it was often the first topic of conversation, but I still wasn't ready to answer some of the questions openly. Later that night I described my reluctance to Bev in different words: "I don't like to bleed in public."

The final bond to break was my relationship to Northwest Hospital. As a busy surgeon, I had spent more time in the operating rooms, the ER and on the orthopaedic floor there than I did at my office. My term as Chief of Staff added even more time in the administration wing, until I felt like I lived at the hospital and my office was only a remote address that I occasionally visited.

In August, when questions about discontinuing surgery loomed large in the night, I remembered the hospital policy our ethics committee wrote in 1994. In early October I went to the hospital to review the policy's terms. It had originally defined the obligations of doctors with the AIDS virus. At the medical staff office I discovered that in 1997, after I had stepped down, the board of trustees had extended the policy to include any health care provider with hepatitis-C.

Its wording was unequivocal. "Seropositive health care workers shall not perform procedures identified by the Hospital as exposure-prone without consent from the Hospital and the specific written informed consent of the patient." Reading those words was like hearing the click of a closing door. Three-quarters of what I did was exposure-prone. All the total joint replacements, all the trauma work, all the power instruments and sharp fragments—they all put patients at risk. Anybody in the OR who looked at a printout of my cases would know it. Once the word got out, the hospital would require me to inform each of those patients explicitly about what I had and what it meant. I had no illusions about what would happen then. Unless I had kept my condition completely hidden, the policy I once helped to write would end my surgical career.

Dr. Greg Schroedl, an emergency room physician by training, was a colleague in the ER and a friend with whom I worked side-by-side when I was Chief of Staff and he was Chief of Staff-Elect. He had since become Vice-President for Medical Affairs, and his office was right around the corner from the medical staff office. After I read the policy I sat for a long moment. Then I asked the medical staff director, "Is Dr. Schroedl in his office this afternoon?"

She replied, "I believe so."

I happened to glance at a large clock on the wall. As the second hand swept around, the same tightness I felt before telling Bob Clawson crept back into my gut. Greg was a good friend, but this would be a visit to an officer of the hospital. As soon as I said what I had to say, he would have to put into motion the policy I had just read. When I talked with Bob, I ended my role as a surgeon. With Greg, I would end my relationship with my workplace. I watched the clock for another minute and then went to his door and knocked. A voice answered, "Come in."

Greg smiled when I entered and rose to greet me from behind his desk. "Hi, Bill. How's it going?"

"Fine," I lied. "Got a minute?"

"Sure. What's on your mind?"

I sat down heavily in the chair across from him. "You know we've brought in a new guy, Bruce Thomas?"

"Yes," he replied. "We credentialed him a few months ago."

"Well, I've decided to taper down. I'm going to be turning over my surgical caseload to him."

"Really…" Greg looked at me quizzically. "Well, sooner or later everybody has to deal with the stresses." I smiled ruefully at the truth of that observation.

"True. That's one explanation…. Now let me tell you what the real reason is."

I talked about facts that were known and then about a future that wasn't. Greg listened with the understanding that it could've happened to him. Another ER doctor had recently suffered a needle stick from an HIV-positive patient.

I told him I was aware of what had to happen next. We talked over the process stipulated by the policy. As I got up to go, he put his hand on my shoulder. "You had a remarkable career here, Bill. It shouldn't have ended this way."

"I know," I replied quietly. "Sometimes I can't believe it's over. There's something surreal about what's happening. It shouldn't have ended this way, but it did."

The official meeting stipulated by the policy convened around a polished mahogany table in the Chief of Staff's office. Present were the medical staff officers and the chief of surgery, all former colleagues. Now they, along with the hospital attorney, constituted an expert review committee, and I was on the other side of the table. I had put myself there, but the changed relationships at the meeting heightened the surreal feeling I had described to Greg.

Later, I received a letter confirming the legal process:

> This is to inform you that the Governing Board formed an expert review committee as authorized by Northwest Hospital's policy concerning HIV and HCV positive health care workers. After reviewing your situation, the review committee, acting for the Quality Standards Committee, recommends that, because of the highly infectious nature of your medical condition and the high-risk orthopaedic surgery which you typically perform, your privileges in orthopaedic surgery are hereby revoked.

> The expert review committee wishes to thank you for voluntarily curtailing your surgical practice and timely notifying us of your condition. Regretfully we must implement the measures as noted above in the interest of patient safety and welfare.

I set the letter down slowly. "Your privileges in orthopaedic surgery are hereby revoked." The outcome of the meeting was a foregone conclusion, but seeing the edict in print felt like looking at the pieces of a broken world.

It was difficult enough to restructure a surgical practice, but altering its economics appeared impossible. Surgical reimbursements produced three-quarters of our total revenues. Fixed overhead consumed forty-five percent of it. Rent and utilities for our office space, salaries and benefits for twenty-three employees, premiums for multiple insurance policies, and the operational expenses of two x-ray rooms and an MRI all had to be paid every month. Only after the bills were paid did the doctors get to divide what was left.

It didn't take a terribly sharp pencil to figure out that without the surgical revenue, reimbursement from office practice didn't come close to covering my expenses, much less produce any income. The math of staying in practice was simple. I had to augment my revenues and decrease my expenses.

It had taken years to build my identity as an orthopaedist; it was impossible to discard it in a few short weeks. Alternative revenue sources such as doing disability examinations, consulting work, or medical administration seemed foreign to me and held no appeal. I could no longer be a surgeon, but I wanted at least to try to remain a clinician, so I clung to caring for orthopaedic patients, even if it was only in the office.

Office practice, however, required a radically different patient mix. Before September, most of my patients were sent from the ER, referred for surgery, or seen as follow-ups post-operatively. Within a month all of those appointments would disappear. I had recognized interests in non-operative areas such as fall prevention, osteoporosis treatment and sports medicine for seniors, but I needed time to transform that expertise into a viable office practice.

It was time I didn't have. Our office overhead was a voracious machine that ate big bites of money every month, whether the revenue was there or not. I spent four weeks trying to trim costs, reducing my operating expenses a little, and my insurance premiums a lot, but there was no fat to trim from monthly rent or office salaries. Up until mid-October, payment from prior cases provided some revenue, but after that I had no income, and my partners started paying my bills.

All of the partners carried both overhead and disability insurance that we hoped would protect us from financial disaster. It soon became obvious that these policies were the only realistic way I could augment my revenue. An overhead policy from CNA was supposed to help pay my share of the clinic's bills. A disability policy from AIG was supposed to help me pay my own. In early October I submitted completed claims to both companies. They would not determine benefits for at least thirty days. Without these benefits I would soon be in a negative cash flow from which I alone couldn't possibly extricate myself. In the business world that process is called a death spiral.

In the midst of a disintegrating practice I received a letter from Mark. In early July he had fallen and sustained a laceration on his chin. Despite immediate antibiotics, three weeks later his right knee became inflamed and was at clear risk for re-infection. If that happened, he knew salvage would be impossible.

Sept. 19, 1999

Dear Dr. Gruber,

I am sorry that I have not provided you with an update of my medical status, but I just now got my computer set up.

I have been hospitalized three times recently for a red and swollen right knee. Three orthopedic doctors saw me in the hospital at the behest of my rheumatologist and infectious disease physicians. They are all trying hard to save the right knee prosthesis. They originally had me on a Vancomycin/gentamyacin combination but the latter caused nausea and kidney dysfunction, so I was put on Vancomycin by itself and for three weeks now have tolerated it well.

They have aspirated the right knee about 8 times so far but no bacteria appear present. The orthopedic physician has referred me to the Hospital of Special Surgery in Manhattan. He felt I needed special attention because of my history and the fact that I've already had revisions.

I hope they can save the right knee hardware and also preserve all the hard work you put into my knee(s). I would never have walked again had it not been for you Dr. Gruber, and I am forever grateful. I might return to the Pacific Northwest one day and if so, I'd like you and Dr. Carlin to be my doctors again.

Please give my regards to Dr. Carlin. Tell him that they suspended the Enbrel while I am on the antibiotic but so far I am feeling relatively good. Maybe it's the climate. Also, please say hello to Linda, John, all the other doctors and all your staff. I was always treated extremely well by everyone in your office.

All in all, except for a few minor pains in my knees when I first get up, I'm fine. I get around well with my cane and recently walked around the Staten Island Zoo for two hours. I'm going to Montauk, Long Island next week, mainly for the three-hour train ride, but I will get in some walking exercise there as well.

I miss Seattle, Washington State and driving trains but am in the process of starting on a model train layout in the basement. So I'll get in my kicks one way or another.

I will ask my new orthopedic doctor to send you his notes per your request.

Yours truly,

Mark

In October, I received follow-up notes from his orthopaedist. Three knee aspirations at weekly intervals all showed only few white cells in the fluid and no growth of bacteria. His doctors stopped the antibiotics and watched him closely, just as I had done. Eventually, the swelling went away. From then on, Mark's knees never bothered him again.

Even in the face of a disastrous threat, his letter revealed the remarkable spirit that I had once watched in person. I kept the print he gave me in my office and looked often at its locomotives, pulling uphill through the mountain pass. Somehow, I was not surprised when his letter showed up. It seemed more than a coincidence. I wrote him back:

Dear Mark,

Thanks for your wonderful letter. I enjoyed hearing from you and appreciate your thoughtfulness in keeping me up-to-date. I have forwarded a copy of it to Dr. Carlin.

It sounds like you are getting very good care with respect to your knee. I have forwarded all of our clinic information. If I can be of any other help, via phone call or fax, please don't hesitate to have your attending physicians be in touch.

I admire the way you are continuing to get out and do things. You have a truly indomitable spirit. I think of you every time I look at the picture you gave me of the train. I think you are as indomitable as that locomotive.

Warmest regards,

Bill

The days of autumn were ending. Out in our yard, a tall maple was gradually losing its large yellow leaves. During the summer its green canopy had provided shelter and shade. Now, one by one, the leaves were drifting downward, dried, curled and turning to brown, until they rested on the ground in scattered disarray and only bare branches remained.

During the days of autumn, I dismantled a work pattern that had served me for two decades. I turned over my surgeries to Bruce, severed my relationship with my referring physicians, had my privileges revoked at the hospital that had been my home and cut what I could from my office overhead. One by one the familiar routines that defined my professional life drifted away. Without their comfortable structure, the world around me, unable any longer to reassure me about who I was, began to feel empty and strange. The identity of orthopaedic surgeon was slipping away, but I had nothing else I could put in its place.

During those days, Mark often appeared in my thoughts. When I read his letter, I felt sad that I could no longer help him. Whatever might happen to his knees, he would have to get by without me. He was in good hands. All of my patients were in good hands, but that wasn't the point. His letter reminded me of all of the patients I could no longer help.

I remembered the desolate moment when Mark knew he could no longer drive trains. Now I would have to let go as he did. My recollection wasn't a comparison; I faced only a fraction of all that he had confronted. Instead, it was a lesson. If he could do it, I could do it.

In early November I planned to spend a special time with my parents and my two brothers. Whatever was going to happen next would have to wait until I returned.

Retreat

Bill Gruber was a monk.

He was also my uncle. Born in 1921 in Cincinnati, he was the youngest of seven children and the namesake of his father, William D. Gruber. He was a brilliant student in college and studied to be an electrical engineer, but while serving in the armed forces occupying Japan after the war he saw devastation around him that was deeply dissatisfying. Upon his return, he struggled to find a path that was more fulfilling. He felt he had a calling to the clergy and initially sought out the Jesuits, but even that life was too involved with the world, so shortly thereafter he transferred to the Trappist monastery at Gethsemani, near Lexington, Kentucky. Within that religious community he initially studied for the priesthood, but later chose the simpler vows of a brother monk, and took the name Brother Cyprian.

The Trappists, also known as the Cistercian Order of the Strict Observance, derive their name from their parent monastery of La Trapp in Normandy, France and live under a rule written by St. Benedict in the sixth century. Through five hundred years of reform, the Trappists have sought to strip away everything that is irrelevant to a life of absolute simplicity. The monks seek their spiritual destiny in a cloistered community, devoting themselves to work, study and prayer without going out into the world. Manual labor makes the monastery self-supporting, silent meditation defines its spirituality and within its liturgies echoes the ancient beauty of Gregorian chant.

Bill remained at Gethsemani until 1951, when the abbot asked him to help with the founding of a new monastery near Buffalo, New York. In 1977 the abbot asked him to move again, this time to help found a monastery at Campo do Tenente, near Curitiba, Brazil. He died there of cancer in 1989.

Our family visited Bill every year while I was growing up. From my father, I learned how to make my way in the world. From my mother, I learned social graces. From my early schooling, I learned the rigid Catholicism of the fifties. From Bill, I learned the value of an inner life.

From 1991 on, a series of yearly reunions drew my extended family closer together. In 1998 we gathered to celebrate my father's ninetieth birthday. At the time, it wasn't clear how many more reunions his age might allow, so in the spring of 1999 we decided to reunite in a different way. My middle brother Don scheduled a family retreat for the five of us at Mepkin Abbey, a Trappist monastery in South Carolina, for late October.

On October 28 I flew to Cincinnati, where Don lived, and together we drove to South Carolina through rolling Appalachian hills covered in autumn foliage of scarlet and gold.

I was glad I hadn't flown directly to Charleston. I was still tense and depleted and needed to unwind. During the long drive, Don asked questions about hepatitis and the effect of its diagnosis on my life. He and I were close. Since college we had talked openly to each other. The car trip and the conversations with him gave me time to put into better perspective the unrelenting upheaval of the past two months.

The next morning we arrived at the small town of Moncks Corners, near Charleston. A few miles down a country road, my oldest brother Ken and my parents had already arrived at the monastery. Don and I joined them at the guesthouse and visited for a while.

The monastery was originally a plantation that belonged to the Laurens family, one of the most prominent among the landed aristocracy of the pre-Civil War South. A monument just outside the monastery gates described the family's vast wealth, power and prestige. The plantation was later purchased, and then donated to the Trappists, by Henry and Clare Boothe Luce, a family that also valued wealth, power and prestige.

The abbey, in contrast, offered values that were diametrically different. As I entered the gates and sought to open to those values, I began a journey far different than the car trip from Cincinnati.

Monks have a different sense of time. Within the abbey walls, life is deliberately slowed down. The markers of monastic time are more like those of the first millennium than today's demanding clocks and digital appointment calendars. There are fewer sharp edges to the pace of the day. Instead of the beep of a pager, church bells mark the passing of the hours and work in the fields marks the passing of the seasons. Slow simplicity becomes a lens through which to see life in greater depth.

The life there is simple, but it is not easy. The monk's day is divided into liturgical hours, beginning with Vigil at 3:20 a.m. and ending with the Compline service at 7:30 p.m. We convened in the abbey church for Sext, the sixth hour, the midday prayer just before lunch. It was November 1, celebrated as All Saints

Day. The readings for the noon service spoke of the departed souls: "Teach us, Oh Lord, to cherish the time we have been given." It was a reading about our priorities in life. My partners and I sometimes talked about that; we just phrased it differently: "Nobody ever went to their grave wishing they had spent more time at the office."

Such an ancient routine might seem odd to the uninitiated, but to me it felt familiar. I was back in a setting I had known a long time ago. In my senior year of high school I went on a weekend retreat to an abbey older than this one, the Trappist monastery at Gethsemani, where my uncle had begun his journey. The lessons of his life spoke to me there, but soon after that I buried myself in college, medical school, residency, and then the duties of family and career. In the midst of all of adulthood's tasks, I never seemed to have enough time to pause and reconnect with those lessons.

Now I wanted to make the time. That afternoon I went for a long walk by myself, seeking to experience fully the setting of Mepkin Abbey. The old plantation was filled with ancient live oaks, whose branches spread outward fifty feet and were hung with a silver drapery of Spanish moss. Footpaths that allowed walking contemplation meandered under them. Benches here and there invited a moment of rest. The lovingly restored gardens of Clare Boothe Luce furnished fragrance to the afternoon air. Ripples of a turtle disappearing from its log were all that broke the peace of a pond beside the path. The abbey garden sloped down to the banks of the Cooper River, where redwing blackbirds warbled in the cattails and tranquil views of low-country marshlands stretched out into the hazy distance.

I left far behind me the stress of overload and walked instead along a path where time slowed to stillness. In this ageless place the voice I had no time for would no longer be dismissed. It was the voice of the inner life I had left behind long ago. The quiet here allowed it to emerge, as if another person was appearing out of a mist. In my solitude, the voice within began a silent conversation.

Why are you here?

"To say goodbye."

To whom will you say goodbye?

"I need to say goodbye to my father."

How will you do that?

"I need to thank him for what he has meant in my life. And I need to let go of him. In doing so, I will be saying goodbye."

What is the task?

"The task is to stay open to what might be."

We began Tuesday morning with the monks at Lauds, the morning prayer at 5:30, followed by breakfast at 6:00, and then by the Eucharist service at 7:30. After the services I went for a walk with my dad. The early dawn became a brilliant day. The moss in the oaks filtered beams of sunlight that lit our path and warmed us as we walked.

He asked, "What's your program?"

My dad had asked me this question for as long as I could remember. I always felt there was more to it than just curiosity. Instead, I projected into it an unspoken expectation about what I was accomplishing, or perhaps what I was supposed to be accomplishing.

Rather than waiting for my answer, he began to talk about the future. "There is so much out there.... There are so many opportunities.... There were so many things that I could have done."

At first I listened as I had in the past, so all I heard was another projection of his expectations for me. Then something changed. I began to listen differently. This was no ordinary talk about accomplishments. He wasn't talking about me. He was talking about himself. Even at age 91, he saw so many opportunities, but now he recognized that he would never take part in them. "I'm an old man," he said. But he could still see them, and they took his spirit to a distant horizon.

He was, in his own way, talking about dying—his dying.

"I feel so inadequate, like I missed so many opportunities growing up. I wanted to learn Latin. My dad never suggested it. I trudged up the street in the dark to serve six-thirty Mass. I remember thinking that the Lord was sure to reward this sort of thing. And He truly has. The Lord has been good to me."

The monastic liturgies had a warm familiarity to him from years of visiting Bill. He talked about how he could see his brother in each of the monks. "I can feel Billy's presence during the services."

He wondered what would happen at the time of his death. "I hope to see the Lord face-to-face. But then I want to see Billy again. That is so important to me. I miss him very much. It's been ten years now. Then I want to see my mom. She was so warm and so wonderful to us kids. She would bake cinnamon buns and make wonderful meals for us. We took it all for granted. She got so depressed in her later years. She just wanted to end it all. I'd go for walks with her and try to make things better, but I'm not sure I ever helped."

In the urgency of his voice I began to hear his message. He was trying to tell me about what really mattered to him, as if he had just discovered it inside and needed to tell me all of it today. When he paused I replied, "Dad, your life has many lessons that will remain alive in each of us."

After our walk the family went into the church for Sext and sat quietly.

Sitting there, listening to the liturgy, I flooded repeatedly, awash in an intense awareness I can't name. I have found no words that describe this feeling well. It is neither grief nor joy. It is not an emotion evoked at will, but instead moves through me, unbidden, like a brief saturating wave that spreads outward from somewhere deep inside and then is gone. At that moment the feeling flooded me with a vivid appreciation that events around me had significance far beyond their surface appearances. Being at the monastery with my family was the work I was supposed to be doing.

High in the front wall of the church there was a circular window of unstained glass. Within the glass was a frame that formed a cross. Within the beam of white sunlight streaming downward from the window my parents sat in quiet contemplation. As I watched them both softly enveloped in the light, the monks rose as one and began to chant the divine office. The waves of flooding continued. Being present became more important than anything I could imagine.

After the noon service, in the monastic tradition, we ate lunch silently. It was simple vegetarian fare, but I concentrated on each bite and savored each taste. Each of us had our own thoughts, and yet we were together as a family. I thought, "What's happening here? We're just sitting here, eating silently, yet something is happening. What is it?"

That afternoon I walked again. It was a walk like the ones I took in late July and early August, an aimless attempt to sort through questions that arose from a place beyond thought. The voice within continued its silent conversation:

Why are you here?

"I need to let go."

Of what?

"My father's expectations for me."

How will you do that?

"I don't know. But that's the real issue. It isn't just saying goodbye to him. It's letting go of what he represents, of what got ingrained into me a long time ago."

You can't be his hero anymore?

"No…I can't." That simple acknowledgment stabbed at me.

Who is Dr. Gruber?

"He's the hero. He's the personification of all of my father's expectations for me. 'My father' and 'Dr. Gruber' are roles that are intertwined, as if each one lives within the other."

What did Dr. Gruber give to your life?

"Acceptance. Being a doctor was a good profession. It was a good living. It was a way of helping people. But way down deep what I did was a way to guarantee acceptance. It was the role by which I connected to the world."

To whom will you say goodbye?

"I need to say goodbye to Dr. Gruber."

If you let go, will you still be loved?

"I don't know. That's where all the turmoil is really coming from. It's the fear of letting go of the white coat. The role is like a magic mask. What will be left if I take it off and toss it away? That's what I'm afraid of. I don't know who's behind the mask."

What is the task?

"The task is to stay open to what might be there."

I walked until the day faded into dusk.

At 6 p.m. the bells in the church tower called the monks to Vespers, the evening prayer, offered in thanksgiving for the day each of us had been given. The liturgy of Vespers, celebrated in monasteries like this for more than fifteen centuries, is a series of chanted psalms, between which there are readings from scripture. After the liturgy the monks dimmed the lights in the church and left for an hour of contemplation. In solitude and stillness they reflected on the evening's reading. It was a familiar one. "He who keeps his life shall lose it. But he that loses his life for My sake shall gain eternal life."

Sitting there in the dim light I heard the words in a different way. "If I cling to my old life, I'll die inside. There's nothing there anymore. There's no life to it. I'd just be going through the motions, clinging to what was out of fear of letting go. If I did that there'd be nothing left but a false self. But what's the alternative? Can I just accept what is happening to me? I could be completely out of a job. How do I get past that? Where do I find the strength to do that?"

This time no voice answered me.

After an hour the monks returned for the Compline service, the final prayer of the day. The Compline liturgy always ends with the prayer of the abbot, "May the almighty and merciful Lord grant us a restful night." The monks traditionally respond, "And a peaceful death. Amen" As each monk leaves, he bows and receives a blessing from the abbot. One of the monks beckoned for us to participate. I watched my father walk slowly forward and bow as the abbot blessed him. After Compline, the grand silence began. Without saying a word, the family walked the few hundred yards from the church to the guesthouse. The day had ended.

Even without an alarm clock, at 3 a.m. I found myself wide-awake. I dressed quietly and walked back to the church by myself. The night was clear and the air crisp. Orion shone brilliantly overhead and a quarter moon rose in the east. Soon after I arrived the monks entered in silence and sat in the darkened church for a short time, meditating. At 3:20 the abbot turned up lights along the side walls and the monks began Vigil. The words of Psalm 133, floating on the simple rhythm of plainchant, resonated through the church. "How good and pleasant it is when brothers live in unity." Sitting there, I reflected about my family, my priorities, and the people who were important in my life.

After Vigil the monks separated and spent the next hour in individual contemplation. Given the hour, I expected to be sleepy. Instead, the opposite was true; surrounded by silence, I felt intensely alive.

I gradually noticed a faint light flickering on the walls of the church. It seemed to come from a narrow vertical opening in the wall next to me. Looking further, I saw that the opening connected the main area of the church, where I was, to a sanctuary, at the front of which was a small alcove. Next to it burned a single candle, whose soft glow bathed the sanctuary and then spread outward through the opening to dance dimly on the walls of the darkened church. Sitting quietly, I focused on the life of the dancing light and the flame within the sanctuary from which it came. Time disappeared. All that remained was awareness of the light.

Eventually I heard the soft shuffle of the monks returning. As one of them brightened the room lights, the subtle dancing light of the candle retreated into the sanctuary. The liturgy of Lauds began.

After breakfast the monks began their day's work. Normally there are conferences for the retreatants during this time, but because of my parent's age we chose to leave the hours unstructured. After getting up so early I anticipated needing a nap, but by mid-morning I felt invigorated, so instead I went for a walk along a meandering path that went down to the garden. The autumn air was brisk and fresh. Sunshine radiated through dew-dampened moss hanging from the trees and dissipated the last remaining patches of morning mist. All around me I sensed both tranquility and beauty.

The path eventually took me past the garden to the riverbank. Next to an old oak, a wrought-iron bench on a small level area faced out over the water. I sat down, watched the river flow by for a while, and then opened a book about life transitions that Bev had given me. In it was a poem about the difficulty of finding one's way:

Mad with thirst, he can't drink from the stream
running so close by his face.

He's like a pearl
on the deep bottom, wondering inside his rigid shell,
"Where is the ocean?"

His mental questionings
form the barrier. His physical eyesight
bandages his knowing.
Self consciousness
plugs his ears.

Stay bewildered in God,
and only that.

—Jelaluddun Rumi (1207–1273)

I read the poem several times and then sat quietly for a while. The poet had written those words in the thirteenth century, but he was speaking to me. The retreat started out about my father, but now it felt larger than that, as if I was being carried on a current I couldn't see.

Dad had asked the guestmaster if he could add a petition to the prayer of the faithful during the Eucharist service. Uncertain of his memory, Dad carefully wrote his petition out ahead of time: "In memory of my dear brother, Cyprian, a Trappist monk for most of his life, who died ten years ago at Novo Mundo Abbey in Brazil. He was my youngest brother, a wonderful man and very dear to me. Please pray for him, as I am sure he is praying for all of us." As Dad struggled through the last words, tears came to his eyes and his voice wavered. In unison, the gathered monks replied with the traditional refrain, "Oh Lord, hear our prayer."

As the family reconvened and walked to lunch, Dad said how uncertain and insecure he felt when he spoke up about Bill. I replied, "It was terribly important for you to say that. We're glad you did." To my surprise, he went on to admit that he actually didn't know Bill well while they were growing up. Dad was twelve years older and went off to college when Bill was still a young boy. The deep bond began later, when Bill entered the monastery. I wondered to myself, "What does Uncle Bill mean to you? He's more than just a younger brother or a pious person. He symbolizes something far more important."

The answer appeared unexpectedly. Dad was an executive. He was famous. All of his life, "doing" defined him. Now he could no longer do, provide, accomplish, achieve. That life was dying. He felt old. Bill was just the opposite. He let go of doing. That's what he symbolized. His life was about letting go of the world's prizes. If the monastery said anything, it said that.

Suddenly, unbidden, words appeared, as if a voice were talking to Dad. *Let go of achieving. Awaken to the reality that you are loved without having to do anything.*

Slowly, I realized that the words were not only about my father.

In the afternoon, while my parents rested, Ken and I went for a walk around the plantation. This visit was my first opportunity to answer his questions about hep-C and the upheavals of August. I hoped that walking and talking with him would help me sort through my own questions as well. After we finished I realized that the opposite was true. Talking with others helped me to sort through events, but the meanings within the events only appeared when I was alone. "That's why they emphasize silence here," I thought. "In the silence are the answers."

The monks supported themselves by revenues from a chicken farm, from which they sold the eggs. The family was invited to see the egg-processing plant later that afternoon. I excused myself from the tour and instead wrote for a while about the nature of work in monastic life.

What made me feel alive here? Where did the monk's contentment come from? Most people I knew seemed to work harder and harder just to buy more and more stuff. After a while their pattern appeared pointless and unfulfilling; their needs seemed to chain them to their jobs. Monastic work stood in striking contrast. Jobs didn't consume these men, or even define them. The monks weren't attached to endless growth, working until their egg business was so big that it took away time for an inner life. They didn't work to compete or achieve; they worked to give balance to their lives.

The morning's scripture reading came to mind. "What does it profit a man if he gains the whole world, but loses his soul?" As I thought about that reading, the phrase changed into words I heard one night in August. "What if you keep your practice, your role, your authority, your income? What if you keep it all, and everything it brings, but in doing so, lose what keeps you alive inside?"

The rest of the family returned from the tour. We sat together in the warm afternoon sun in the guesthouse courtyard, reminiscing as only close families can and telling jokes on ourselves that no one else could hear.

Brother Nicolas, who had conducted the tour of the egg factory, invited us all to the back corner of the plantation to visit the graveyard of the Laurens family. Late on a November afternoon the overgrown graveyard set a somber mood. A broken brick wall and a rusted iron gate surrounded a dozen weathered headstones. This was all that remained of a family that was once one of the most powerful in the southern colonies—privileged oligarchs who ruled in a manner I couldn't imagine. Brother Nicolas entertained us with stories about the family's triumphs and tragedies, the long history of the land, and the brief history of the plantation.

"What was their struggle worth?" I asked myself. "Their wealth and power have vanished. They are all dust to dust and ashes to ashes. There are only weeds growing here now, and even those will pass with time." Fallen leaves rustled at my feet. As the shadows grew long, the rest of the family returned to the guesthouse. I went by myself down to the river to watch the sunset and then, as distant bells rang in the gathering twilight, walked back along the path to Vespers.

The next day was our last at the monastery. I awoke again at 3 a.m., but this time my body argued with me about getting out of bed so early. "Oh, get up," I thought. "You have three hundred and sixty-two days in which to do your sleeping. You have only three days here in which to be awake." As I walked to Vigil in the crisp night air, I was glad I had gotten up.

This time I sought out the experience of the candle. I sat silently in the darkened church, aware of the flickering light, wondering if I could disappear into its presence. The silent questions began again.

What is happening to you?

"My father is failing. A world of comfortable familiarity is crumbling around me. A part of the world I knew is dying. Perhaps a part of me is dying, too. I don't know."

Are you afraid?

"Yes…but not as much as I was."

Why is that?

"Somehow I know now that there is something larger to my life than just the mask. I can sense it all around me here. I have no words for it. I simply know that if I let go…I won't disappear." I began to flood intensely.

After Lauds I walked over to the refectory, the dining hall for the monks and retreatants. There was always a pot of hot coffee there, and by then I needed some. Sitting at the table in the darkness, I curled my hands around the warm mug and sipped slowly, letting my thoughts wander wherever they would. Gradually the darkness gave way to the vague light of early morning. The shadows of other monks sitting by themselves became apparent. One of them nearby looked at me. It was Br. Nicolas.

He asked softly, "Are you okay?"

"Yes," I replied. "At least, I think so." I paused for a moment, and then told him briefly about Uncle Bill, about why my family was here, and why I was.

"That's a lot," he said. "How's it going?"

"I guess okay. I'm just trying to let whatever is going to happen inside…happen."

"Sometimes the simplicity of the life here helps that."

"How does it work?"

He looked at me quietly. "Over the ages a lot of people have tried to answer that question. When I try, a passage from scripture always seems to come to my mind…'Seek and you shall find. Knock and it shall be opened to you.'"

"Thank you," I whispered. The words seemed terribly inadequate for the gratitude I felt.

He gently asked, "Can I help you?"

"I think you already have," I replied. "Please keep us in your prayers."

After the morning services we packed up and loaded the cars. On the way out of the monastery I stopped at its bookstore. Books are my favorite souvenirs, and I was looking for something to take with me that captured the message of Mepkin Abbey. As I browsed through a book that attempted to describe the deeper meaning of the monastic life, my eyes fastened on a sentence that spoke to me: "It is a journey of the heart."

Winter

After the intense experience of Mepkin Abbey, the family relaxed for a few days at Ken's home on Hilton Head Island in South Carolina. Then I returned to Seattle.

I re-entered a different universe. The tranquility of the Carolina monastery disappeared into the dreariness of a Northwest winter. Heavy clouds, hanging low across the November horizon, dimmed each day to a drizzly gray. Chilly air condensed into drifting mist and then into steady rain. Nightfall came earlier with each passing week until there was no evening at all, only a workday from which I drove home in darkness.

During my first week back in the office, instead of seeing the usual twenty-five patients a day, I saw five. Surgical referrals, hospital consultations and ER patients had evaporated from a schedule once crammed full. Pages in the December appointment book were empty. My practice was collapsing. I could not survive like this much longer.

In September, before writing to my referral base, I had carefully analyzed the possibility of a non-surgical office practice. In October, like a man hanging over a cliff, I still clung to the belief that such a practice was possible. I had an established reputation in the community; surely I could think of something, market myself hard enough, and find an answer somewhere. Long computer printouts listed established patients who might still see me for their non-operative problems. Detailed spreadsheets analyzed variable after variable. If only I could come up with enough possibilities I believed that one of them would rescue me. The reams of data were testimony to my faith in analytical problem solving.

It didn't work. Possibilities didn't pay the bills. My share of our overhead was a spiraling auger that dug me deeper into debt at the rate of $17,000 a month, and the months were adding up quickly. If I could rebuild some sort of practice I could dig myself out. If I couldn't, my partners would be stuck with my operating expenses until I could pay them off personally.

The spreadsheets were worthless. Too many unknowns prevented a prediction of when I would reach a positive cash flow. I couldn't determine how long it would take before possibilities became revenue, or how long before revenue would cover expenses. Worst of all, I didn't know when I would hear from the insurance companies. Without that information my practice was in a financial fogbank.

I had a shrinking amount of time to prove that I could survive. I couldn't keep accruing debt indefinitely. Our corporate bylaws prohibited carrying debt into the next year. That was only six weeks away. On December 27 we had to pay off all overhead expenses, balance the books and send them to our accountant. I had to come up with some kind of revenue by then or my partners would have to pay my share of overhead out of their year-end bonuses.

The CNA overhead policy was supposed to pay my operating expenses until I could get back on my feet financially. On Friday, November 19, the week before Thanksgiving, I got an answer: CNA denied the overhead claim.

> "Medical documentation does not support total disability at this time." "Testing does not confirm any lack of abilities or deficits or limitations that would preclude return to surgery."
>
> "Barrier methods of protection such as gloves should be used to prevent transmission to patients."
>
> "You have the right to appeal." "The Appeals Committee will issue a ruling within sixty days of receipt of your appeal. The Committee may need an additional sixty days to reach a decision if necessary."

Six weeks of calculations, expectations and tension exploded into disbelief. The conclusion from this letter was inescapable. Without overhead benefits I was out of practice and deeply in debt.

I had desperately sought some remnant, some shred of clinical orthopaedics to which I could still cling. Perhaps it was because I trained for so many years to do it. Perhaps it was because I did it well. Perhaps it was because I received so much gratification from it. Perhaps I was just clinging to a familiar world because I couldn't imagine a different one. Whatever the reasons might be, now there was no shred left. The words I had spoken to Bev came back to haunt me. In August I had stepped off a diving board and began hurtling downward. With this news I learned that there would be no watery cushion between me and the concrete. A practice built up over twenty years was going to disintegrate in six weeks.

The medical uncertainties of August were at least familiar concepts. By comparison, the opaque terms of the insurance contract were as confusing as a foreign language. That weekend I examined every aspect of the denial, trying to see through its opacity and analyze its weaknesses. Monday morning I began making phone calls. The CNA agent was no help at all. An attorney who had done prior work for us was familiar with insurance issues and felt he could help me. Tuesday I faxed him all my relevant materials.

Because of the upcoming Thanksgiving holiday, his reply wouldn't arrive until the following Monday. The lost time backed me into a corner. My profession, my practice, and my solvency were all on the line. The denial letter stated that CNA could take months to decide my appeal. I didn't have months. Like a blinking neon sign, the calendar reminded me of how little time I had left until December 31. The Friday after Thanksgiving I began writing the appeal letter myself.

The company denied the claim because "testing did not confirm any lack of abilities or deficits or limitations that would preclude return to surgery." Lab tests proved I had a high level of hepatitis-C virus. I was contagious as hell, my caseload put patients at risk and my surgical privileges had been revoked. If that didn't preclude return to surgery, I didn't know what did. And thank you, ma'am, for the suggestion to prevent transmission by using gloves, but I was living proof that even two pair weren't enough. The denial's assertions and evasions pushed my disbelief into smoldering rage.

My life lessons told me that just getting angry didn't solve anything. All my life I feared that anger alone robbed me of the rationality I needed to solve problems and that only thinking and working would get me through. I suppressed the injustice in the letter and instead, with surgical intensity, focused every analytical skill I had on the flaws in the company's denial. Instead of using a scalpel, I dissected each fallacy with logic: "This is an assertion, not a fact." "This is an inaccurate inference." The rebuttals were as aggressive as any operation: "This assumption is unfounded; therefore this conclusion is not valid." "This point is irrelevant."

Fueled by anger and desperation, I could outwork anybody. From Friday to Sunday I wrote all day and late into the night. After Bev reviewed a draft, I went back and wrote it again. Perfectionism drove me to refute every allegation, overturn every objection, and make every point as incisive as possible. On November 29 I faxed the final draft to my attorney. He added information about Washington state law. The next day the hospital attorney added input about hospital policy. I added documentation from my gastroenterologist. Within a week I faxed the completed appeal to CNA. There was nothing left to do then but put a lid on my anger and wait.

The absence of any news from AIG about disability coverage for my own bills soon made waiting unbearable. In early October our insurance agent for AIG had described the claim as "thorough and complete." In early November he blandly reassured me that "the claim was being worked on." On December 6 he confidently repeated that "things looked favorable." By December 10 he had heard nothing further. On December 16 I told him bluntly that time was up and that I needed information from the company immediately. The next day a claims adjudicator told him that the claim "was still being processed," the company's medical department "needed more information," and after that they would make a decision and "get back to us." It was a bogus stall; all the data I had carefully assembled was sitting in a stack of files somewhere, awaiting a glance by a paperpusher with other priorities. I became livid at the time being lost.

By December 17, at our Friday morning meeting, we had to deal with the claim denial. The clock was ticking down to zero. There were only five working days left. The following Monday Sandy would have to begin balancing the year's revenues and expenses. The following Friday the office would be closed for Christmas Eve. On the Monday after that, December 27, we would meet to finalize bonuses. The accountant had to have the books by the 29th in order to file corporate returns by the end of the year.

Everyone reviewed the spreadsheet numbers. They didn't work, and without insurance payments nothing could make them work. To expect a reply from either insurance company within five days appeared hopelessly unrealistic. With growing gloom we talked the alternatives to death and found no solutions. For the first time Herb brought up in public the possibility that at the end of December I might have to leave.

"Bill, can you see any way out of this?"

I paused for a long moment and then shook my head. "No, not really."

"You're $44,000 in the hole for this quarter and $69,000 in the hole for the year. Are you going to be able to come up with that by next week?"

"I guess I'll have to."

"Why are you doing this to yourself? Why not just leave?"

Herb's questions hit with an almost physical impact, as if he had thumped me on the chest. Since August, leaving practice completely had been an option, but always on the bottom of my list, like an analytical afterthought. I didn't know how I'd make a living if I left. Now, escalating indebtedness left me little choice. With hesitant equivocation I answered, "At first, it was because...I wanted to stay in practice. Now, I'm not so sure why I'm doing it."

After the meeting the other partners went to the OR for surgery or to the clinic to see patients. I had no patients to see. I spent the rest of Friday with the accountant, the insurance agent, and the attorney, firing faxes back and forth to the insurance companies. After that there was nothing more to do, so halfway through the day I went home.

That Friday evening we held our office Christmas party in a private room at one of Seattle's sumptuous waterfront restaurants. The partners, plus John, Sandy, and our spouses welcomed Bruce Thomas and his wife. Outside the large picture windows the colors of twinkling Christmas lights reflected off the still water of the darkened lake. The scent of festive greenery freshened the room. Everyone was elegantly dressed; in the background, laughter came up from the main dining room and holiday music played softly in the background. The surface images froze into a montage of nostalgia.

Below the surface there was a surreal quality to the evening, as if in the middle of the room there stood a thousand-pound gorilla of anxiety that everybody knew was there but nobody could talk about. All through the evening we chatted, laughed, raised toasts, and ignored the gorilla.

Saturday morning the anxiety cornered me in my cage. Caught in its grip, I began to lose my ability to solve anything. The day disappeared into phone calls, faxes, and more meetings with the attorney and the accountant. Overwork and chronic insomnia blended into emotional exhaustion. My thinking blurred and my effectiveness faded. Possibilities and decisions that once seemed clear and crisp no longer made much sense.

That Saturday, in the midst of chaos, I received Christmas cards from Mark and his mother. Mark wrote that his knees "seemed to have dodged the bullet this time" and wished me a hearty Merry Christmas. Zita wrote:

Dear Dr. Gruber,

Mark had a bout of Staph, but thank God, that has cleared up. Dr. Bryan Nestor at the Hospital for Special Surgery is Mark's orthopedist here. He is a kind, caring person such as you and we were very fortunate to find him.

Mark is now able to enjoy going to operas and concerts. We have heard two Mozart operas at the Met and a number of New York Philharmonic concerts. All of these places have entrances for handicapped people and thus Mark can attend.

I want to thank you again for everything you did for my son. He would not be alive today if it were not for you and the wonderful care you gave him. I am very grateful. Take care of yourself. You are a valuable person to society.

Sincerely,

Mark's Mom, Zita

I read both cards repeatedly. The caring in their messages touched me deeply and for a moment took me far away from my problems.

It was only a brief respite. My gratitude for the kindness of friends soon sank beneath an urgent need to deal with CNA. On Sunday afternoon I faxed their claims adjudicator:

On December 8, I sent by fax and priority Federal Express a comprehensive appeal to your denial letter of November 19. I have not received a reply.

It has been three months since the onset of the disability, two months since the submission of all forms and six weeks from when we supplied you with all the additional information you requested. You write that it could take up to four more months for a committee to rule on my appeal.

Attached financial records show that, without overhead benefits, I will have a projected deficit of nearly $70,000 for this fiscal year. If I have to wait four more months without benefits, or indeed without even a determination of those benefits, I will incur ruinous debt.

At a meeting scheduled for 5 p.m. on 12/20, we will close our corporate books for the fiscal year and decide whether I can remain in practice. I must have financial information from CNA for those meetings.

Please call me if you can resolve these issues by then. Without some resolution, I will suffer substantial loss, and must seek the support of the Office of Insurance Commissioner to expedite the processing of this claim.

On Monday morning, December 20, the office received a faxed reply, confirming that my appeal had arrived, that I might get an answer as early as a month from now, and that "Your claim is currently being reviewed and we will keep you updated on its status."

It was a non-answer. I gathered up my files and went home to work, away from the distractions of the office. I now had every reason to believe that adjudicating this claim was going to be a long legal struggle. An advocate in the Insurance Commissioner's office spent much of their morning on the phone with me, sorting through the mess. In the meantime, I stared at a growing mountain of losses.

At 3 p.m., two hours before our meeting, Sandy called me at home, her voice spilling over with excitement. She announced that she had just gotten off the phone with CNA. "The adjudicator acknowledged all the points in your appeal! The company is going to accept the claim!" The company would issue checks covering prior expenses within two days. The money would be here in time for next Monday's meeting. It sounded great. She hung up on an upbeat note.

It was such welcome news and hit me with such surprise that it took a while for the darker implications to sink in. CNA's benefits would cover about sixty percent of my overhead. That meant patient revenues would have to cover the other forty percent just to keep me from accruing more debt each month. I would have to see twice as many patients to generate that revenue, and even then, I wouldn't have anything left over. Overhead benefits could keep me in the office, but without disability coverage I wouldn't have any income. I had drawn half my salary in September and October and none since then. Even with CNA's payments, the situation was still unsustainable.

With only forty-five minutes remaining before the meeting, I couldn't calculate a solution. Once we convened, the partners couldn't either. For three hours we struggled to balance the books with the promised payouts, but by 8 p.m. the discussion ground down to weary frustration. CNA's benefits were an essential start, but without any word from AIG they weren't a solution. We adjourned the meeting.

For weeks I had tossed in restless half-sleep. Now I stayed wide-eyed awake all night long, completely conscious, yet strangely numb. I was blankly incapable of analytic thinking. In the blackness of the bedroom I stared at everything but saw nothing. Careful logic and persistence had convinced CNA. What would I have to do to convince AIG? In the darkness, I heard no answers. I was beyond the brink of my ability to solve anything.

On Tuesday morning I called the claims adjudicator at AIG. She gave me the same shuffle I had heard the week before; they "were working on the claim," but "might need more information." I faxed back a reply:

In response to my question about delays, you replied that your medical director needed clarification of specific questions regarding my condition.

The medical facts are very clear. I have a viremia. Because of that, I am contagious and will be for the indefinite future. My hospital has a policy about this. They revoked my surgical privileges. My coverage with you is specific for the practice of surgery. I can't do that anymore. You have received specific and extensive objective documentation of each and every one of these points.

Two months after receiving the claim, you are asking for clarification. This suggests that your medical department did not even begin to review this claim until recently. Even now, you have given me no notification of when processing may be complete.

The standard in the state of Washington for determination of benefits after a claim has been submitted is thirty days. The Office of the Insurance Commissioner has informed me that this situation is a grossly inappropriate way to conduct a claims investigation.

You have not communicated with me in a reasonable and timely fashion. I would like you to send me by fax before close of business tomorrow an estimate of when you will render a determination of benefits.

By Wednesday afternoon there was no reply.

I had nothing left to try. There were no more magic rabbits in the insurance hat. I grew vaguely indifferent to thinking up solutions. Numbness disconnected me from trying anymore. All the weeks of weighing and balancing started to look stupid. I felt like someone in a bar who doesn't really care that he can no longer find his way home.

On Thursday, December 23, I shuffled through a small morning clinic for the few patients I had to see before the holidays. The afternoon was empty. The next day, Christmas Eve, I didn't plan to come in at all. After seeing the last patient I retreated to my back office, made an appointment with my accountant for the following Monday before the year-end meeting, and then began the drudgery of the day's dictation. At 12:30 the receptionist asked by overhead page if I would take a call from AIG.

It was the claims adjudicator. I listened blankly as she told me they had reviewed all of the findings. Then she announced, "Dr. Gruber, I am calling to tell you that AIG has accepted your claim for disability coverage."

I sat there, blinking as if a flashbulb had suddenly gone off in my face, but I had no emotional response to her news at all. With a completely flat affect I took down the details of the acceptance, thanked her, hung up the phone and continued my dictation.

I didn't tell anyone about the call. Perhaps I was numb because the news came out of the blue. Perhaps I felt deflated because their payout was a lot less than our agent had projected. Or perhaps I was a limp balloon, with absolutely no feeling left in me. The reasons didn't matter. I had marched to the point of emotional exhaustion and now, like a dazed soldier, I could only concentrate on putting one foot in front of the other. I had to finish my dictation before I could leave, so that's what I did.

Bev heard the news from the insurance agent. She called me forty minutes later, incredulous that I hadn't called her, and even more incredulous to hear not a shred of interest in my voice. In reply, I mumbled something inane about explaining it all when I got home. Sandy heard from the agent next and hurried into my office, asking excitedly if I had heard the news. With a faint smile of indifference I replied, "Yes, I found out a little while ago." She couldn't believe my response.

I should have told them. I should have shouted the news to everyone. I should have danced out the damn door singing "Merry Christmas!" to the whole office at the top of my lungs. Instead, I placed the stack of completed dictation into my outbox, gathered up my papers, and disappeared.

I desperately needed to get out of there. I fled to Greenlake, an urban park near the office. Light fog over the lake masked the setting sun of an early winter evening. I turned my collar up against the chill and began to walk the three-mile path that circles the lake.

The phone call had been life-defining news. I had income. I could pay my bills. I could even leave if I wanted to. Everyone else expected me to react with a flood of relief. Instead, the news pushed me into intense isolation, an emotional exile in which I could neither feel anything nor talk to anyone. I couldn't think and I couldn't cry. Whatever was walled off inside wouldn't come out. I went walking as if I needed to get away from something, but I couldn't grasp what it was. I remembered Mark as he had tried to escape the realization that he would never drive trains again. Now here I was, walking and walking, perhaps running as well, trying to escape as he had.

The Empty Place

AIG's announcement was so sudden it swept me away, as if I'd been buried by an avalanche. The news relieved my fear of financial failure, but I couldn't get beyond that. I needed the walk around Greenlake to dig out from under its impact.

My thoughts about the future didn't become any clearer that afternoon, but the time alone helped ease the emotional frenzy of the past five days. As I walked, the numbness of my anxiety receded. That night I sank into restful sleep for the first time in weeks. The next day our daughter Cathy arrived for the holidays. Saturday we celebrated Christmas as a family. As I watched the warmth of my wife and daughter in the glow of the Christmas tree in the living room, I remembered the priorities I had appreciated at Mepkin Abbey.

Monday morning I met with my accountant to review spreadsheet information prior to the partners' meeting that evening. I gave him the variables, and this time, working with hard data instead of guesses, he quickly computed the answers. He pointed out unappealing consequences of staying in practice that I hadn't considered. When he finished explaining them I asked, "Jack, what do you think my long-term options are?"

I had considered that question several times in the autumn, but until AIG accepted the claim, answering it had been impossible. Jack had all of our personal financial information in his files. Now he could make firm projections. He began busily entering the data into spreadsheets, but then paused, leaned back in his chair, and looked at me.

"Let me ask you a question first."

"Okay."

"What does Bill want out of all of this?"

I hesitated for a long moment, and then replied softly, "I'm not sure."

He was probing priorities that had quietly shifted. In September I wanted desperately to stay in practice. Ten days ago, when my partners asked me why, I couldn't give them a good reason. A need that was once compelling now felt empty, even a bit stupid. My desire to stay in practice had bled to death.

"I don't have an answer. I'm really torn between staying or doing something different. When you look at the numbers, what do you think? What would happen to us financially if I left?"

I knew our financial situation. Every year I did projections for my retirement plan. I didn't need his numbers. I needed his permission. He was the detached analyst, the objective reviewer, the financial father-figure. I needed him to say, "You're not just running away, Bill. You've met your responsibilities. You can stop now. You don't have to provide anymore."

Accountants have a way of disappearing into their numbers when they're working. It took ten minutes for Jack to pull together relevant information from our file and do his computations. Then he looked up, smiled a bit, and said, "Bill, you're in good shape. If you want to, you can leave."

The partners met at 5 p.m. In several hours, with hard numbers in hand, we hammered out an agreement, balanced the books and closed out the year. 1999 was over. After months of thrashing through alternatives, it all felt anticlimactic.

Reaching a solution lightened my load, but it left me with no illusions. I survived the fourth quarter only because the overhead checks had arrived. The coming year was a different story. Our salary formula wouldn't work for me. It was based on surgical revenues, and if I didn't do surgery, no matter how big an office practice I might build I would never again generate enough revenue to participate as a partner. The numbers were obvious to all of us. Even with overhead benefits I was no longer playing on a level field.

Everybody was bone-weary of dealing with this problem. Allan felt that building a new practice wasn't going to work. Bob suggested that I would be better off leaving. Herb concurred. Nobody wanted to change the formula. Nobody stepped forward and said, "You still have value here. Please stay." This was a business. After everyone had spoken, I realized that I wasn't a part of it anymore. The meeting adjourned.

That night, after Bev and Cathy went to bed, I took a long, hot shower, put on my robe and sank into my favorite chair in the living room. Reclining there, I watched the flames in the fireplace slowly die to embers. As the firelight faded, the room darkened and became quiet. Sitting alone in the silence, I realized that I was going to leave medicine.

It wasn't an analytical decision about leaving the clinic or private practice, or even leaving orthopaedics. Instead, I awakened to an awareness that had probably been there since my walk, but now appeared as an accomplished certainty, beyond rational rebuttal. I could no longer be a doctor. Countless reasons rattled through my mind, like boxcars passing through a crossing, but where they were going no longer mattered. I wasn't on the train anymore.

I had to leave because I couldn't heal patients. That was the center of it all. Four dissatisfying months in the clinic told me that treating people non-operatively left me cold. I saw what needed to be fixed, but then I had to transfer the patient to a partner to fix it. Watching others operate on my patients alienated me intensely. I gained no satisfaction from my surgical skills and no gratification when a patient got better. A sense of disconnection told me I didn't belong in the clinic anymore.

I thought of Mark and all the patients like him whose problems I had once solved. My ability to do that was gone. It was gone when I got the virus, and nothing I could do would ever bring it back.

In August I had realized that if I kept operating I wouldn't be helping people, I'd be placing them at risk because I needed to hang on to doing surgery. In September the same needfulness had pushed me to try practicing in the office. It didn't place patients at risk, but I wasn't healing anybody. I was just kidding myself, clinging to a white coat while the weeks went by. Eventually the emptiness of it all sucked the enthusiasm out of me, until all that was left was a hollow shell propped up by insurance payments. I didn't want to lead that kind of life.

Losing my identity as a doctor was a fearful thought. Fear had fueled all my clinging, and the turmoil that went with it. Fear kept me running for five months, dodging this moment, trying to evade this realization. Nevertheless, whether I liked it or not, something had died inside. The professional part of my life was over.

The next morning I found Bev in the kitchen, baking special cookies that Cathy liked. From the oven came the smell of warm chocolate and sugar coatings. Over cups of coffee, we discussed my decision. Bev had seen the toll the struggle had taken. She responded with relief and gave me the reassurance I needed.

Cathy, twenty-six, lived near Albany, NY. During the autumn's events I had called her and written several long letters, but this was our first chance to talk in person. That afternoon we went for a walk at one of her favorite places, the beach at Discovery Park. The low tide exposed sand bars that sloped outward from the dunes to waves gently lapping in the distance. In the low winter sun, ripples of sand glistened with diamond-points of light. We walked together along the curve of the beach out to West Point and watched the lighthouse blink its white and red beacon out over the sound. Sitting next to her on a bleached piece of driftwood, I described my decision and all that had gone into it. She listened quietly and held my hand.

During the week that ended the millennium I called members of my extended family. I gave Sandy and my partners the news after the holiday ended. In clinic that week I told patients whom I had known for years that I wouldn't be there to see them any more. The hardest bonds to break were the ones with Linda and John. When I scrubbed with John for the last time, I was leaving surgery. Now I was leaving the practice altogether, ending professional relationships that had connected us for years. Telling them left a lingering feeling of desolation.

The front desk receptionist drew an X through the following Thursday's schedule. She asked what to do about the inevitable questions that established patients would ask when she told them there would be no appointments after that. It was time to be open about information I once considered intensely private and kept carefully hidden. I instructed her to give a straightforward answer: "Dr. Gruber acquired hepatitis-C and had to close his practice."

Sandy shut down the less visible parts of the practice. She canceled dues and premiums, terminated tax numbers, ended memberships in organizations and resigned my hospital privileges. On January 12 I saw my last patient. The next day I cleaned out my desk completely, deciding book by book what to take home and what to throw away. Over the subsequent week I said goodbye to nurses in the OR and day-surgery unit, staff on the orthopaedic floor and friends in the clinic building. On January 25 the office held a farewell potluck lunch.

Parting with a daily routine and a deeply ingrained identity felt like a friend's description of getting a divorce after twenty-five years of marriage. In January I felt euphorically free, unburdened from stress in a way I hadn't known since the irresponsible days of college. I had no schedule. Workdays and weekends were all the same. I had no duties, no meetings, and no one turned to me for answers. I was free of demands to produce and responsibilities to provide, and no one held me liable for anything. At the deepest level, I was free of a role I had assumed in residency, a role I had worn for so long that I had come to believe it was the real me.

After the initial euphoria came the sticky negotiations that always accompany a separation of assets. After slogging through misunderstandings and moments of frustration and anxiety, in mid-April we signed papers dissolving my partnership.

After the dissolution of our contract, the final phase of parting appeared. It was an aching emptiness where the role of Dr. Gruber used to be. Every time I said goodbye to someone the emptiness worsened.

When I explained this feeling to friends, I called it "a people hole." My work-days had been filled with people from early in the morning until late at night. I had interacted with nurses on the orthopaedic floor, colleagues in the operating room, hospital administrators, office employees, and medical assistants. Patients had filled my clinic and families waited after surgery. People, more than anything else, had defined my professional life. Now they all vanished, as if they had disap-peared down a hole, and with them went a deep sense of connectedness to a world that was disappearing into my past. I despaired that any other work could ever replace that world.

Autumn allowed me valuable time to separate slowly from surgical patients. As I did so, I learned that saying goodbye to them was a sad but essential part of clo-sure; without doing so I felt cut off, isolated, even embarrassed. Now I had to say goodbye to all of my professional relationships. I wrote my referring doctors, this time explaining openly why I was ending my practice altogether. I couldn't write every patient I had ever seen, but I wanted at least to write to long-term patients whom I had treated in the last two years for an active problem. Using those two search criteria, the office computer generated a long list of names. Everyone on that list got a letter. One of the names was Mark Smetko.

March 3, 2000

Dear Mark,

It has taken me far too long to reply to your kind Christmas note. Unfortunately, over the past eight months I have joined the ranks of being a patient. In late July my internist told me that I have active hepatitis-C. The most likely source was a surgical needle stick. The consequences of that have been far-reaching.

In August I had a liver biopsy and a second opinion at the University. The virus I have does not respond to current treatment and could be transmitted to patients during surgery. Under those circumstances, I decided to end my surgi-cal practice. I did my last case on August 26.

September to December was a transition time. Psychologically it was a period of letting go. I am grateful that this was not an abrupt event, and that I had this time to transition gradually away from being a surgeon. Clinically, I used that period to determine whether office practice was feasible. Apparently I was not cut out to be an internist. Working in the office wasn't worthwhile. Economi-cally, the best time to conclude matters was at the end of the year. In December I decided that the best course from all perspectives was to discontinue practice.

In the course of all of this I have thought of you often. What I have gone through is nothing compared to what you have struggled with for years. The forbearance with which you endured every episode of your illness will remain a constant inspiration to me. One of the hardest things I had to leave was the opportunity to help people such as you.

I truly hope this finds your health stable and your knees continuing to function. Please give my regards to your mom.

Warmest regards,

Bill

I received kind replies from many colleagues, and more than fifty cards and notes from former patients. Whenever depressing thoughts appeared I reread their messages. The appreciation of others cut through my isolation and touched me in a way I could not have imagined. Zita's reply was typical:

April 8, 2000

Dear Dr. Gruber,

I can never thank you enough for everything you did for Mark in the many years that he was your patient. That you are now a patient has upset me so much that I hardly know what to say.

Mark has a fine orthopedic surgeon here at Cornell University but he said many times, "If I need to have any more surgery, I will fly back to Seattle to Dr. Gruber." The hundreds of times that you have been able to fix what was wrong should sustain you for the rest of your life. I am sure that few surgeons have accomplished what you have in twenty-one years of practice. Perhaps you can write a book someday about your experiences.

I can't begin to tell you how sad I am about your situation. That your work put you at risk of contracting diseases makes you a real hero in my eyes. You knew the dangers and yet your desire to help people kept you at it. I want you to know that all of us in the Smetko family care for you deeply and also have great respect and admiration for you. Mark just came out of the hospital a few days ago. He has kidney failure but hopefully he will not have to go on dialysis. He will write to you as soon as he feels stronger.

With many thanks from me, I will close for now.

Sincerely,

Zita

A short time later I heard from Mark. He was too sick to write me himself, so he dictated a letter to his mother from his hospital bed.

April 13, 2000

Dear Dr. Gruber,

This is Mark. I am sorry that I cannot sit down to write a letter to you. I am upset about your illness and I can only tell you that it is the worst news I have heard. I cannot get you out of my mind for long. I remember all your kindness to me and it is only due to you that I am able to walk and function as I have for the past years. Dr. Nestor at Cornell and all my physicians here in Staten Island are amazed at the way I can walk. I have you to thank for this and I am sure there are many, many others whom you have helped in the same way. I can only hope and pray that you will get better.

I do not know if I am saying that in correct medical terms, but I have vasculitis in the kidneys—also in my lungs and other organs. Last week the urologist did a kidney biopsy. The report said my kidneys are functioning at only 20 percent. I am to get chemotherapy for this once a month for six months but that is on hold because I have pneumonia for which I am getting antibiotics.

I have a ticket to visit my brother Carl in California on May 9, but that is also on hold. I have had fevers and in general have not been feeling well. The doctors don't want me to leave until I have had at least three chemo treatments. I can understand this, but needless to say I am very disappointed, as it was something to look forward to. Maybe I will be able to go later in the summer.

My brother Paul takes me to concerts and operas but I really want to go somewhere and do something different. But every time I make plans, I get sick. This hospital stay is the fourth one since the beginning of March. Hopefully I will go home at the end of this week.

I will write to you as soon as I can. I am deeply sorry about your situation and wish such bad things did not happen to good people like you. If there is anything my family and I can do for you, please let us know. We can ask a friend in

Wenatchee to send you apples if you would like this. Just let us know what we can do for you.

With grateful thoughts,

Mark

By mid-April Mark had recovered enough that he could go home from the hospital. He required maximum chemotherapy to keep the vasculitis under control, but when he could finally write to me on his own, he did so as if his medical complications didn't matter. What mattered to him lived beyond his illness.

April 19, 2000

Dear Bill,

I finally feel well enough to sit down, and type out a letter to you personally. I had to dictate the last letter to my mom because when your letter arrived, I was in the hospital again and had more tubes and lines going in me than an Indianapolis race car. My left eye had fogged up on me and I needed her to read your letter to me. I just stared at the ceiling and to be honest, she got very emotional at times as well. In fact, the nurse came in to give me my medication and asked, "What's wrong?"

I am still dismayed, shocked and saddened by your medical problems. I don't want to belabor the point, but I am really at a loss for words in this regard. This is a very difficult reality for me personally. I still consider you 'Dr Gruber', and MY doctor. I have great physicians on my case here but they are all fill-ins. They wouldn't have anyone to work with had you not pulled me through all that mess that I got myself in. I hope and pray that you will get well again.

My joints feel fine. My rheumatoid arthritis remains quiet. I am not on any arthritis medication because they don't want to overload my system. Unfortunately, I have other problems. I've developed a severe case (what else for me), of vasculitis and necrotizing glomerulonephritis. The doctor wrote it down as "P-ANCA vasculitis, Titer >1000" I think it means I have developed antibodies to my own white cells. I have to go in once a month for chemo for six months and am being closely monitored. Still, I remain upbeat. I'll get through this somehow as well.

I am flattered you look to me as one source of inspiration. For what it is worth, I find it helpful to keep in contact with my family and friends. I also need to keep specific goals in mind. I miss the railroad, probably as much as you do surgery, so I am designing a huge model railroad layout for the basement in this house. I have 28 boxes of model locomotives and cars (about 125 locomotives and perhaps 700 cars) stored away and it's time to get them up and running. If I can't run the real ones, I'll get my kicks this way. Besides, I have a 2½ year-old nephew to build it with. I still have goals and plans and they sustain me. The hardest part is that I wanted to go to Hawaii and also California this summer but now must wait until September.

Whatever you decide to do Dr. Gruber, you will be good at it. Just remember, time is a great healer. For me it took almost two years for the reality to sink in that I was no longer able to do what I loved, live where I wanted and just have everything return to the way it once was. But I've made the adjustment. The door closed on that life but a new door to a new life opened up for me as well.

Well Bill, I better get this in the mail to you. I hope this letter finds you feeling better and getting stronger by the day. Please keep me informed of how you are managing. I will let you know as things develop with me. I will also keep you in my daily thoughts and prayers. Please say hello to Linda and Dr. Carlin for me. Most of all, get well!

With warmest regards,

Mark

Mark's transcendence was remarkable. He knew he had Barrett's esophagitis, and knew its eventual consequences. He knew his vasculitis was worsening. "Necrotizing glomerulonephritis" meant that areas of his kidneys were dying because of the inflamed and clogged vessels. He had only a fraction of his kidney function left and teetered on the edge of dialysis. The vasculitis was spreading into his lungs. His antibodies were attacking his own white cells. His doctors were running out of options. Despite knowing all of this, he fought to stay upbeat. He did whatever he could to preserve the little strength he had. He reached out to others. He kept his dreams alive. Above all, he accepted his life for what it was, and each day tried to rise above the suffering that sought to drag him down. In doing so, he taught me how to handle anything that life could hand out.

The payout of disability and overhead benefits settled my financial worries. By mid-April I resolved residual issues about health and malpractice insurance and dissolved my contract with our parent corporation. Northwest Hospital assigned me to emeritus status; in late April I went to the annual dinner meeting of the medical staff for the first time as a retired doctor. As I sat through administrators' updates and after-dinner speeches that no longer pertained to me, I realized that my colleagues, the organization I once led, and the daily commerce of the medical community would go on quite well without me. It was a moment of closure.

April 20 was Holy Thursday, the beginning of the Easter liturgy. I hadn't attended the evening service for years. When I was in practice I never got off work in time. This year, something tugged at me to go downtown to St. James, the archdiocese cathedral. It felt odd, because I didn't know the church at all. I had never even been inside it.

That evening's liturgy is structured around the symbols of the Last Supper—symbols that had powerful meaning for me from when I had served this solemn liturgy as a boy. As I entered St. James, candles everywhere bathed the cathedral in light. The celebrants, entering from the rear of the church in elaborate procession, passed by me in ornate white and gold vestments. Incense floated in the air. From the loft, the great organ filled the vault with reverberating music, while from the apse at the opposite end of the church the choir answered in intricate polyphony. Accompanied by the auxiliary bishop and the pastor, the archbishop, with his miter and crosier[1], walked slowly down the center aisle to the high altar. It is a procession intended to symbolize the entry of Jesus into Jerusalem. To me it also symbolized the power of position and wealth in the world.

Bit by bit the liturgy extinguished every aspect of pomp and glory. After ringing continuously through the "Gloria in excelsis Deo," the bells—and then the organ—fell silent. For the rest of the service only *a cappella* voices echoed throughout the church. After the scripture readings and sermon, the archbishop set aside his elaborate vestments. Wearing only the plain white linen garments called an alb and stole, he knelt and washed the feet of his parishioners. After the Eucharist service the celebrants removed the host in solemn procession to a separate sanctuary, and then departed.

From the rear of the church a lone male voice began in plainchant the canticles of lamentation: "They divided my garments among them, and for my vesture they cast lots." Acolytes in black cassocks snuffed out, one-by-one, each of the tall altar candles and removed them. Silent figures slowly stripped the altar of its splendor, removing linens and lace until only a bare stone table remained. Carefully, the servers draped a red shroud over the large central crucifix, covering it

---

1.   The miter is the peaked hat. The crosier is a staff with a curled top. Together they symbolize the bishop's authority.

from view. The overhead lights were lowered until only dim shapes and shadows remained. As a final symbol one man bent over and extinguished the solitary light of the sanctuary candle.

I knelt alone in the back of the church, surrounded by the symbolism of overwhelming emptiness, and flooded intensely. Wave after wave of utter aloneness washed over me. I knew why I had come. Nothing remained of what once was—absolutely nothing at all.

I didn't return three days later for the Easter service.

For most of May Beverly was out of the country on business. Alone in the house, I watched the person I once was ebb away. The identity through which I had functioned in the world was gone, as if I had been disembodied. Without familiar life landmarks, I couldn't tell who I was. Nothing defined me. Instead, emptiness surrounded me like a dimensionless void. Clinically, the diagnosis would have been acute situational depression, but in simpler terms, a part of me had died, and I needed that time to grieve for it, and then eventually to let it go.

PART III
Teacher

The Letters of Summer

The word "doctor" comes from a word that means "to teach." In 1991, when my relationship with Mark began, I was the doctor and he was the patient. In 2000, in ways I never expected, our roles reversed. I was no longer a doctor. Instead, as he gradually opened up, Mark became my teacher. From him I slowly learned to recognize the path I was traveling.

The word "patient" comes from a word that means "to suffer." As patients, Mark and I couldn't have been more different. There was no comparison between what he went through medically and what I did. The lessons I learned from him weren't about physical pain. Instead, he taught me about the suffering of being trapped within walls, the difficulty of breaking out of them, and the freedom that came from finally doing so.

Residency created my identity as an orthopaedic surgeon. It also trained me to repress everything else. Through long hours and late nights we were taught that feelings interfered with surgical focus. Surgeons soldier on. Hard work wins the game. The toughest and the smartest make it. It was a Faustian bargain.

Mine wasn't the hardened armor that Mark had formed in childhood, but it was a role that gave me security and respect—a mask I fought to keep and was afraid to relinquish. For years I had watched Mark fight to escape his fate. "If only I can keep my knees, I can still work on the railroad." In the autumn of 1999 I did the same thing. For months I clung to the status quo, fighting to find a way to stay in practice. "If only I can practice in the office, I can still be a doctor." "If only…If only…" They were the futile words of our fight to preserve identities that had become illusions.

As 1999 ended, I discovered how draining the struggle to hang on had been for me. Over the next several months I read about its toll on others. Through the web site of the American Academy of Orthopaedic Surgeons, that winter I helped form a support group for other orthopaedists who struggled against hep-C. Colleagues wrote about their fatigue, about fighting to preserve their practice, and continuing to work despite the erosive effects of Interferon. They wrote about wrecked relationships, failing marriages, and inner emptiness. They wrote anonymously to me about their fear of discovery because they had no one else they

131

could trust. They wrote because they were desperately looking for someone who would understand. In their anxiety and depression I recognized the isolation and slow suffocation of leading such a life.

As I watched Mark's struggle, then my own, and then my colleagues', I realized how difficult it is to let go of an acquired identity. "If I'm not what I do, then who am I?" We hung on to what was, not because of reasons, but because of fear—fear that ancient warnings might be true. "What if everyone only relates to the mask, and when it's gone they all leave?" "What if, when the identity disappears, there is nothing else there?" Letting go of an identity touched the primordial fear of abandonment and annihilation.

As I struggled to detach from my prior life, Mark had already detached from his. It was not easy.

In June 1999, three months after Steve died and a month before my diagnosis, Zita and Mark moved from Wenatchee, and Paul and Diana moved from Brooklyn to a large house on Staten Island that Paul had purchased with pooled money. Suddenly three generations had to learn to live together under one roof. The first six months together were a time of immense stress and transformation for them all.

Mark, already resentful about his circumstances, now had to cope with more life changes. He missed life in the West. He had nowhere to go with his feelings about his father. He had only one room in the house to himself. He feared for his knees. That autumn he was on antibiotics for months and knew what would happen if the revisions got infected. All of this upheaval fed resentment and recrimination, which Mark routinely projected onto those around him. For the first six months after the move he regularly created chaos.

Zita, despite her unshakable appearance, was worn down by the year's woes. She had lost her husband, left her only sister and her many friends in Wenatchee and moved across the continent to a house that wasn't hers, a strange neighborhood and a huge city. Despite her age and heart problems, she struggled every day to care for Mark's physical needs and avoid his anger. She bore her greatest worry silently. It was a vague but growing realization that despite her best efforts, her son's illness was getting worse.

Paul had his own stresses. In addition to moving into a new house he was starting a new family with Diana. They had an energetic two-year-old son, Stefan. During the week Paul directed a mental health department, supervised care in a foster child agency, taught college students, and had a clinical therapy practice. On his weekends he arranged to see Cecille, his preadolescent daughter by a prior marriage. Like Zita, he also bore a silent worry. He was a passionate pianist who had recently seen a specialist for increasing pain and stiffness in the joints of his hands.

By the autumn of 1999 Mark's rantings had become intolerable. Paul told him bluntly, "You're acting just like your father did! It's the same outbursts, the same criticisms, the same silent withdrawals! I'm not going to be treated that way." They had several angry exchanges, but unlike the experiences with his father, Mark now lived with a man who didn't distance himself. Paul was both a brother and a psychologist who helped Mark realize that his rage and resentments came from long ago. "Paul did the work with Mark that Mark couldn't do with his dad," Diana said. "The relationship grew very deep."

Within the kindness of a caring family, Mark no longer felt isolated by his ancient hurts. By the spring of 2000 a remarkable transformation was taking place. Medically he remained ill but psychologically he felt safe, possibly for the first time in his life. His defensive walls began to crumble. In April he wrote, "For me it took almost two years for the reality to sink in that I was no longer able to do what I loved, live where I wanted and just have everything return to the way it once was. But I've made the adjustment. The door closed on that life but a new door to a new life opened up...."

In his letters to me that summer he shed the shell that had once walled him off from others. Eventually he showed me how liberating it was to live an open life. That openness drew others to him, and through it he found the strength to continue his journey.

His letters in April created a connection that I wanted to continue. To break out of my emptiness I needed to reach out and reply to him. At first we wrote about familiar topics, such as music or trains, but like our conversations long ago on evening rounds, our letters that summer gradually created a deeper connection.

Mark inherited Zita's love of music; my mother gave me the same gift. Family hardships ended my mother's violin lessons early, but what she lacked in mastery she passed on in appreciation. She collected recordings of classical music. She took me to concerts and operas. On Saturday afternoons in the winter, Metropolitan Opera performances filled our house with the radio voice of Milton Cross.

I didn't have a player's technical mastery of concert music, but I loved its beauty. I wanted to audit an introductory music class in college, but pre-med courses crowded it out. Medical school, specialty training and then private practice left even less time.

When I retired, I put the intensity of that life behind me. In the spring I looked for lectures on music appreciation. In April my mother sent me a check for my birthday. I instantly knew what I wanted to do with it.

April 28, 2000

Dear Mark,

Your comments about my abilities and accomplishments in your letter of April 19, and the note you dictated to your mom, touched me deeply. Your concerns and thoughtfulness meant a lot.

First, some reassurances:

Physically I'm doing okay. My only symptom is fatigue. I had to stop surgery because I am contagious, not because I am sick. I didn't require heavy chemotherapy and my laboratory values are improving. So physically, this has not been a major burden, certainly nothing compared to what you have borne for so long.

Professionally, everything has to end eventually. I did surgery for thirty years. Now it is time to set that aside. I have a variety of other interests. Something else will turn up. Many years ago, when I was an orthopaedic resident at a hospital for handicapped children, the teenage boys challenged us to a basketball game in wheelchairs. They beat us badly. Afterward, one of the boys, a congenital amputee, came up and said to me, "Doc, there are no disabilities. There are only new learning opportunities."

I have never forgotten his words. The process he described is exactly what you described when you shifted from running trains to operating models of them. It's the same message. Now it's up to me to put that message to work in my life. I need to look for new learning opportunities.

My family and friends, in an effort to be supportive, reassured me, "Bill, you can always teach. You can be an administrator. You can do research. There are lots of new roles you can have." What they say is true and I appreciate their encouragement. From my past, I know that I have the abilities to do any of those things.

But those abilities notwithstanding, for me right now there is loss. It is more than the loss of being able to solve a problem surgically. It is the loss of a people-to-people connection, the loss of my ability to help others through their suffering. In no other role is the emotional connection present that your letters so eloquently describe. In no other role are the words I once heard at the bedside: "Doctor, my leg pain is all gone." "My hip works." "I can walk again." "Thanks, Doc, for helping me." This is the loss I am working through.

You are right. Time is a great healer. This sense of loss will pass. I know that. But what I need to tell you here is that your letters are deeply appreciated because they are helping me to let go of this loss. I read them and I smile, because they make me glad that at one time, I could help.

So I want you to know that your words, coming from someone I admire a lot, have meant more than I can adequately express. They have helped me in the one area where I have needed help. With your thoughts and good wishes, an empty place will begin to heal. Thank you.

In the second part of this letter, I would like to reach out to you in return. I remembered that you loved to listen to music when you were in the hospital. Since you moved to New York, I suspect that your hospitalizations have limited your access to performances.

Recently I discovered a company that distributes taped lectures by the country's top teachers. Professor Robert Greenberg of the San Francisco Conservatory taped an introductory course on concert music for them. He has both a mastery of his material and a witty and fascinating lecture style.

Sometime soon, you will receive audiotapes by Professor Greenberg on "How to Listen To and Understand Opera." I thought these lectures might allow you to enjoy music even though your mobility is limited, and hope they yield a deeper appreciation of operas you will someday be able to see.

I look forward to hearing about your train layout. As you may remember, I had a model train when I was growing up and loved it.

I'm also glad you began your recent letter with "Dear Bill." It's time now to let go of Dr Gruber. From now on, it will be just Bill.

Warmest Regards,

Bill

The Greenberg lectures were a small gift, but they opened a large door. We began writing regularly. Our correspondence revealed aspects and interests we hadn't shared before. Mark replied,

May 11, 2000

Dear Bill,

Thank you very much for Professor Greenberg's tapes. They are outstanding and extremely informative. You can tell he is really into his subject because he points out things about opera that we peons just take for granted. The lectures make listening to operas much more meaningful and enjoyable for me now than in the past. I am learning a lot beyond merely knowing the plots and enjoying the music. While I have a way to go to complete all of the lectures, I am listening to each tape several times to make sure I don't miss something.

When my brothers and I were growing up my parents always had classical music blasting through the house. My mom was a concert violinist who won three music scholarships when she was young, so it was inevitable that her sons would be into music as well. John played the flute, Paul played the piano (and still does and is excellent on it), while my oldest brother Carl is a baritone. I studied violin and played the Bach Double Violin Concerto with my mom for a well-known Chicagoan at an award dinner years ago. Unfortunately, I stopped playing when baseball became more important, but we never lost our appreciation for Mozart, Bach and Puccini. I am all set for the fall lineup at the Met. My brother here is an opera nut so he gets my tickets because he knows what I like. Now, with these tapes you so kindly sent me, I'll be a real connoisseur each time I go. Thank you again.

That kid in the wheelchair hit it right on the head. There really "are no disabilities." It's all in how you look at it. I keep thinking of Stephen Hawking and all that he has accomplished. He has only his mind to work with, but what a mind! Maybe you can't do surgery anymore but there are hundreds of people, including myself, who are getting along fine because of your surgical skills. If you don't forget that, you will no doubt remain positive and upbeat. The options opening up to you now are really just different manifestations of the same thing: helping others. I still want to make a positive contribution. As soon as the highly *dis*organized lady coordinator gets organized, I want to tutor disadvantaged kids here on Staten Island.

The chemo treatments have me captive for six months. I go next week for my second round, which the doctor said will be a stronger dose of cytoxan. They said my blood test results were good and there has been improvement in my kidney function. All I know is that it makes me a little nauseated and fatigued. I still have all my hair though.

Last week my brother and I stopped for gas in Perth Amboy and I heard the familiar rumble of a diesel locomotive idling nearby. I started talking to the Conrail crew and once they knew I was a railroader, it was like old times for me. If I could've climbed up the ladder, I'd have done some of the running (driving) for the hoghead (engineer). They invited me up but that is beyond me now. It was great just to talk to rail guys again though. It works for me.

I am still thinking out my future railroad layout. It will be a model of the Great Northern railroad, centered on the Whitefish Mountain area and depicting the Havre Mountain to Spokane mainline. With all the rolling equipment I have though, I may have to revise it to include the entire United States. I got out of control a few times along the way and purchased enough trains to fill Yankee Stadium!

Overall, I am still feeling fairly well. I keep myself occupied reading, listening to music, taping history and scientific documentaries and playing with my computer. I need to exercise more. I won't lie to you and say I've ridden my Aerodyne when I have not but, with the cool weather, I'll be on it everyday from now on. Chemotherapy notwithstanding, I need to build up my stamina.

Well Bill, I'd best close. Thank you a million for Professor Greenberg's wonderful tapes. I am going outside into the garden now with my Walkman and the next lecture. I hope this letter finds you well and content with your newfound activities.

All the best,
Your friend,

Mark

Years ago in the hospital, our talks like this transformed a doctor-patient relationship into a friendship. In our letters this summer I sensed another transformation. Mark had changed. All that I as a doctor once focused on, he by now had left behind. He wasn't in denial. He didn't avoid writing about his disease or his limitations. They simply took second place to something else he had found that was more important to him. He saw each day as a gift.

June 2, 2000

Dear Bill,

I have been meaning to write to you sooner but this chemotherapy had me wiped out most of the time. They put me on iron supplements and now I am getting peppier.

The opera tapes are great. I never knew how little I knew about opera until I began listening to the lectures. I am about half way through the whole series and will no doubt re-listen to them quite a few times.

The good professor's tapes have put me into an opera mood all the time now. As I type this, I am listening to Ponchielli's *La Gioconda*. It's a trip back in time for me. That opera was in my CD player when I got so ill in September of 1997 and ended up on life support. After that hospitalization my family just packed up all my things and moved them out here. I only recently set up my CD player again and the same opera was still in it. So here I am nearly three years later, opening up a time capsule of sorts.

I am looking forward to my first real vacation in four years. In three weeks I am going to Gettysburg! I will meet some Chicago buddies there and get a thorough guided tour of the battlefield. I read all I can on the Civil War, but my friends are real fanatics and they know everything I need to fill in the gaps. I am reading a great book written in 1958 by Glenn Tucker, *High Tide at Gettysburg*. It tells how close the South really came to winning that battle. By reading the book and fighting the battle on my computer I'll be better informed and it will be much more meaningful when I go there. I'm glad I'm going with my brother and two of my best friends. They'll shove my wheel chair around if I get into any tight spots.

I am going to join the YMCA and go swimming every day with my brother. You always encouraged me to swim, remember? I did a lot in Wenatchee after the ankle fusions and also when I had the knee spacers in. I remember how well I felt when I did that. I hope that you are getting enough exercise. I am not the one to look to for inspiration on that score though.

The cytoxan has been both a blessing and a curse. I think the iron supplements will help me deal with the grogginess it causes. I just need to fight the urge to sleep. Does your hepatitis make you tired all the time? My other problem is lack of endurance and stamina. The swimming sessions will take care of that. Don't worry about me, I will not let your handiwork and surgical labors go to waste. As I stated before, Dr. Nestor and all my physicians are determined that I stay out of the operating room and in particular that I keep my present knees. They are astounded that I can walk as well as I do.

What are you doing with your time? I hope this letter finds you active, happy, in good health and in a positive frame of mind. I'll keep you updated on my progress. Write when you have the opportunity.

All the best,

Mark

Mark wanted to know what I was doing with my time. His concern helped me to open to him. I decided to go beyond descriptions of daily activities and write instead about the deeper currents of my life. That was risky for me. In my past, such overtures had sometimes proved too uncomfortable to others and had ended the conversation.

June 5, 2000

Hi Mark,

I thoroughly enjoyed your letter of May 11. I love writing like this!

I share your love of music. Greenberg discusses ancient Greek ideas about why good music has the power to arouse feelings far beyond just enjoyment. Music can be magic. I'm glad you are enjoying the tapes. If you are interested in other lectures by him that I already have, I will copy representative tapes for you to preview. That way you can determine for yourself if you want to buy them.

You asked what I am doing. Right now I'm reading *The Tibetan Book of Living and Dying*. I am fascinated by a comparison of its description of Bardo and the dictionary's description of retirement.

In Tibetan Buddhism, Bardo is the place between lives where souls rest before reincarnating into a next life. For me, not exactly raised Buddhist, Bardo is instead a useful metaphor to describe what I am doing now.

In the dictionary, the first definition of the verb "to retire" is not to leave the work force. The first definition is "to go to a quiet place and rest." Many people ask me, "What are you doing since you retired?" The answer is that I am resting. I'm pausing between lives. I let go of one life; at some point another one will begin. In the metaphor of Bardo, if I use this period of rest for growth and insight, my next life will be better than the one I left. If I don't, I will probably just repeat the pattern of the prior one over again. It is an interesting metaphor to explore just now.

I'm struck by how forward-looking you remain, how generous you are in your desire to help others, how creative you are in discussing your plans for a model railroad and how realistic you are in telling me about how you let go of being a railroad engineer but didn't let go of what it meant to you. You're right. It is all relative. We come into this world rich man, poor man, beggar man or thief as they say, but the real issue is not what we do. What matters is how well we use the time we are given.

Letters are only brief connections. In between letters, I hope you know that I am with you in spirit during all of your efforts. Your mom says you are struggling to regain weight after your chemo. I hope that has improved by now.

Warmest regards,

Bill

After months of chemotherapy, the doctors determined that Mark was in remission. His kidney condition was controlled, his lab values were stable and he didn't need dialysis. That meant Mark wasn't tethered to a machine, and that in turn meant, like long ago, that he was free to roam.

June 21, 2000

Dear Bill,

Well, I'm leaving for Gettysburg on Sunday. I can't wait to see the place where so much history and drama played itself out 137 years ago. I've done a lot of reading about this battle but there are many gaps in my knowledge. A guide will show us around. I will pick his brains with questions. I will also go to the Gettysburg Military Book Store and get you some publications. Trust me, I'll get you what you need to enhance your knowledge.

The experience of seeing this place will certainly have a profound affect upon me. When my girlfriend and I saw Verdun in France in 1972, we both felt a real connection to what happened there so many years before. We were overcome with sadness. Gettysburg will no doubt move me in the same manner.

I will accept your offer of some of the Greenberg lectures. If you would be so kind as to dub the tapes comparing the Beethoven and Mozart piano concertos and perhaps the lectures on the Beethoven symphonies, I would greatly appreciate it. After hearing Beethoven's piano concerto, I'd like to hear Greenberg's take on the two styles.

I have been a great fan of Mozart's piano concertos. I particularly like Rudolf Serkin's performances produced by Deutsche Gramophone. I never tire of hearing them. I have them all, on tape and CD. Recently I was at Avery Fisher Hall and the great Alfred Brendel played Mozart's piano concerto #22. It was incredible! That is my favorite.

I agree with you. Nothing wakes up the senses so profoundly as music. We were lucky that as kids, my folks exposed us to good music. It's kind of sad that many others are not so fortunate.

I find your study of the Buddhist concept of Bardo very interesting. I feel the same way you do. After a period of rest and contemplation, it is time to go on. Life is change and one must go along with the changes. It is good for the mind, it is good for the body, and it is good for the soul. As I recall, Buddhist teachings use the metaphor of a twig that has fallen into a stream. As the twig gently meanders along with the flow of the stream, so should we with our lives.

I will delve into *The Tibetan Book of Living and Dying* once I dig it out. It is still in my unpacked stuff. My mom has read a lot of Thomas Merton, a Trappist monk, poet, and author of many books. One of the best is his *Asian Journals*, which was published after his sudden death in Bangkok in 1968. He was the main speaker at a symposium of Eastern (Buddhist/Zen) and Western (Benedictine/Cistercian) contemplative monks. He believed in the combination of Eastern and Western thought.

You will be happy to know that, per your instructions in 1996–1998, I am back to swimming. I get up at the crack of dawn with my brother and 85-year old mother and head for the Staten Island YMCA. My bum shoulders are a hindrance but I am nevertheless getting along fine. In particular I need to get my legs stronger. It's ridiculous that if I fall down, I am down forever unless somebody helps me up. I am determined to eliminate that in the future. As long as I am alive, there is no reason to remain infirm. Besides, improving oneself is blocked only by one thing—inertia.

I had my third chemo treatment last week. I seem to be tolerating the chemo well and my kidneys are improving. They also gave me two units of blood. I was anemic again and that explains in part why I was so fatigued. You will be interested to know that everyone knows me at St Vincent's Hospital now, just like they did at Northwest. I go down the halls, and it's "Hi Mark!!" They know me on every floor except the maternity ward.

I hope that you are feeling well and keeping your dreams alive. They do indeed come true. There is really no reason to get down or depressed. Life lies in another direction. I had to learn that myself. Know that you are always in my thoughts and my prayers.

All the best and until later, keep faith in yourself.

Mark

Mark had a safe and enjoyable trip to Gettysburg. Shortly after he returned I received a large package, filled to overflowing with National Park pamphlets, battlefield maps and tour books. No wonder people said "Hi" to him in the hospital halls. His enthusiasm and generosity flowed outward to all he met. A man who had once wanted his hospital door closed and the covers drawn up over his head now opened to embrace everyone. His promise, "Trust me, I'll get you what you need to enhance your knowledge," was probably more accurate than he realized.

After the package arrived I wrote him back.

July 23, 2000

Hi Mark,

First, a note of apology for not getting back to you promptly after your wonderful presents and letter from Gettysburg. I was trying to copy the Greenberg lectures you selected but it didn't work out well. I'll just send you the originals. Listen to them, duplicate them if you wish, and then send them back to me. I will be traveling this fall, and won't listen to them for some time anyway. I look forward to your comments on Greenberg's comparison of the Mozart and Beethoven concertos.

I was moved by your description of the Gettysburg battlefield. You saw so much more there than just faded photos and stone monuments. You are aware of what took place there in a way that makes it all come alive.

I believe that trying to capture this "sense of the place" adds a lot to a visit. When I saw Gettysburg many years ago, I camped out near the old road down which the Confederate divisions marched toward the town. I deliberately broke camp early and walked in the predawn stillness along their path to Seminary Ridge. As dawn began to break, I stood on the Confederate side of the battle of the third day. There were no other tourists present yet. I was there in solitude and silence. In the half-light, stone statues of soldiers seemed to speak, cannon seemed aimed and one could imagine the sounds of distant bugles and drums. A shallow mist lay in the low field that stretched out to Cemetery Hill, the field across which those soldiers would soon resolutely advance. I felt as if ghosts were still there, the spirits of thousands of men looking out across that space, listening to those bugles and waiting.

The crowds and noise and heat of the day soon drowned out the stillness and yanked me back into the twentieth century. I toured the other sites and read the relevant facts, but the emotional connection of the early morning is the experience I can't forget. There was something of reverence about it. From your letter, I think you know what I'm talking about.

We seem to have yet another common interest, Eastern and Western contemplative thought. After you dig out *The Tibetan Book of Living and Dying*, let me know more about your thoughts on Bardo. I found the book influential, as were the books by Merton that you mentioned. He seems to be another interest that we share. You see, my uncle was a Trappist monk and contemporary of Merton's for a while at Gethsemani. Recently, my readings have centered on exactly the issue you mention, namely, the wisdom shared between Eastern and Western contemplative traditions. When I ended my medical practice, I began meditation, something I previously didn't have time for. It has helped me substantially.

When your passenger train arrives, I would love to see photos. What is the scale of this train? It sounds big.

I hope your chemo is going well. You likewise are in my thoughts and prayers. Thanks again for the package. Say hi to your mom for me.

   Bill

By late July Mark had obtained an Internet provider service, so we switched our correspondence from letters to e-mail. Without the delay of surface mail our exchanges began to feel more like a conversation than a correspondence. At one point I suggested Instant Messaging. That wasn't a good idea. Caught up in cyber-spontaneity, I had forgotten the extent of Mark's physical limitations. The arthritic deformities in his hands and wrists allowed him to type with only one finger.

7/30/00

Hello Bill,

Thanks for the tapes. I'll listen to them and get them back to you ASAP.

I've been anemic, so they are putting me on Procrit, a medicine to build up my blood count. Other than that, my health and kidneys are fine. How is your health coming along?

I found my *The Tibetan Book of Living and Dying*. I've begun to read about Bardo but my left eye is going bad on me. I'll let you know later what I think about it.

My all-brass Great Northern Empire Builder passenger train will arrive sometime this year. I ordered it five years ago and it is finally coming. I have seven big passenger steam locomotives capable of handling such a heavy train. I also have a Great Northern 10-car baggage & mail train coming. They are exact brass replicas as well. Once they all arrive I'll line up the cars and photograph them for you.

Some day you will have to see my railroad—once it is up and running. My brass locomotive fleet is nearly all Great Northern prototypes. There was a period of time (1944–1957), when steam and diesel power overlapped on the American railroad scene and the Great Northern was no exception. Since these trains may have been heavier than one steam engine could handle, I have several early versions of 4-unit diesel sets ready to take over. The cars have custom interiors and 'grain of wheat bulb' interior lighting. I had to order this train five years ago because they only produce maybe forty or fifty sets of them. I was lucky. All the rest sold out long ago.

I can't wait to set up my railroad. My two and a half year-old nephew will get all this once I pass on. But not before! And for obvious reasons: he throws temper tantrums when his toy trains derail, screams at them and beats himself on the head with his engine. It is an absolute riot!

Your friend,

Mark

It was characteristic that Mark wrote revealingly about himself, but rarely about his family. His brief comments about Stefan were only a small glimpse into all that was happening in their house.

As Mark's relationship to the children brightened, however, other aspects of his life dimmed. A new shadow was floating across the small and shrinking world still left to him. He was losing the sight in his left eye.

8/14/00

Dear Bill,

I am in a writing mood at the moment and catching up on all my correspondence. It's been very Seattle-like in New York this summer, with cool, rainy, gray skies. It reminds me of my previous home. I love it!

I started to read about Bardo in *The Tibetan Book of Living and Dying*. However, my bum left eye made it difficult to read anything. I have to close that eye to read and it puts an undue strain on my right eye. It's hard reading with one eye shut all the time. The ophthalmologist changed my prescription and said if that didn't work I might need membrane laser surgery. All my physicians prefer not to operate on me because of my medical problems, but that may be a moot point. Reading is one of my most important activities. Now that I have most of my books unpacked and my library set up just like in my Seattle house, I need to be able to read unencumbered.

I was interested and enlightened by the little bit I was able to read in the Tibetan book. Now, more than ever, I want to dig deeper into it. I got interested in Tibetan culture and Eastern contemplative thought in an indirect way. I bought a book about 18 years ago, *Himalayas*, with photographs by Yoshikazu Shirakawa. The photos of the various mountains were awesome, but there was one particular mountain that I became obsessed with, Ama Dablam. It wasn't the highest peak by any stretch, but it was incredibly beautiful. It is a sacred mountain to the Buddhists. I thought, "What a fabulous place this was for the monks to do their meditations and gain insight." I wonder if Thomas Merton ever visited there. If he did, I'm sure he couldn't help but be inspired by it.

My mom finds the news about your uncle very interesting. She said she will write to you about this. I am going to read Merton myself and should probably begin with *The Seven Storey Mountain. The Tibetan Book of Living and Dying*, as written by Rinpoche, seems a bit easier to understand and digest. But anyway, Tibetan and Buddhist culture and the mountains in Nepal all seem to bring together a whole new aspect of thought that needs exploring.

As for me, if I can work around this week's chemo session, my brother and I might head for Baltimore and a baseball game between the O's and White Sox. We saw two games between the Cubs and Phillies in Philadelphia. I also want to go to Lincoln Center this week for the Mostly Mozart Festival featuring Andre Watts on the piano and Julia Fischer on violin. Next week, they feature a Bach celebration with the Mass in B minor, then the complete Bach sonatas and finally the closing night celebration of Mozart's Mass in C minor.

I understand you are traveling this coming fall. When are you going and where? I hope it is someplace beautiful, inspiring and relaxing. You definitely owe it to yourself. Let me know where you are traveling, as I am interested. Once I finish with chemotherapy in mid-September, I'm going to travel too. In October I am going to California to hike with my brother Carl in the Sierras and on Catalina Island. Ever since I heard that song "26 Miles Across the Sea..." I've been fascinated with Catalina. My brother will give me a ride in his jazzed up Mustang race car. Then in November, I am going to D.C. to visit the Smithsonian, Library of Congress, and perhaps Congress itself to tell them what I think of them, a lifelong quest. That, plus several Mozart operas at the Met, the Notre Dame/Rutgers football game at Piscataway, a Chicago Bears/Giants game and hopefully no hospital detours. Outside of the chemo and eye problems, this month looks mighty fine!

I need to be able to look forward to all these activities and events in order to keep my depression at bay. I wish I was still working and being more productive, but my chosen profession is out of my hands now. However, as you well know, that does not mean that life has become empty. Consequently, I also have plans for Hawaii and Ireland in my near future.

I am still listening to the Greenberg tapes and will return them to you as soon as I am finished. I keep thinking about how passionate Professor Greenberg is with his subjects and that is a jewel in itself. Thank you again for sharing these tapes with me. I'll comment on them in more detail once I finish them and am able to piece together all my thoughts.

How have you been feeling these days? My mom, brothers and I are concerned about this. Also, how is your support group coming along? I have often thought of going into a support group myself, but I don't do well in those kinds of settings. If I could do it over the Internet in an arthritis chat room for example, perhaps that would be my way to go.

Anyway, my problem isn't so much my illness as it is my loss of control and independence. I often dream that I am back at work, out there on the mainline, but then when I wake up, I get a little morose and nostalgic because after all, it was just a dream. In my afterlife though, I know exactly where I want to be—in an engine cab "highballing down the high iron."

Well, I better close. Best wishes to you and your family and until the next time,

Your friend,

Mark

"In an engine cab, highballing down the high iron." That's where Mark wanted to be in the afterlife. The destinations he wanted to visit mirrored the freedom he once knew in his trains, freedom he longed to feel again.

Physically, he was not doing well. His brother Carl, who had visited in July, said "He had aged a lot. He looked puffier. He needed a cane. He wanted to be by himself more. He seemed depressed."

How then could Mark write that "this month looked mighty fine"? Was he in denial? The medical facts that he mentioned in his letters suggested that he knew he would never recover, but I listened differently now than I once did as a doctor. I believe he wrote as he did because he realized that no matter what his disease threw at him, he alone determined his attitude about it.

Even as he put his hopes for travel down on paper, however, little eddies of sadness swirled around his sentences. There was so much out there that he would never see, and he knew it. "I need to be able to look forward to all these activities and events in order to keep my depression at bay." I believe he chose to look at life as "mighty fine" because the alternative was a darkness he had lived in far too long.

August slipped by before I wrote my next letter. On the surface, the month was filled with guests and outdoor summer activities. Below the surface, I was changing.

9/4/00

Hi Mark!

This is long overdue, but not out of neglect. I have been traveling, perhaps in more ways than one.

In the conventional sense of traveling, I just returned from Alaska. I helped a friend bring his boat from Glacier Bay to Ketchikan. If you are so inclined, I will send you the narrative of the trip from my journal.

I am on a journey within as well. The signposts aren't quite as easy to discern, but I sense that healing is happening and I am finally letting go of a life that is receding into my past. Your example and your encouragement in this process have meant more than you might guess. I truly appreciate your counsel.

I enjoyed your comments about Merton. I hope his writings are a source of strength for you and your mom.

I also enjoyed the photos of your model trains. I can relate to the details of your railroad cars. I used to build models and was also a fanatic about getting the details right. (Not a bad trait for a surgeon!) It once took me a year to build a detailed model of a clipper ship that had working running rigging. So I smiled when I read about your excitement over building your railroad. Stay with it. I agree with you. Dreams do indeed keep us alive.

I will send you Greenberg's lectures on Beethoven's symphonies next. There is no rush to return them. My wife Beverly has been leading cooking tours to Italy for five years. In the past, because of work, I wasn't able to take the time to travel like she does. Now I can, so I will be in Italy from September 23 to October 24. For most of November we plan to visit my parents and my oldest brother in South Carolina, so you need send nothing back until December 1.

My health remains good. You mentioned that you had another important eye appointment coming up. I hope that went well and that your eyesight has improved.

Warmest regards,

Bill

9/5/00

Dear Bill,

I must confess I was a bit worried when I hadn't heard from you that perhaps you were ill or even worse, in the hospital. Thankfully, you were traveling and having a ball. Believe me Bill, you owe it to yourself to do that. Operating on me between 8 a.m. and 4 p.m. and then taking on somebody else until midnight, getting awakened during the night and then having office hours the next day takes its toll. I always marveled at how you handled that. You deserve the change of pace.

I would love to read your journal from your Alaskan trip. Alaska has always held a fascination with me even though I've never traveled there. I might get my chance next summer. My cousin in Gig Harbor wants me to go with him on his boat up there. I can't wait. I'll pay you a visit while I am back in my beloved Pacific Northwest.

I would also love to see a photo of your clipper ship. I remember a model boat shop in Evanston, Illinois that had hundreds of ships such as you described. A person could build a Bounty, a clipper, a British 4-stacker, a tugboat, liberty ship—you name it! They had brass fittings and parts innumerable. I was enthralled in that shop. Were I not into trains, I would've been building up a fleet by now.

Have you ever visited the Museum of Science & Industry in Chicago? In the area where you can enter the German U-boat, they have scores of ship models, displayed in exquisite detail. Growing up in Chicago, I went there often and I always made a beeline to the huge Santa Fe Railway layout and the ship models.

Most of my books are finally unpacked. I am literally living in a library now, but I am forced to use space judiciously, like on a nuclear submarine. I had much more room in my modest home in Seattle but even there, I was swamped. Here I can't afford to waste any space whatsoever. I have scores of railroad prints, paintings and Winslow Homer prints, but little space to display them. I may have to rotate them.

I'll get you color pix of my trains once they arrive. Some will be painted Pullman green and gold while others will be Great Northern orange and olive green. The mail train will be ten baggage and mail cars plus one coach car. Railroads tried to discourage people from riding their mail & express trains but provided a second class coach for the diehards. I love these kinds of trains. They were not as glamorous as the named trains and Limiteds, but they ran like the wind.

Every railroad had a fast mail train. The company's best motive power was always assigned to them and woe to anybody who caused their delay. I caught them occasionally when my name came up next on the crew board. They were preferred assignments and we had priority over everything, even Amtrak. It was green signals all the way. When I worked for the Santa Fe back in the 1970's, I occasionally got assigned to the "Red Balls." Those were 80-mph freight trains. The Santa Fe was one "highballing railroad."

I look forward to the Beethoven tapes and will send them back to you in a timely manner. In Greenberg's analysis of Mozart's 25th piano concerto, the fourth theme in the first movement is what I consider 'goose bump' music. It is so beautiful and simple that it gives me goose bumps. It is hard to put into words, although Greenberg does the best job of anybody. I love the way he takes music apart and analyzes each segment. He is as much a master as the composers themselves. Wouldn't you agree?

I am happy for you that you are going to Italy. I was there years ago and consider Italy one of the world's most beautiful countries. If you are going to Milan, I am sure you will be seeing both the Cathedral and La Scala. Mark Twain describes the incredible beauty of the Milan Cathedral in *Innocents Abroad* (1869). My maternal grandmother taught German to Italian children in an exclusive school there before 1900. She went to Mass at the Milan Cathedral where singers from the La Scala Opera, singing either solo or in the chorus, often sang the Mass. My grandmother loved opera. In any case, you will love Italy.

The eye doctor gave me a new prescription and if that doesn't work, I'll need laser surgery on the membrane. Nobody wants to operate on me except as a last resort. In Seattle, as you know, there was no other alternative. All in all though, I feel fine. I am also happy to hear your liver function is satisfactory. My mom and I pray for your well being daily.

Keep healthy! Keep traveling! And keep yourself happy. All the best and best wishes to you and your wife on your upcoming travels.

Your friend,

Mark

I sent the journal notes of my Alaskan trip. I was concerned that descriptions of far-away places might add to Mark's frustration about his limits. I needn't have worried.

9/16/00

Bill,

Thanks for the Beethoven tapes. I will begin listening to them after today's baseball game and return them to you by Dec 1. Also, thanks for sending your journal on your Alaskan trip. Now that's what I call living! I am determined to take a similar one myself now. I've always wanted to take a cruise up there. I'll have my opportunity next year with either my cousin or my brother.

I wanted to wish you and your wife Beverly a wonderful trip to Italy. Try to get to Milan if time allows. You'll love La Scala and the cathedral.

All the best and until next time,

Mark

This was Mark, through the window of his own words. His letters reveal his optimism, his enthusiasm and his breadth of interests. They illustrate how, in the face of physical adversity, he reached beyond his own fate to care about others.

The person himself had not morphed into some placid personality. Make no mistake—Mark's life was not idyllic and he was often not easy to live with. As he struggled to emerge from his past, he could be moody, cantankerous, hurtful or depressed, and was sometimes all of those at once. Nevertheless, surrounded by people who continued to care, he gradually tamed the tempests of his prior world. By the time he wrote his letters in the summer of 2000, the hardened armor that had shielded him was disintegrating. A man once broken was becoming whole. His was not a state of bliss, but during those months he began to find a state of joy.

How did the real Mark break through?

The word "shame" comes from a word that means "to hide." Few people break out of a shame-hardened shell by themselves. Some try to run. Most choose to hide. Mark changed because he could neither run nor hide. Fate put him into a corner like an unyielding teacher and didn't let him out. He couldn't hide from his physical deterioration. He knew the limits of his life expectancy. He had nearly died twice. No one returns from those experiences unchanged.

After those episodes he no longer cowered in the corner. I believe that, instead, Mark made several difficult but deliberate choices that lifted him out of his past and pointed him toward a path of personal transformation.

His relationship with his father might have ended in frozen rage, recrimination, and a life of barely suppressed bitterness. Instead, in the hardest of all conscious choices, he had asked his father for forgiveness, and when Steve died, Mark, with a kiss, in turn forgave him. I believe that Mark's acts of forgiveness began a profound transformation. Steve's death ended a physical presence. Mark's forgiveness ended a relationship. For the first time in his life he was free of the fear his father symbolized.

I believe he changed because he lived within an extended family whose members openly cared for one another. For the first time in his adult life, he routinely had children around him. Stefan was spontaneous and wanted to play. One night he was lonely, so he toddled downstairs, curled up, and went to sleep on Uncle Mark's lap. Mark beamed in surprise and delight. Diana said, "It was like an epiphany." A relationship with Cecille came more slowly. At first a preadolescent girl brought out Mark's awkwardness, but in time they both overcame their reservations. Gradually, both Stefan and Cecille wormed their way past Mark's walls and drew him out; faced with their openness, he could no longer contain feelings of affection he had hidden for so long. The children taught his solitary soul how to play, and in return he learned to love them.

Once he felt safe, I believe Mark changed because he chose to open to others. He could have stayed cooped up in his room reading his books. Instead, he gradually unpacked his possessions and recreated his interests. He set up his computer and used the Internet to widen his world. He looked forward to tutoring children. He resumed traveling. His correspondence grew. As he opened outwardly, Mark revealed the caring inner person he had long ago hidden away.

I believe that in the letters he wrote to me that summer, this once-hidden person found his voice. In his letters he revealed his dreams, his compassion and his empathy. These were not predetermined attitudes or foregone conclusions. In the face of relentless disease and daily disabilities, these attributes shone because they were conscious choices he fought for every day, deliberate decisions he made about how he would face the world. He faltered often, but he always returned to them. If nothing else, his letters are testimony to that.

As the real Mark emerged, I believe he began the final part of his journey; he began to help others. Many were drawn into the expanding circle of his openness. I was fortunate to be one of them. Someone I had once helped was now helping me—in ways I could never before have imagined. Despite the disparity of our diseases, he wrote to me as if we were in this together. I believe he knew that in the largest sense, we were.

On September 23, Beverly and I left for Italy. Shortly afterward, Mark left on his long-awaited trip to California to visit his brother Carl.

Transformed

If highballing down the high iron in a diesel locomotive was Mark's idea of heaven, screaming around a Formula 1 race course in a hot car was a close second. Willow Springs International Raceway was a 2.5-mile course in southern California that Carl raced at regularly in a red Mustang Cobra. The car was supercharged and intercooled to 580 horsepower, and it wasn't afraid of the curves. Strapped tightly into the passenger seat by a racing harness buckled across his chest, Mark roared around again with his big brother, just as they had when they were growing up. In the pits, he hung out with car guys and talked muscle machines, just as he had once hung out with railroaders and talked steam locomotives. Out on the course, as Carl pushed the accelerator to the limits of his brother's safety, Mark grinned in the wind with euphoria for speed that he hadn't felt for a long time.

He was out West again—out where he still heard the siren song of open spaces that had seduced him as a youth. Zita had taken him to the Swiss Alps with his brothers when he was eighteen; his love for the mountains took him from there. He climbed in Germany and Colorado, and after he moved to Seattle he took walks in the Cascades whenever he could. In 1982, despite painful knees, he managed 3000 feet of elevation gain in the Tetons with Carl and Paul. His disease wore him down, but the lure never left him.

Now his stride was stiff and cautious. He needed a cane to steady himself. He could barely climb stairs. None of that mattered to him. Regardless of what he could no longer do, Mark was back where he wanted to be. As he wrote me, "It's all relative." Being out West was a breathtaking vista compared to the walled confinement of a Staten Island hospital room.

For Mark the West was not a place—it was a state of mind. In it he could climb above his life's limits and gaze at a wider vision. He wanted to see Catalina Island because "I know it's out there and I want to go there." He yearned to be in Hawaii next year, Alaska after that, and countless countries beyond. His trip out West was a symbol of his dream to be free, and there were no limits to the destinations in his dreams.

During the same period, I was emerging from the narrow world I had known. During the summer of 2000 I came out of a tunnel of intellectual confinement. Greenberg's lectures were only part of a long list of interests previously prohibited by the pressures of practice. I began to read extensively, meditate regularly, keep a journal, visit with my extended family, stroll through galleries, and crew on a friend's boat in Alaska for as long as he needed me. In October, while Mark was visiting Carl, I went to Italy for four weeks. During that trip I came out of a tunnel of a different kind: a tunnel of time.

Beverly taught cooking and loved Italy. When Cathy left the nest, Bev began leading cooking tours to Tuscany, and by 1995 made it her main business. I envied her. While I was in practice, I couldn't feel comfortable taking off enough time to travel like that. All too often a tight schedule transformed my trips into forced marches, an ongoing effort to cram too many activities into too little time. Like the white rabbit in Alice's Wonderland, I was always in a hurry, burdened by a clock that never had enough hours.

Until my trip to Italy I had no idea how work had shaped my perception of time. Since the days of Isaac Newton, the Western world has conceptualized time as a line, along which every event has a beginning, a duration, and an end. I had accepted this concept as an absolute. The sequence seemed so essential as to be intrinsic, as if time couldn't be otherwise. There appeared to be no alternative to an appointment book that determined the weekdays I worked and the weekends I didn't. Because time was always scheduled, it was always scarce.

I didn't realize how confining this artificial absolute was until I was free of it. Relieved of choices forced by call schedules and the constraints of paying office overhead, I went abroad for a month and then went to Hilton Head for another three weeks. When I did so, I was free in a way that would have been unthinkable in my past.

In Italy I deliberately traveled slowly. Mine was a pedestrian's pace. In Florence I wandered at whim through its cultural treasures, marveling at the legacy left by the Renaissance. In Rome I walked amid the monuments of an eternal city, read inscriptions in once-familiar Latin and reexamined the roots of my upbringing. Near Venice I biked for a week along back roads, stopping at out-of-the-way places to have a cappuccino or gelato or to make new friends. North of Rome I sat in on one of Beverly's cooking tours at a villa overlooking the rolling hills of Civitavecchia.

I wasn't traveling to get away from it all. I had no agenda, no list of sights I was supposed to see. Instead, I traveled to become more aware. I paused often to gain the sense of a place or to write about my impressions. Spontaneity made life lighter. The time I took seemed altered, as if it were endless. When I came home from Italy I looked differently at my days.

When Mark returned from California on October 30, he wasn't well. In a few days he started vomiting. His worsening weakness kept him from his few remaining pleasures. He could no longer read or work at his computer. He became pale and withdrawn, staring from his chair or staying in his bed. Lethargic, dehydrated and unable to keep anything down, he went back to St. Vincent Hospital, a mile from where he lived.

On admission, his doctors determined that his chemotherapy was no longer suppressing his disease. His vasculitis had broken out of remission, attacked his already-marginal kidneys, and was ravaging his lungs. Within a week he was in the ICU with severe pneumonia. He began coughing up blood. A lung biopsy revealed Wegener's Granulomatosis, in which lung tissue around blocked vessels dies from lack of blood supply. The condition worsened Mark's pneumonia. By Sunday, November 12, his kidneys were failing. He stopped eating. He told Zita that he wanted to die.

Through all the crises of the past, Zita had never called me directly. Although often present when I talked to Mark, she had usually stayed in the background. This time she hunted me down in Hilton Head. In a voice tight-pitched with worry she said, "Mark is in the Intensive Care Unit, Bill. It doesn't look good."

Once again, the doctors were doing all they could for her son in the ICU, but this time Zita measured the moment with the sure sense of a mother and knew it was different. The resilience that always pulled Mark through was failing. He told her, "Mom...I can't keep going..." When she called me, Zita asked haltingly if there was anything more that anyone could do.

I had no idea how to answer her. In the past, when she had turned to me for medical solutions, I had always come up with something. Now that was impossible. I promised her an e-mail the following day that she could print and read to Mark.

That night, after Bev went to bed, I sat quietly in the living room, saddened and distressed by Zita's news. I couldn't rid my mind of the image of Mark, lying alone in an ICU, confined by protruding tubes and surrounded by blinking monitors. My friend was far away, flickering on the edge of existence, and I felt powerless to help him. I wanted to reach out to him, but I didn't know how. Sorrow surrounded me like a flooding tide washing over a solitary pebble.

The next morning I wrote to him. Words poured out without thought or deliberation, and with them, so did tears. The e-mail reached Zita before she left for the hospital.

11/13/00

Hi Mark!

I sent a copy of this to your e-mail address, but I know that the best route will be to send it to Zita so she can print it and read it to you today. I will also try to call. The probability of reaching you by phone in the ICU is small, but I will use anything I can to try to reach you.

And I think I will. I think that somehow I will reach you. Quite which technology gets me through to you is beside the point. The point is that I believe you will hear me. I believe this based not only on my spiritual beliefs but also from years of professional encounters.

For years I managed patients in the ICU. Yes, I had to make decisions about their lines and tubes and whether or not to operate. That was important. But beyond all those decisions, I made it a point each day on rounds to reach out and, for a moment, hold each patient's hand.

Sometimes they were conscious and returned my touch. Sometimes they were no longer conscious, but even then, I believe that they could sense the connection that came from touching. I came to believe that this sense of connectedness has power far beyond lines and tubes, indeed, a power far beyond my ability to find words to express it.

Because my words seem inadequate, I will call upon an image from the Sistine Chapel, which I just visited. If you can, I want you to bring to mind the image on the ceiling there of the Creation scene. In it, God reaches out, and with one finger, touches Adam. What Michelangelo was expressing was the divine spark, the gift that transforms us from dust and clay into human beings. This reaching out and touching is somehow at the core of our humanity.

I have come to believe that reaching out and touching has a power far different from what scientific medicine can provide. Your medical state is terribly important. Sadly, I can't provide help with it anymore. But I can still reach out to you. I can still try to touch you. So as Zita reads this to you, I want you to try to imagine me sitting there next to you, reaching out and holding your hand.

I am just a voice now. Which technology gets my voice to you doesn't matter. I believe that somehow it will reach you. I believe that to the very core of my being. And I am just one of many voices reaching out to you.

The reason we are all out here and the reason we are all reaching out to you is that you have reached out to all of us. Captured in a physical body stricken with disease, you nevertheless have a boundless spirit. I am not just rambling on. I know this. I have your letters. I have the words you wrote me this summer. In a body with knees of plastic and metal is a soul who knows no limits, who even now wanders freely over silent fields at Gettysburg and sunny islands in California. Burdened by depression and physical limitation is a spirit that can nonetheless still soar in rapture to the beauty of Mozart and smile in excitement at the rumbling sound of a diesel locomotive.

Others may see only the stigmata of a terrible disease in a human body wasted with illness. I don't. All those who know you don't. We see a soul free and unfettered.

I am reaching out to you, because you have reached out to me. You have touched me. You have held my hand, in a way that I can never fully express, at a time when I needed it very much.

Diseases are awful. They are crippling, depressing, limiting, and sometimes lethal. Mine doesn't physically limit me as yours does. Rest assured about that. But it took away something that was important to me. I almost fell into a very bad place about that.

You taught me, at a moment when I needed it, that at the deepest level the limitations of a disease don't matter. We all get something sooner or later. We all have limitations sooner or later. But by your example, you taught me that what matters is to transcend those limitations. What matters is to break free of our chains, whatever their form. At the deepest level, you have helped me to understand that what matters is reaching out and touching.

Rest now. Rest quietly and deeply. Rest and dream. Dream of me, dream of all of us, sitting by your bedside, holding your hand. Hold that image in your mind, and smile. You are loved.

Peace be with you.
Your friend,

Bill

In this letter, I saw for the first time how I had changed. It was as if I had come out of a long dark tunnel, stood in the sunlight, and could finally see. That evening Zita replied:

11/13/00

Dear Bill,

Thank you for the beautiful letter you wrote to Mark. When I read it, I wept as I have not been able to do since Mark became ill this time. It released all the tension and stress that had built up in me.

I had felt as though everything had turned against me and that somehow, somewhere, sometime in his 56 years, I failed my son. Why did he have to suffer such illness when I am healthy and, at 85, able to do things which he can't because of this distressing illness? Your letter opened wide a door that I have kept shut for quite a long time. I realize that Mark is serving a true purpose in life through his illness and that I need to thank God for sending you to show me how to think about this in the proper way.

Mark was sitting up when I visited him in the ICU this afternoon. He had the oxygen mask on but his breathing was not as labored as it had been Sunday. He is getting different antibiotics now and has been fever-free today.

Needless to say, Mark was very happy when I read the letter to him. It caused him to retract what he had said to the nurse. He said, "Mom, I didn't really mean that I don't want to go on anymore. I just felt sick and weak when I said that. I do want to live and now, with Bill's letter to guide me, I'm strong again."

Thank you again for writing this letter to Mark. It meant so very much to him and to me. I don't know how to tell you adequately just what it did for him, but he was a different person when I left.

Zita

In its own peculiar way, the spark had reached him. Maybe it was just the words in a letter. Maybe it was something larger. Whatever it was, it reached across time and space; it touched him and it helped.

That evening I sat quietly again. To my amazement, the loneliness and isolation of the night before had disappeared. I felt connected to my friend. The power of reaching out was present in both directions. The metaphor in the letter, the image of touching that I wanted to give him, was real for me as well. In the stillness of the evening, familiar words filled my mind—"It is in giving that we receive."

11/15/00

Dear Bill,

Here is an update on Mark's condition.

The renal specialist told me that Mark's creatinine was over 6 when he arrived in the emergency room, but with the IV's they poured into him it has gone down to 2.4. Unfortunately, then his lungs started filling up. I was really very fearful when I saw him last Sunday, as was his internist. That's when I called you.

During the course of the day, five specialists came in to examine him. A bronchoscopy verified what they suspected all along. He has vasculitis in the lungs. The doctors were frank with Mark and today told him that this is serious.

Despite it all Mark never loses his sense of humor. When the bronchoscopy procedure was finished, he asked the doctor where that "torture instrument" was invented. "It must have come from Nazi Germany!" He has been an inspiration to the doctors caring for him here. He never complains and talks to them about so many things. His primary care doctor spends a lot of time with Mark. In the course of this illness they have become friends.

Mark told me to tell you that he has a great team of physicians working on him, and that you are part of that team in his heart and mind. His heart is strong. He knows that you are there with him. He wants you to know this, Bill. Your letter came to him at the right time, and I thank you again for giving him the courage to go on and fulfill his mission in life.

Zita

My connection with Mark reawakened perceptions I had experienced at Mepkin Abbey. I felt a split between interactions with my family at one level of existence and my interaction with Mark at a completely different one. Each day I talked with Bev about her Italy trip or walked the beach with Ken, visited with my parents or chatted about the evening news. Each night, as I sat alone in stillness, all of that faded away, as if it had no significance at all. Despite a lifetime of family closeness, our activities during the day seemed like those of people floating in a boat on the surface of the sea, while at night, in the depths below, something profoundly important was happening to me that I struggled to understand.

All my life, understanding had been important to me. Now I sensed that understanding was not enough. "What's happening here?" It was a question asked not about daily events but about a different awareness of them. Whatever was happening was beyond the safe and familiar realm of intellectual comprehension. I couldn't tell my family about what was happening with Mark and Zita because I wasn't sure myself.

In that state of uncertainty, Zita's replies became extraordinarily important to me. They reassured me that, however strange and unsettling I might feel, what I wrote was helping Mark. Without that reassurance, I would have felt uncertain, hesitant, a bit lost and perhaps a little crazy. I probably would have retreated from writing so openly. Her letters encouraged me to continue.

11/16/00

Hi Zita,

Thanks so much for your kind reply to my note and for bringing me up to date about Mark.

Medically, I know this is serious. The diagnosis of vasculitis in the lungs is indeed worrisome. Part of me, the trained medical part that I used in the past to help Mark, feels frustrated that Dr. Gruber can't be there and contribute clinically to his care. Part of me still yearns to do that for Mark.

But I am in a different place now. As you know, last spring, in the course of our correspondence, I wrote Mark that I was glad he addressed his letter to Bill rather than to Dr. Gruber. Dr. Gruber is gone. I didn't choose to be where I am now, but I am here nonetheless. Although there is a certain amount of sadness to that, in a peculiar way I am accepting, even glad about what has happened. It has opened a door to a new part of my life.

My mother's mother suffered for years from severe rheumatoid arthritis. My mother would try, as you have, to understand why. "Why does suffering happen to someone I love?" To this day, I remember the only phrase that she could find to explain it—"God writes straight with crooked lines." I use that line now for myself. I no longer ask "Why?" It is no longer mine to understand what is happening intellectually. Instead, what is opening to me now is a journey of the heart.

I first encountered that phrase last November. In the midst of the medical and professional decisions of last fall, I made a retreat with my family at Mepkin Abbey, a Trappist monastery in South Carolina. A book I read there described the inner life of contemplation at the monastery in just those words.

It is an unfamiliar path for me. For years, I used my "head tools," my analytical and decision-making skills. This is what I was trained to do. I did it well. I plated and rodded and cemented lots of bones back together. I solved peoples' problems.

Now I am trying to learn about the tools of the heart. They are very different and unfamiliar to me. I am unsure of myself with them, just as I was unsure of my medical skills when I was only an intern. Often I am apprehensive that I will say something that is inappropriate. Nevertheless, I am on that journey.

But my uncertainties notwithstanding, one thing I am sure of is that all of this is real. I had no reason to know how my message would reach Mark. I simply sensed that it would. I was not sure which words to use. Call it the divine spark, call it energy, call it grace, call it love, call it whatever you will. But whatever it is, it is real, and it is powerful. It is quite possibly the most real thing there is. I knew, without knowing how I knew, that he would sense that someone was touching him, and that somehow that would help.

In return, Mark is helping me more than he knows. Through your feedback, you are helping me as well. So I will make you an offer in return. Write me if you want to worry or weep. Call at any time if you just want to talk. I will try to be here when you reach out.

Peace be with you,

Bill

My relationship with Zita was growing far beyond medical explanations and professional reassurance. I had no medical facts to explain. I had only a meager idea of what was happening to Mark. Instead, doors of a different kind were opening with her. As our e-mails flew back and forth, she revealed a deeper dimension of her distress. Mark was not her only son who was suffering.

11/18/00

Dear Bill,

You must know that your letter touched me very deeply. Thank you for the offer of instant contact with you when I need help with my problems. I will never forget your kindness. You know much about healing the human spirit.

Right now, I am trying to come to terms as to why my youngest son, Paul, with whom we live, has also been diagnosed with rheumatoid arthritis.

He is an accomplished pianist with a degree in piano performance. About three years ago, he noticed that his fingers became stiff and painful when he played.

Other joints became affected. He finally saw Mark's rheumatologist and after extensive testing, was given the bad news. I just don't understand this illness at all. I keep wondering why two of my sons have RA.

I will cut this short now as I am going to the hospital. I will write another e-mail when I return.

All the best to you. I know that Mark thought of you yesterday very much and had you with him the whole time.

Zita

11/20/00

Hi Zita,

I have been thinking about the anguish present in your comments about Paul and his diagnosis.

First, let me respond to your statement "I just don't understand this disease." Perhaps I can at least help with the "how" questions—"How does it happen?" Call me and we can talk about the facts of the disease.

Having said that, I know explanations can't change the feelings in your heart. I realize that such explanations do little to answer the darker question of "why?" "Why Paul? Why did it happen to Mark and then Paul?" "Why" questions are always much harder to answer than "how" questions. Apprehension, discouragement, bewilderment, and anguish are not easy things to explain away. Perhaps sharing something that I learned may help you.

I knew a doctor friend who had hep-C for a long time. When I was first diagnosed, I went to see him. His condition was advanced and caused him terrible stress and depression. I jumped to the conclusion that my situation was going to be like his. After my evaluation, it became clear that my disease was recent, much less advanced, and had a completely different outlook. The conclusions that I jumped to prematurely caused me anguish that, as it turned out, wasn't at all justified.

A diagnosis of rheumatoid arthritis is serious. Worry for one's sons can never be set aside. Nonetheless, the addition of anxiety and bewilderment can make the burden a lot heavier than it might otherwise be. I made the mistakes of taking on anxiety that I didn't need to. I had some friends who helped me separate out what was really there from what I had projected onto it. It made a big difference to me. If I can help you in a similar way, I'll feel good about that.

Bill

11/22/00

Dear Bill,

Paul has probably had RA for about two years. I believe that with his recent onset he will have less involvement and fewer complications than Mark. He follows a good exercise program and does work at the piano to keep his fingers in shape. He starts with scales, works through some Bach and Mozart Sonatas and finishes off with Chopin for technique. He swims with me in the morning and then after he finishes teaching at Wagner College he swims again in the pool there. Celebrex helps when the going gets bad and he is on Enbrel, a twice-weekly injection. As time goes, on there will other medications. In coming years he will have the advantages of all the new research and medications.

I wanted to send you and your family a Thanksgiving wish. We have much to be thankful for this year. Mark is doing very well indeed, considering that just a short while ago he had such a difficult time with breathing. We owe much to you, Bill, that Mark is with us and again I will say that I am so very grateful. This Thanksgiving will be a special one and you will be with us as we celebrate.

Your journey of the heart will be as important a career for you as your medical one was. Few travel that path. Many people out there need someone like you. That you encountered this phrase at Mepkin was indeed a blessing for you, and to the many souls you will meet on the journey on which you have embarked.

You should not in any way be unsure of your skills in this new direction in your life. Do not be afraid that you will say something inappropriate. You couldn't possibly! Mark needed your heart skills this time, just as before he needed your medical skills. He came out of his depression and hopelessness.

I hope I have reassured you in this whole concept of your new role in life. I need you, and will use the phone if I am confused, which I sometimes am. I meditate and pray, but occasionally am overwhelmed with problems and sometimes don't see a way out of the maze.

Paul heard a superb concert Monday night at Carnegie Hall. It was chamber music with Barenboim, Perlman, Zuckerman, and Yo-Yo Ma. They played Schumann and Brahms Piano Quintets, but Paul was particularly impressed with a contemporary piece by a French composer, Olivier Messiaen, who lived from 1908 to 1992. The work Paul heard was "Quartet for the End of Time." I will quote from the program notes:

"This quartet is one of the finest manifestations both of Messiaen's musical invention and spiritual attitude. It also has the grim distinction of being one of the few chamber music masterpieces, if not the only one, written in a concentration camp....

"The third movement is called "Abyss of the Birds" for clarinet alone: "The abyss is Time, with its sadness, its weariness. The birds are the opposite of Time: they are our longing for light, for stars, for rainbows and for jubilant streams of song...."

I am sorry to be so verbal, but the above program notes reminded me so much of what you have had to say to us in your wonderful own words of hope and peace.

Sincerely,

Zita

As the days passed, family events at Hilton Head kept me busy. Our wedding anniversary was November 18, Cathy arrived for the holiday on November 21, the extended family planned Thanksgiving together on the 23rd, and the 24th was Beverly's birthday. In the midst of all of those arrangements, Zita called. "Mark has improved!" she announced with jubilation. "He is coming home for Thanksgiving!" When I heard that news, gratitude and joy made me feel like turning cartwheels. Since I probably wouldn't have survived one of those, I just told her instead how happy I was for all of them.

I called Mark on Thanksgiving. His weakness precluded a long conversation, but it was good to hear his voice again. He was frail and thin and his weight loss worried Zita, but true to form, he joked about it. "Bill," he said, "don't worry. I'm going to eat like a horse. I'll get it all back."

The following Sunday Mark sent his first e-mail since his hospitalization. Zita told me it took him two days to write it.

11/26/00

Hello Bill,

I am feeling more spiffy now and getting my strength and energy back. I am eating well and had a great Thanksgiving dinner. I thought I was going to have to resort to hospital fare, but Dr Sidlow got me home in time. My brother is good at everything he does and he put out a masterpiece of a feast.

I want to thank you for your supportive e-mails and calls during my illness. The doctors were very concerned there for awhile. Your letter made a huge differ-ence at a moment when I was at a real low. I felt better almost immediately. I rallied and improved to the point where all my values were back to normal. You were instrumental in that and I cannot thank you enough.

You see, you are still part of my team. You are still my doctor and will always be my doctor. When I was in the OR and they were about to put me out for the biopsy I instinctively looked around for you. I asked my late father, "Dad, go find Dr. Gruber!" Once I sensed your presence, I was fine.

Addressing your email regarding reaching out, this has really resonated with me of late. I was in the Sistine Chapel in 1962 when I was 17 years old. I would appreciate it much more today of course, but I remember the awe that I had for Michelangelo's works even then. Your description and interpretation of God reaching out to us through Adam is beautiful. I really believe that this is a task that the Creator has mandated for all of us.

I really don't think that I would've softened to life and people had I not been stricken with this illness. I am convinced that the RA and all the secondary illness that have resulted from it have had a huge beneficial effect upon me, far outweighing all of the negatives. It has forced me to confront the flaws in my personal life and has burned them off like dross from a piece of gold. It has exposed my soul so that I could align it and my life with a purpose. It has put me back in touch with my humanity and with humanity as a whole.

I am a better friend with my friends now than ever before because I'm a better friend with myself, which is the ultimate beginning point. I'm closer to my brothers and extended family than at any time previously. My mom is my best friend and always was but now I realize it more.

As you said, "God writes straight with crooked lines." I know that you understand what I am talking about here because you have had to confront the same issues.

I also know that you understand that as one chapter in the book of life closes, a new one opens, grander and more enlightening and spectacular. That is the way life is and those people who cannot, do not or will not accept life in all of its manifestations are poorer for it. I try to live my life according to the Buddhist metaphor of the twig falling into the stream and gently meandering down its course, going wherever the stream might take me.

Every time I walk, it is because of you. My whole family is extremely grateful for the super care and consideration you have shown me, both during your days of active practice and now. Of course, I took that to the extreme in September 1997. I waited too long and put you through all that trouble trying to save my life. I am forever grateful for your supreme efforts but I am sorry I made you work so hard.

I would like to ask you a favor. There is a great picture of you in the Chief of Staff display case at Northwest Hospital. Would it be possible to get a copy of that picture? My mom derives much comfort and strength from your communications. Your portrait belongs in the Smetko family household. I have a great photo of me operating a fast freight between Seattle & Portland in the early 80's—back when I was still in "pristine" condition. I'll get a copy of it made and send it to you in return.

They have me on high steroids at the moment to treat my lung problem. My cytoxan treatments resume next month for the kidneys. Despite it all, I'm a lot happier than I have been in a long time. My heart remains strong, as do my spirits. Two of my brothers are going to take me to Hawaii so I need to get into snorkeling shape. My library grows daily as I unload box after box. I love astronomy and am an arm-chair theoretical physicist (without the equations). I am looking forward to the Nutcracker Ballet on Christmas Eve and more turkey, of course. I've decided I need another brass freight locomotive so accordingly, I will place reservations for a Great Northern R-1 class 2-8-8-2.

I hope this e-mail finds you well and happy. Know that your letters are always welcome and that I read your "reaching out" letter all the time. I derive much strength from it. I am on the mend again and hopefully can go awhile without another long detour to St Vinny's.

Best wishes, stay happy and healthy.
Your friend,

Mark

I reread Mark's letter many times. A week before he had been moribund in the ICU, as gray as a bowl of cold oatmeal, tethered to his bed by oxygen lines and monitor leads, gasping with exhaustion on the edge of eternity. A week later he was home with his family, wolfing down Thanksgiving dinner and joking about his plans for more turkey. In this letter he revealed a life transformed beyond either of those circumstances.

"Reaching out is a task that the Creator has mandated for all of us." This wasn't a book belief, something Mark had read somewhere. He'd been at death's door twice and ten days ago was halfway there again. Every time he came back from the edge, a man who had once held back and stayed hidden reached out ever more openly. What had he learned at the edge? What kind of connectedness did he discover there?

"I am convinced that the RA and all the secondary illness that have resulted from it have had a huge beneficial effect upon me, far outweighing all of the negatives." I was Mark's doctor for eight years. I saw him suffer through more pain, depression

and loss than I ever thought it possible for one person to endure, and I didn't see a fraction of the suffering he felt inside. Yet here he was, telling me that this whole catastrophe had a huge beneficial effect, far outweighing all of the negatives? When I first read that, I couldn't believe it. "Perhaps," I later thought, "it's because I don't know how to believe it."

"It has forced me to confront the flaws in my personal life and has burned them off like dross from a piece of gold." His disease forced him to confront his fears and shame. When he at last let go of those, he found the radiance within, the person whose voice I heard in his letters.

"More than ever before, I am a better friend with my friends because I'm a better friend with myself, which is the ultimate beginning point." When fear melted away and he became comfortable with himself, I believe that Mark finally felt the freedom he had looked for all of his life. No longer needing his defenses, he could at last love others openly, without reservation. He was right. It was the beginning point of everything. The Buddhist texts teach that detachment and acceptance become the path to liberation. When I read this letter, I finally understood that teaching. Mark was free.

"I know that you understand what I am talking about here because you have had to confront the same issues." I didn't confront a fraction of what Mark did, but he was right about one thing: if I hadn't gone through what I did, I would never have understood the words he wrote. I'd still be seeing a patient with a list of problems and a poor prognosis, looking with eyes that couldn't see and listening with ears that didn't hear.

Time after time I saw Mark live outside of his disease. How could he transcend this implacable affliction? How did he transcend his own body? If he put his pain and prognosis in second place, what was in first? What was he living for? In this letter I began to see what he was trying to teach me.

I believe that Mark sensed a world within himself of such intense beauty that only a Mozart concerto could convey its majesty. He was aware, with increasing clarity, of a power so energizing that he could only describe it through the metaphor of mighty locomotives. He found a freedom he could only symbolize by the expansive vistas of the West. Within that inner world I believe he found joy so profound that each day it helped him to detach from his trials, his depression, his losses, and his pain.

I believe that when Mark connected to this inner world of beauty, freedom and joy, it sustained him night and day. Within it, he could be open to everyone without fear or defensiveness. In comparison to it, everything else, even the relentless failings of his own body, took a pale second place.

I sent Mark the photo that he asked for, but events kept him from sending me the one of him driving his fast freight on the Seattle to Portland run. Months later, Zita gave it to me. It was a picture of him sitting in the cab of his locomotive, a picture of Mark in his prime as I always imagined him, highballing on the high iron.

It's easy to identify teachers when they appear as a learned professor or supportive therapist, a spiritual counselor or saintly guru. I suppose it helps if a teacher wears white robes, but that wasn't the way it worked for me. My teacher showed up dressed as a railroad engineer.

Reprise

On November 28 Beverly and I returned from Hilton Head to find a wedding invitation waiting for us. Ken's son Michael planned to be married on March 31 in Brooklyn. The family looked forward to it as a gala celebration. I had an additional reason for wanting to go.

12/4/00

Hi Mark!

I'm back in Seattle, slowly catching up. Tell your mom I think of her often and will try to write her soon. I remain deeply moved by her replies to my letters.

Something important is growing inside me as a result of our recent e-mails. I can't describe it well just now, but I sense that what happened to me during our correspondence in November is as important as what happened to you. It is something hard to define, a connectedness for which there are no good words. In time, whatever happened will slowly take form in my thoughts, at which time I hope I can find the right words to describe it, but for now it is simply an awareness of something important.

One manifestation of this "important something" is that I would like to see you again. I want to see your trains, watch you run your model locomotives and hear you tell your train stories. I want to give Zita a hug. I want to meet Paul. We are currently making arrangements to attend a nephew's wedding in Brooklyn on March 31. If possible, I would like to visit with you as well. Does Sunday, April 1 work for you?

There is so much to cover from your letters that I can't seem to write enough. I may call, and we can just visit that way. Either way, the desire to visit is what seems important now. Let me know.

More later,

Bill

12/4/00

Hello Bill,

I am looking forward to your visit already. So is my mom. You are always welcome. April 1 would be great. We'll have a lot to talk about over a great dinner. Please bring your wife and daughter too. Just get on the Staten Island Ferry and we'll pick you up.

I am happy we are keeping in contact. I too have gotten immense value out of your communications with me. My mom does also. To see and visit with you will be great.

My model RR layout is not up and running but I do have some beautiful brass engines already unpacked to show you. Incidentally, Microsoft is working with my old employer, the Burlington Northern Santa Fe RR, to produce a lifelike simulator program of routes all over that system. I'll be able to run trains on my computer over my old routes between Seattle, Wenatchee, Portland and Vancouver. I need to see if I can "re-qualify" on each subdivision. You will get to see how rusty I've gotten.

I loved doing that kind of work. Not the least of reasons is that I am a ham and liked to wave at people and blow the whistle for them at their hand signal requests. It was a challenging and fabulously fun job. I still have dreams about it.

I do not plan on getting felled by another medical setback and end up in the hospital. I will keep from knocking on death's door for sure. I am getting stronger by the day, eating and exercising. I want you to see how well I am walking and getting about, albeit with a cane at times.

Well, I better go exercise so I can ride my bike and get into snorkeling shape. Dinner calls and then a four-year boycott of the national news begins.

Best wishes to you and your family and good health forever.
Your friend,

Mark

Mark's e-mail had the same familiar enthusiasm, curiosity and breadth as did his letters from last summer. They read like a conversation that paused in September and resumed this week. He made no mention of his bleak mood of mid-November. Only a few of his comments suggested that anything at all adverse had happened.

How could he possibly write this way? He knew that his joints were wrecked beyond repair, his immune system was on the attack everywhere and that he had very little kidney function left. He knew that Wegener's Granulomatosis was an advancing form of vasculitis, and that his only chance from now on against fatal pneumonia from it was massive doses of steroids and cytoxan.

The split I recently experienced in my own feelings helped me to understand how he lived outside his disease. I believe that no matter how serious it seemed to others, he saw no great significance in his medical condition, because for him what was truly important each day happened at a different level of living. He separated surface events from deeper issues and chose deliberately to focus on what mattered the most.

It was not hard to see the source of Mark's resilience and determination. At eighty-five, having mastered e-mail, Zita wrote me letters that held few hints of discouragement or fatigue. Instead, she exhibited an abiding concern for others, as if she had tapped into an inexhaustible source. In one letter I acknowledged how much her letters meant to me.

> Your replies to my notes at Thanksgiving were very important to me. They meant more than you might guess. The feedback you gave may not have seemed like much to you, but I am just starting on an uncertain path, and your kind words of support were an enormous encouragement. A phrase my daughter once used comes to mind here: "You give much, and know not that you give at all."
>
> Thank you. I wanted to write you directly to say that.

A day later Mark wrote, describing eagerly all of the interests he could once more pursue.

> 12/15/00
> Subj: Cold Harbor and other topics
>
> Hello Bill,
>
> I just got your e-mail as well as the fine portrait of you. Thank you.
> My mom's cousin from Germany visited last week. She and I went to the Met and heard Wagner's *Flying Dutchman*. My brother and his wife were across the

way at Lincoln Center attending Bach's *Christmas Oratorio*. What a great way to spend a blustery and frigid Friday evening in Manhattan!

Surprisingly, my German language skills are coming back to me. Even though Hilde speaks fluent English, I spoke German to her a lot and I got along quite nicely. She got me a book, *Deutsche Dampf Locomotiven* about, what else, German steam locomotives, and although it is written in German, I can actually understand much of it. I love that book. It is full of great photos down through the years.

I can't wait until Microsoft and the BNSF have their computer simulations on line because I really want to "get back to work." Much of the job was knowing the physical characteristics of the railroad segment you were operating on. You always wanted to think five miles ahead so that you could have your train under control through grades, curves and dips in the track. Seven-thousand-ton freight trains can be very unforgiving if you don't plan ahead, especially up in the Cascades. I know. I had enough white-knuckle experiences to never let me forget that fact. Remind me to tell you about one of them coming down the west side of Stevens Pass.

Our Civil War trip this year is probably to Cold Harbor. Grant was handed his head there by Lee. This time around my friend Karl will be the tour guide. He's a high school teacher from Chicago and came to visit while I was in the hospital a month ago. We've been close friends ever since first grade at St Leonard's in 1950. Karl is into the Civil War the way I'm into railroading. You would really enjoy meeting him some day.

I found your account of Mepkin Abbey very inspiring. I really want to go on a contemplative retreat sometime. At this point in my life, it would have much to offer me, psychologically, emotionally and spiritually. I believe whenever we can tune into the soul of our very being, we grow immensely as a result.

My health has returned in a grand way. I go in Tuesday for my next cytoxan treatment. I have put on weight, probably due to the hunger generated by the 60 mgs of prednisone a day, and am up to 170 lbs now. The chemo will discourage overeating for awhile though. I am exercising and really have not felt this good in a long time. PT gave me all the exercises and I do them religiously. As soon as my leg muscles are stronger, I can get back on the Aerodyne and ride.

Well I better close. My brothers Carl and John, asked me to pass onto you a hearty hello and Christmas Greetings. I have great brothers and they are grateful for what you have done for my family and me. Merry Christmas to you, your wife and daughter and the happiest of holidays.

Your friend,

Mark

P.S. I just found out that Paul and I are going to Avery Fischer Hall tonight to hear Brahms' piano concerto #1.

"My health has returned in a grand way." Sometimes I still doubted that Mark's way of looking at the world could be real, but nobody who was around him did. He drew people to him in a way that doesn't happen when someone is in denial. Paul said "During these days an inner joy radiated from Mark. Nothing could keep him down." Once, while coming out from a concert, Mark fell to the sidewalk and couldn't get up. As people passed him by, he struggled unsuccessfully to roll from the pavement up onto his knees. Finally, someone stopped to help him. Unembarrassed, he joked about his infirmity. "I guess people must have thought I was drunk." He smiled as if a lens focused all of the Christmas spirit in Manhattan into him, and he in return radiated it all back. Paul said, "He was so joyous. It was the happiest time of his life." A person who had once been as wounded and walled off as Ebeneezer Scrooge now knew the joy that made him "…as light as a feather, and as happy as a schoolboy."

I often felt that I could talk with him for days. Beverly asked, "Why don't you just call him up more and talk?" I often did. Our conversations rambled over as many topics as our e-mails, but with one important difference. His letters left a written record. Without them, I could never have described what Mark was trying to teach me.

12/15/00
Subj: Trains on computers at Cold Harbor in German with Brahms on a retreat

Hi Mark!

I think I could spend days replying to all that your e-mails contain. The problem is that my typing speed simply isn't up to it.

Your notes about trains glow with excitement. Don't lose this. Don't let it slip away. Your descriptions help me appreciate the enormous loss you overcame when you had to let go of railroading and the degree to which you still struggle with it. But I also see that you are trying to find other ways to be "at work" on the trains and in doing so, to stay alive.

Often when people can't do things in their accustomed way, ("I can't play golf like I used to." "I can't garden anymore.") they give up, crawl into a corner and stop living. I saw many patients do that. It is easy to do. I almost did it. ("I can't do surgery anymore.") That is the "very bad place" that I mentioned in my e-mail to you when you were in the hospital. People can die from that despondency. It is a dark, ugly hole into which one's soul can disappear and never be seen again. I can remember sitting at your bedside some evenings after rounds. The dark place almost got you a few times too, and with good reason.

But that didn't happen. What comes through in your writing is the message, "There is a lot I can't do, and I miss that. But there is still a lot that I can do that brings me excitement and satisfaction and I'm going to do that!" As I read your letters, I know that in spite of everything, the darkness didn't win.

Mark, that's rare. I have to tell you, it's rare. It's inspirational. That's not just a high-sounding word. I'm not kidding. This is real.

There is a song that has very special meaning to me, called "Lord of the Dance." One of its verses is,

> *"I danced on a Friday when the sky turned black.*
> *It's hard to dance with the devil on your back.*
> *They whipped me and they stripped me and they hung me up high.*
> *…But I am the Dance that will never, never die."*

In the terms of this song, you are still dancing. Or maybe something working through you is dancing. But whatever it is, you had to open yourself to it rather than giving up, closing off and disappearing into the darkness.

I use the word "inspirational" because of what I wrote to you in November—"You helped me at a time when I needed help." Even up to the edge of darkness, you were able to keep dancing, and if you could do it, I knew that I can do it. That is inspirational, and because it is, I say, "Thank you."

Keep writing about trains, man. You're alive when you do that. I don't know much about trains, but I'm learning more and more about being alive.

When are you going to Cold Harbor? If you are thinking about a retreat, I can send you a video that I made while I was at Mepkin Abbey. It is no substitute for being there, but perhaps it might be a first step.

More later,

Bill

I had joked about how slowly I typed. In her next e-mail to me, Zita mentioned how slowly Mark typed. His hands and wrists were by now so arthritic that he tapped out his e-mails, one letter at a time, with a pencil eraser.

Around December 12, Mark started having pain across the left side of his face. Thinking it was an infected tooth, he went to the dentist, who noticed an angry red blotch on his left cheek and suggested immediate referral to a specialist. The pain kept getting worse, but Mark made no mention of that in his reply to me. Instead, he commented about how alive he felt.

12/15/00

Hi Bill,

I think the guys are planning the trip to Cold Harbor around Easter break. My friend Rich may also join us. He's a Chicago firefighter who has non-Hodgkin's lymphoma. He had a kidney removed but is battling back and should be mended by then. He'll survive. He's as upbeat as anyone there is. Paul may come as well. If you'd like to join us, you're most welcome. You won't be bored.

I am glad you like my passion for the "high iron." True, it was tough giving that all up, but I'm alive and in many ways more alive than ever before. I am glad that I have been able to help you through your travails. You certainly have done the same for me.

More later,
Your friend,

Mark

That night Mark fell again. His pain rapidly worsened and spread to his ear. An inflamed, blistering rash rapidly erupted across the left side of his face. The ear, nose and throat specialist took one look and told Mark he had shingles.

Because of Mark's steroids, the shingles virus invaded the nerves across his face unopposed. Its telltale blisters spread into his mouth, his left ear swelled shut and his left eyelid crusted over. Within three days, his pain became excruciating.

By the evening of the 23rd, the lightning-like torment kept him curled up on his couch, moaning. Unwilling to watch him go through the night like that, Paul and Zita took him back to St Vincent. Mark had been looking forward to attending a festive performance of *The Nutcracker* on Christmas Eve; instead, he entered a world far away from a holiday ballet about sugarplum fairies. Fading into a morphine fog, for the fourth time in a row he spent his Christmas in a hospital.

Zita called me. She described the medical details as best she could, but her main worry was that Mark might lose his vision and hearing on his left side. The doctors were doing all they could; I could offer nothing more.

12/24/00

Hi Zita,

I appreciated your phone call. I recognize how much distress this hospitalization is causing. I am sad that I can't be more helpful with advice.

In his last letter, Mark asked to see the videotape I made while I was at Mepkin Abbey last autumn. Tell him that I will get a copy off to him promptly with some notes that I wrote at the time. I truly hope that the serenity of the monastery may be of help to him just now.

Call or write at any time. You are in my prayers. Please give your entire family my regards.

Bill

On Christmas Eve, her hopes for Mark's holiday dashed, Zita replied to my e-mail with resignation.

12/24/00

Dear Bill,

First of all, I want to wish you everything good and peaceful on this Christmas of the year 2000. I hope and pray that the new year for you will mean health of mind, spirit and body and that your many kindnesses to us and to many others will be repaid to you a thousand-fold.

As for Mark, he missed The Nutcracker this afternoon. I really didn't feel like going, but he insisted. He got morphine and slept most of the time once I left him. Paul dropped me back at the hospital after the performance.

Mark is hardly eating. His mouth is sore inside and out. The left side of his face is especially swollen but the entire face and neck show the effects of the steroids he takes. It seems to be a vicious circle. The steroids help the lungs, the chemo helps the kidneys, but both treatments tear him down physically so that his resistance is very low and he is prey to other illnesses. He is getting good care but the doctors are very concerned about him.

Mark will be very happy to get the tape and notes from you about Mepkin. I am afraid I was a bit distraught when I called you about Mark and I apologize for not asking you about your health. I do hope that you are well. Certainly I think of that many times, but I just didn't ask you about it on these two occasions.

Mark and I ordered a box of Fuji apples for you three weeks ago to be delivered this past week. They were shipped last Monday from Wenatchee. If they are delivered while you are gone, please let me know, because I will order a new shipment. Next Tuesday is way too long for apples to be on a truck and we want you to have nice fresh ones. We really wanted you to know, with this little offering, how much you mean to us both. Your words have been an inspiration and we will never forget you.

Have a wonderful day tomorrow.

Sincerely,

Zita

I spent Christmas morning with my family, opening presents. After all the excitement died down and the wrapping paper put away, I sat staring into the fire that flickered quietly in the fireplace, thinking about Christmas at the Smetko house.

12/25/00

Hi Zita!

Yes, the apples made it! They are wonderful! How kind of both of you. In the midst of all of your commitments and distress, the thoughtfulness of sending them is doubly appreciated. Please tell Mark that I said thank you.

It was also very kind of you to ask about my health. It remains reasonable. My liver function studies remain normal. Unfortunately, this December's viral count has almost doubled from last March, to 5.7 million viruses/ml. So the war goes on.

I copied the Mepkin Abbey videotape today and will mail it tomorrow. At the level of the retreat, my lab values don't matter much. As you will see from the journal notes, I learned that an inner life is far more important. Mark taught me about those priorities, but I didn't really begin to understand them until recently.

On this Christmas day, I hope you can find a quiet moment, shut your eyes and breathe deeply. As your breath goes out, if only for one moment, let it take all of your burdens with it. Rest, and be at peace.

Then imagine that the next sound you hear is me with a smile on my face, chomping into one of those Wenatchee apples!

Wishing you a blessed New Year,

Bill

The lab values that I gave to Zita were dry facts to me, of only passing significance. I forwarded them to her because she asked about my health. Then I thought no more of them.

Mark's situation was becoming critical. His headaches had progressed to uncontrollable shaking in his right arm. A head CT scan showed a subdural hematoma—a blood clot between his skull and his brain probably caused by his fall. Some hematomas stabilize, but without surgery an expanding hematoma is fatal. The situation was potentially disastrous. Further bleeding would compress Mark's brain like a fist pushing into a pot of mashed potatoes, but he had little chance of surviving emergency brain surgery either. Zita wrote, "It just never stops for him."

Eventually his condition stabilized. On 12/29, Mark finally came home. Zita wrote again the next day.

12/30/00

Dear Bill,

First of all, I wish you and your family a holy and blessed New Year.

I do not understand about viruses/ml, but the fact that they doubled in the last six months and your comment that it is "unfortunate" is indeed a worry to me. I have not told Mark because it will upset him, too. How do you fight this "war" and what will the doctors do to reverse this situation?

If it is any consolation to you, I want you to know that Mark and I pray together for you every night. Every time I visited him in the hospital, I stopped at the little chapel there and asked God to take care of you and let your virus level go down to where it needs to be. Please keep me informed. You must know that you have become an important person in our lives. You are our inspiration and guide.

The tape arrived Thursday. Thank you! As I went through the journal day by day, it brought tears to my eyes. I felt as though I was making a retreat simply by reading the notes of your journey. Your references to the prayers and rituals brought back my college days in the Thirties when our yearly retreats followed a pattern very similar to what you described. Of course, everything was in Latin back then, but I liked that. I love Gregorian chant and one just doesn't hear that anymore. Perhaps they still sing that way in the monasteries.

Mark remains upbeat and is happy to be home again. We will watch the tape as soon as he is ready. He needs to read your notes first. I will probably have to read them to him, as he cannot read well. His left eye blurs everything now and is practically useless.

It will be a privilege to read the notes to him. They are as inspiring as anything I have read by St. Augustine and Merton. Thank you for sharing your path with us. We continue to keep you in our hearts and prayers.

Sincerely,

Zita

A year ago, when I ended my orthopaedic career, I anticipated a time of transition. As 2000 ended, I thumbed through my journal notes for the past twelve months. Over the New Year's weekend I reflected on all that had happened during that time. Only then did I realize the magnitude of my change.

The year transformed the way I looked at life. In my letters to Mark, I began to realize why. The outer world hadn't changed, but my perception of it had. I was journeying beyond ideas and words that the mind uses to express itself into a realm of awareness where words become inadequate. I was alive now at a level I had never known before and realized ruefully how little of life I had once perceived. I closed the year's journal with Hamlet's words: "There are more things in heaven and on earth, Horatio, than are dreamt of in your philosophy."

In my next letter to Zita, I tried to describe this transformation and the pivotal role both Mark and she had played in it.

1/2/01

Hi Zita,

As is always the case, your e-mail of 12/30 was wonderful. I appreciate all of your thoughts and concerns. I will try to address some of them.

The lab value I gave you means I have 5.7 million viruses in every milliliter of blood. Viruses in the bloodstream don't produce symptoms like bacteria in Mark's bloodstream did. I have only mild symptoms.

You asked, "How do you fight this war?" and "What will the doctors do for you to reverse this situation?" The answer to the first question is that I am doing everything I can medically to fight this war. I follow a specific plan of close observation with lab tests, coupled with measures designed to maximize my resistance.

That is a "head" kind of answer, filled with specific information and directed toward solving a problem. It is an answer that measures results against standards and progress against objectives. It is a language in which I was once very fluent, the language of a world whose rules were comfortably familiar to me. Lab information that may sound very alarming to you is dry and impersonal to me.

"What will the doctors do?" The doctors can't eradicate the virus I have by any medicines currently available. If medicine could cure my disease, I would have gone for the cure. That would have kept me in my comfort zone. Instead, my disease pushed me down a different path.

If all one has are the answers of science, and if in that world there is no solution to a problem, then all that remains is suffering and despair. You and Mark have helped me to realize that the world of the mind is not the only one there is. He has shown me that a medical answer is important, but it is not the only option. You both have taught me that the world of the heart has a place as well. Those lessons have been invaluable to me.

I am just learning about this world. It is a world where I am uncertain, where the signposts are unclear and the shadows are scary. It is a world where the letters from you both mean more than I can express.

I have learned that this is a path that is not out in the world, but within us. The way of the heart is not to analyze, but to let go, not to rationalize but to believe, not to work toward solutions, but to open toward acceptance. The pilgrims I meet along this path seek not to teach me facts or give me knowledge, but rather to reach out and touch a place within me that knows no words.

Is the path of the heart better than the path of the mind? There is no "better" path. Both ways play a role. Both help. Both are appropriate. In the way of the heart however, there is a very different answer to your question, "How do you fight this?"

On that path, I don't fight anymore. Instead, I am trying to let go of the need to fight, to detach instead of cling. Faced with a problem for which there is no solution, I am trying instead to find acceptance.

You wrote that you and Mark pray for me every night. I want to let you know as clearly as I can that your prayers are working. They are not working in the way our minds normally think. I don't expect prayers to eradicate the virus, cure the disease, or solve the problem. Instead, they are working in a way that has nothing to do with thinking at all. They are working in a world of belief, of acceptance, and detachment.

Yes, Zita, your prayers are working. They work the same way the letters from you and Mark work. They let me know that I am not alone. They give me clarity instead of uncertainty. They give me faith that others are on this path. They reach to my heart, and there they have power beyond anything you might guess.

The opposite of disease is healing, but the opposite of dis-ease is harmony. This is where Mark's example and your prayers are helping me. Both of you are helping me to gain harmony and peace. The task, as I wrote at Mepkin, is to let go of what was, and to be open instead to what might be. In that task, you are helping me more than you know. Thank you.

More later,

Bill

I worried that perhaps that letter was too long, too abstract, perhaps even too absorbed in my own issues. Five days later Zita wrote to tell me that Mark's condition had deteriorated.

1/7/01

Dear Bill,

I am sorry I couldn't write a longer letter in response to yours of January 2. Mark is in the hospital. His shingles caused so much pain that at 2 a.m. Saturday Paul and I took him back to the ER. They kept him there because his left eye looked bad. That is where the pain was concentrated. He said it felt like hot knives stabbing him. He was in such pain that we couldn't do anything else. He can't read because of his eye. His blood pressure was very high. Right now they are giving him morphine. I expect he will come home soon, but I hope with stronger pain pills.

As soon as he comes home we will watch your Mepkin tape. I am anxious to see it and want to watch it together with Mark. I thank you very much for sending it to us.

Your letter helped allay some of my concerns about your health because I know that you are doing everything possible with the help and advice of your doctors. If I may offer you any advice at all, it is that you should take some time to rest everyday.

I did smile from ear to ear and said, "Thanks Lord. You helped my friend, Bill. I don't want him to feel uncertain. Please help him understand that he has found his path in life and is helping others to find their way through all the darkness."

As human beings we all face uncertainty, but I feel so strongly that you have found the harmony you mentioned. You have found a way of life which, even though it is not the way you had chosen in the beginning, I am certain will fulfill every aspiration. You fulfilled your mission as a wonderful surgeon, and now you are helping others in a way that will be truly as important. To accept the good and the bad in our lives creates the harmony that makes life bearable. You will find peace because you are strong enough to "let go and have faith."

You have that, Bill. Please take care of yourself.

Sincerely,

Zita

My letters with Zita stopped for a while. Mark's condition was becoming too complicated to cover in correspondence, so instead I called her often. When we finished discussing Mark's medical status, she closed the calls as she did her letters, by inquiring about my health. She often asked if I was getting enough rest.

In the all-too-brief period after Christmas when Mark was home and not incapacitated by facial pain, he tediously typed out a New Year's message to me. In that letter, as if for the last time, he laid out the testament of his life.

12/31/00

Hello Bill,

I want to wish you and your family a very happy New Year. I feel I know them better now after my mom read me your notes from Mepkin Abbey.

I have been having trouble reading lately because my eyes have changed. After the shingles, my eye doctor determined that I will need membrane surgery on my left eye. I want to get this done ASAP. Reading is one of my favorite pastimes. I got three railroad books, two astronomy books and a Civil War book for Christmas, so the sooner the better.

I hope you had a wonderful and blessed Christmas. Mine of course was spent in isolation at St Vincent's but I am accustomed to Christmas in the hospital. I am home now, with horrendous scabs on the left side of my face, but feeling better. It would have been better had I not had the cytoxan treatment because that set everything off. Just a case of bad timing.

Fortunately, I have super physicians on my case. I have been blessed with great doctors all through my travails in Seattle, Wenatchee, and now here. God has been good to me. I pray He shines brightly upon you as well. Trust in Him. He will give you the strength and the will to go on.

I really was inspired with your experience at Mepkin and your interaction with your father and brothers. I was also very moved by your father's memory of his brother and the void he must feel that he is no longer with him. We tend to measure our feelings, responses and emotions in purely human terms. This is why loss brings such sorrow. But I believe we are spiritual beings having a human experience and when we can focus on the spiritual aspect, then we come to realize that a grander world awaits us all once our human journey ends.

I always wanted to meet my maternal grandfather. He passed away in 1941, three years before I was born, but there is a connection between us that goes far beyond the fact he is my mom's father. I talk to him often. I know that I will meet him one day. In the spiritual sense, I feel I have already. It's a real feeling that I have, a feeling that transcends time and space or life and death.

I understand that your thoughts, fears and questions are unique to you and that only you can fully understand the impact that your retreat had on your life. Yet when I listened to my mom reading your notes, I can place myself on a parallel path. They make me think on a deeper level about my own situation.

My mind is too muddled right now to do justice to what I really want to say, but I certainly want to meditate more. I find that when I do go into deep meditation, I enter a world which is less threatening, more peaceful and far more meaningful. Answers to my life's questions become so clear that it boggles my mind that I don't do this more often. I will go on a retreat one day and experience the peace and serenity that a monastery affords. But in a practical sense, our daily lives ought to be directed by the belief that we can remain in such a state whether on a retreat or not, whether at work or at play, in sickness or in health. I don't know if I am making much sense here, but I know what I want to say and hope you can understand my perhaps clumsy way of expressing it.

It is our reactions to life's situations that count, not the actual situations themselves. Loss of a career, health, a loved one, etc. are all jolts but our reactions to them, our adaptability, our acceptance and our hope in a better future, if not in this life then certainly in the next, is what matters. That springs eternal.

This is what motivates me to go on. I don't really let my medical problems bother me that much because, other than the fact it would make me more miserable than usual, and everyone around me as well, I can still do things. I have my books, my music, my trains, my videos, my family, great friends and a will to overcome whatever life's curves throw at me. It has made a huge difference in my life.

I don't really need much more. I have a sense of deep love and respect for my Creator and trust in His plan for me. Ultimately, that is the most important aspect in all of our lives, provided we embrace it. Sometimes it takes a loss of some sort to put us in touch with what is truly important in life.

I hope you can call up those locomotive pictures I sent by e-mail. I must have 5,000 of them already downloaded on my hard drive.

Well I better close. Best wishes for the coming New Year and I hope your health improves. I will let you know if and when we plan the Cold Harbor trip.

Your friend,

Mark

What was the physical state of the man who wrote this letter? I imagined him, weak but determined, sitting at his computer hour after hour, struggling to find words for the wisdom distilled from twenty years of suffering. Crusted scabs covered the left side of his cheek and the inside of his mouth. His left eye was stuck half shut and his left ear drained fluid. He sought to make sense with a mind muddled by pain medication. Morphine and cytoxan left him nauseated. Lancinating pain pierced his face, and his head throbbed. He apologized for the clumsiness of his thoughts while a hematoma pressed on his brain. He had to prop up his unstable shoulder and wrist and then patiently pecked out his words with a pencil eraser.

What words did he find?

"It is our reactions to life's situations that count, not the actual situations themselves." When everything in the material world had been relentlessly stripped away, when constant physical suffering seemed insurmountable, and when even the most meager expectations for the future were lost, what remained? *"I have been blessed..."* Mark's message reminded me of Viktor Frankl's experiences as a Jewish prisoner at Auschwitz. Even while watching others go daily to their deaths or to the depths of despair, Frankl believed there was only one thing that kept his own humanity alive: the freedom to choose his attitude about life. Even in the face of unmitigated suffering, he believed that nothing could take this freedom away from him—absolutely nothing—unless he let it. In a daily crisis of choice, Mark was alive inside because he would not allow his disease to vanquish his attitude. *"I have...a will to overcome whatever life's curves throw at me. It has made a huge difference in my life."* He refused to give in to the darkness. He was alive inside because he chose to be alive.

"God has been good to me. Trust in Him. He will give you the strength and the will to go on." His letter is sublime testimony to the perseverance of spiritual life in the face of incredible physical adversity. I pictured him as he wrote to me, a man relentlessly being dragged into the vortex of an advancing vasculitis, who nevertheless believed that *"Sometimes it takes a loss of some sort to put us in touch with what is truly important in life."* It was not a message from a distant author about a distant time. It was from a patient who had become my friend and then taught me about the path he chose to travel. *"I don't really need much more. I have a sense of deep love and respect for my Creator and trust in His plan for me."*

He closed his letter by talking once again about trains. He was still sending me pictures of huge locomotives. By now I knew what they meant.

By January 6, six days after this letter, Mark's facial pain became intolerable. His left ear, swollen shut, became infected. His blood pressure went so high the doctors worried that he might re-bleed into his head. They readmitted him for pain control and his ear infection. A repeat CT scan showed no change in the subdural hematoma, so he went back home on the 11th. Over the next week, in an effort to determine the source of his facial pain, he saw the dentist, the ENT doctor, and was due to see the neurologist. Just before that appointment, Zita found him curled up in bed, holding his head and clenching his teeth, with a silent scream of agony written across his face. For the fourth time in as many weeks she called an ambulance. He was admitted again.

By January 24 Mark was comfortable in the hospital on oral pain medication. He laughed a bit and joked with his doctors. They discharged him that morning. That afternoon he called his brothers from home. He reminisced for hours with them and kidded about the mischief they had all gotten into in their past.

That evening Mark fell again, hitting his right arm and his head. He told his sister-in-law, "I was arrogant and walked to the bathroom without my cane." The pain in his arm got so bad it forced him to sit up in bed rather than lie down to rest. Diana and Paul stayed up with him until 2 a.m. They wanted to take him to the ER and have his arm evaluated, but Mark said he had had enough of hospitals and he was sure there was nothing wrong. He said he was happy, he wanted to sleep, and told them to go to bed.

The next morning Zita opened the door to his bedroom and found him comatose.

Into the Depths

It was not clear exactly when Mark became unconscious or why, but sometime during that night he vomited and aspirated into his lungs. On admission to St. Vincent he had raging pneumonia, a painful right elbow fracture, and a critically low blood pressure that threatened his already-borderline kidney function. His fall may have started new bleeding around his brain, but no one knew for certain, because he was too unstable to go to CT for a head scan.

On January 27, 2001 Zita called me, her voice weighed down with weariness. Despite three months of constantly caring for her son, she was remorseful that she had not checked on him in the middle of the night. It was painful to hear her say, "If only I had..." and know that nothing she might have done would have made any difference. The moment Mark aspirated, the damage was done. Vasculitis had already ravaged his lungs. Stomach acid on fragile lung tissue produces an instant chemical burn. Half-digested food is loaded with bacteria. His coma kept him from coughing, and his medications prevented a host response. Life-threatening pneumonia was inevitable.

Over the next two weeks, as Mark's condition worsened, Zita and I talked almost daily, sorting through the medical meaning of each new development. Even as I tried to reassure her, I knew that her son was descending a spiral of complications that couldn't continue indefinitely.

Gradually, Zita's conversations changed. She talked about Mark's boyhood, his love of trains, and how he stayed true to that love. Nostalgia crept into her stories, as if, like fondly putting a young boy to bed, she was starting to tuck Mark into her memories.

By February 5 he teetered on the brink of physiologic collapse. He remained unresponsive and ventilator-dependent. He required a tracheostomy, a quarter-sized hole in his throat, through which a tube was passed to protect his airway from repeated aspiration. He developed a methicillin-resistant Staph infection in his lungs. His kidney function deteriorated. By the 7th he appeared to be developing multiple organ system failure. Everywhere in his body vital processes were shutting down. The doctors were running out of treatments. When Zita called me that evening her voice was desperate with apprehension. "Bill," she said, "I think we're losing Mark."

The family met with the medical team for an end-of-life conference. Despite months of watching Mark's condition deteriorate, Zita had never before faced those kinds of choices. In anguish, she called to ask me how a mother could make decisions like that. I listened to her fears and discussed her alternatives, but the answer could only come from her.

2/8/01

Dear Bill,

When I arrived this a.m., Mark was having trouble breathing and his heart was beating very fast. His kidney function is deteriorating. His renal specialist told me he needed dialysis.

While we talked, the doctor looked at Mark and said sadly, "We are doing everything we can. We all love him." That was very heartwarming. When I left the hospital this evening, Mark was still in a deep sleep. I wonder what I will see tomorrow.

Thank you for helping me yesterday when I called. I have given much thought to all you said to me, and I am most grateful to you. I hope that if the time should come for a decision, I will have the strength to do what is best for Mark. I never thought that I would ever be faced with such a decision, but I guess life was never meant to be easy for any of us.

Sincerely,

Zita

Every morning I set aside time to meditate. In the words of Mark's last letter, "I enter a world which is less threatening, more peaceful and far more meaningful. Answers to my life's questions become so clear...."

The answers were always there, but for years I had been too busy to listen to them. It took the quiet of Mepkin Abbey for me to hear my inner conversations clearly. Now, meditation recreated that quiet. Each morning, within the stillness, a different awareness arose. Sometimes it came in the form of questions that invited me to go beyond an obvious answer. Sometimes it was an awareness of truth, an answer I knew to be true without knowing how or why, indeed without cognitively knowing at all.

The next morning as I meditated, Zita's words—like a stream of bubbles breaking the surface from below—came into my thoughts: "I think we're losing Mark." I felt far away from him, as I had in November when he was critically ill, but this time the feeling was even more oppressive. Silent questions began.

What will you do?

"Maybe I should get a night flight to New York…just to be there with him…but that doesn't feel right."

Why not?

"I don't know. He's unconscious. I wouldn't be able to talk to him. I can't give Zita anything more than I already have. I could only stay a few days without becoming a burden."

What did he teach you?

"He taught me…that miles don't matter. That's what I learned in November. That's what he showed me in his writings. He taught me that the real task is to reach out from within."

The image of a hand resting at the side of a bed came unbidden into my thoughts. I saw my hand reach out and rest on it, as if I was sitting beside the bed. There were no faces in the image, no voices, and no motion. Each morning as I sat, my thoughts returned to that image. All I saw was one hand resting on top of another. From then on, I tried to be that hand.

On February 9 Zita called again. Mark had remained stable through the night but had little strength left. She was numb with the awareness that he might not be there the next day. All I could do in reply was to tell her about the image of two hands touching. I asked her to write in big letters the message "Bill is here with you, Mark" on a piece of cardboard and put it in his line of sight.

After her call I sat down and began to write.

2/9/01

Hi Zita,

My prayer for both Mark and you is what I spoke to you about, the prayer you learned long ago: Rest in Peace.

How can I pray for peace at a time of such turmoil? As I wrote once before, where others might see a body devastated by disease, I see, with ever-increasing understanding, a soul who has become free. That understanding has been

Mark's great gift to me. On the outside, he appears to have lost so much. But it is the life within that really matters and he has lost none of that. And if faith teaches us anything, it teaches that the life within will not die.

I see a soul free to be excited. He has boundless enthusiasm for his dreams. Some people see only the limitations of life. They are people with chains on their souls, who, regardless of their health or wealth haven't felt once what Mark feels every day. In his letters, I see instead a sense of curiosity, compassion, and excitement that overcomes his physical limitations.

I see a soul free to feel joy. Everyone who knows Mark knows this joy. Everyone in the hospital comments about it, and always has. His doctor spoke for all of us when he described how everyone loves Mark. Why? Because in loving him we all are drawn to the best that is in each of us.

I see a soul free to experience incredible beauty. Mozart's music is the manifestation of beauty that Mark experiences all along. I believe Paul did well to play the Mozart CD's for him at his bedside. I bet it broke through the isolation of the ICU. The music helped Mark reconnect, both to its beauty and to all of you, his family. The music tells him that you hear the beauty he hears, that you understand it and share it. That is the level at which hearts connect.

I see a soul free to experience unbelievable power. Mark kept sending me pictures of the most powerful locomotives he knew. I believe he sent those pictures because he was telling me something, not only about his past but also about himself. Mark loved huge locomotives because their power and freedom expressed what he experiences inside. His soul was talking to me in those pictures. Tell him for me that I heard him.

I see a soul free to be at peace. He wrote me, "I see everything so much more clearly now. I cherish my Mom more each day. I am a better friend to my friends, because I am a better friend to myself." This is the place we all seek. This is the place of deep acceptance, the place of peace. Regardless of what happens in the next days or weeks, I believe Mark made it to that place.

I have come to realize how terribly hard the journey of acceptance is. "It is easier for a camel to pass through the eye of a needle..." than for a person attached to all the things of this world to let go and enter into the place of acceptance, the place of peace.

It is in this sense that I pray for you as well. I pray for you to rest in that place of peace. For a mother to accept the suffering of her son is beyond my experience. To let go like that is more than I can even imagine. You are teaching me the depth of that emotion but I have no words for it. All that comes to my mind is the image of Michelangelo's *Pietà*.

May both of you rest in that place of peace. In the Latin of long ago that you love, "Requiescat in pace."

Bill

Writing the letter drained me. Zita's suffering arose from a bond she couldn't relinquish. I could only hope that my e-mail would help her. Eighteen hours later, she wrote back:

2/11/01

Dear Bill,

It is hard to find words to tell you just what your letter meant to me. Perhaps the best way I can do this is by saying that today Mark opened his eyes when I spoke to him. This time they seemed aware and not hazy as they were last Sunday.

It was then that I told him the wonderful words you wrote about him. I pleaded with him to get well so that I could read the whole letter to him. I believe that he heard me. I believe that with your letter, you reached out to him and touched his hand, and he responded. He blinked several times and he moved his lips. For him, this was something tremendous indeed. I hope that this will give you some idea of what your letter has done for us both. He is so very sick, but you were there and he knew it. Thank you.

Mark is a little better but still critical. The doctor said it could still go either way. Last Sunday they almost lost him and it could happen again. The big problem is that his immune system is so compromised. They are worried about some other bacteria hitting him because of his poor general condition. They feed him through a tube but that isn't working very well. A yellow liquid food caused his sugar to go up and now he has to have insulin. It is one problem compounded upon another. Thus it goes on, day after day.

Please know that I am very grateful to you Bill. You were in my thoughts and prayers at Mass today in the hospital chapel.

Zita

Exhausted physically and emotionally, Zita called me on February 13 with more bad news; Mark was bleeding from his bowel. Memories of his massive bleed in Wenatchee haunted her. Surgery had solved his bleeding then, but everyone knew he couldn't survive similar surgery this time. All the doctors could do was keep giving him blood. As Mark's feeble pulse waited for each transfusion, they knew that either the bleeding had to stop soon, or Mark would. Despair crept into Zita's voice. "Bill, last night the nurse told me they don't think he's going to make it." We were at the bottom of the barrel.

I labored to say something encouraging. "Zita, I know it's been one complication after another. I don't blame them for thinking Mark can't possibly make it through all of this. If he were an ordinary patient, I'd think that way too. But Mark is no ordinary patient. I don't say that out of fondness or false assurance. I took care of him for eight years, and I've personally seen him come through stuff that I never saw anybody else survive! He's been at death's door three times now, and every time he's pulled through. I don't know how he does it. I just know it's true and so do you. If anybody can make it through this, Mark can."

I could say that with complete conviction. All of it was true. But it wasn't enough. What mattered now was to allow Zita's sorrow to surface without self-reproach. It was an impossible task. How could she detach from her son without the anguished guilt of abandonment?

After we finished talking I went for a walk in the damp air of a winter afternoon, trying to cope with my own feelings of sorrow and loss. Mark had indeed survived unbelievable battering before. His spirit surmounted pneumonia in November and shingles in December. In the midst of that suffering he wrote letters of incredible faith, his words shining like a beacon that beckoned everyone to him.

Now that beacon was lost in the gray fog of my own grief. The peace I had wished for Zita abandoned me. Clinical experience told me that Mark couldn't keep going like this. I thought, "Why is his suffering going on and on? Why doesn't it end? What more is there left to learn?"

I needed to reach out, but I couldn't talk to Mark, and I didn't want to burden Zita. Instead, I wrote to a close friend.

I am losing one of the people with whom I have corresponded at the deepest level I know. My friend Mark Smetko has been in the hospital three times since Christmas. It seems unlikely now that he will survive.

His journey of letting go has been beyond my power to describe. It was he who, by his example, helped me work through the loss of my doctor persona. I always felt that if he could let go, I could too.

> But now that his journey is coming to an end, it is very hard for me to let go of him. When he goes, there will be silence where once there was a voice.

I stopped writing. "There will be silence." Emotion swept through me like a tidal wave rising up from the ocean and flooding the shore.

Who is Mark?

"I don't know! He was a patient once. Now he's so much more, as if I've known him all my life."

What does he mean to you?

"I hid once, behind the mask of Dr. Gruber. I was afraid that if I took it off I'd have no connection with anyone. There would only be silence. I felt that silence last year, when I lost the connection with all my patients. It was terrible. I felt alone, cut off. Mark reached out to me in that place. That's why I'm so grateful.

"I'm afraid that if I lose him, I'll be cut off again. I'll lose a connection to life itself. I don't want to be in that place. He helped me break out of it. Now he's alone. That's why I want to reach out to him. This whole journey is about reaching out. For me, the nature of the journey is connectedness."

Will you lose him?

"No...I'm afraid of that, but...something tells me that I won't. The connectedness is inside now. Somehow I sense that I'll never lose it. I want to believe that...but he's dying. My belief keeps fading away. If he goes, will I still have what he gave me?"

What do you fear?

"I need to let go of my fear...of the silence."

When those words appeared, the flooding feelings inside reached a crescendo and then strangely, started to subside. It wasn't a wrung-out collapse. Instead, it was tranquility, as if the peace I wanted for Zita had suddenly returned to me. Perhaps Mark had responded to me. That didn't make any sense. I knew he was nearly comatose, barely responsive to anything. Nevertheless, the calm I felt was real.

The next morning as I meditated, my Uncle Bill appeared in my thoughts. What did his life mean to me? Why did I still feel connected to him? I could no longer write Zita about medical matters, so I wrote to her about Bill.

2/14/01

Hi Zita,

You've been on my mind a lot since we talked about Mark's medical situation. There isn't much more I can say there, but if I can at least give some comfort to you, then I will feel that I have helped.

It is with that in mind that I will tell you a story.

I've mentioned my Uncle Bill. You know now from the notes at Mepkin Abbey what an important role he played in who I became and the journey I am now on.

When he joined the Trappists and became Br. Cyprian, Bill let go of all of his material possessions, even his name. When he took his vow of obedience, he let go of his independence. When he volunteered to help start a new monastery in Brazil, he let go again, this time of his homeland and all of his family.

Now I will tell you the rest of his story.

On Ash Wednesday in 1989 the doctor told him he had incurable cancer. The abbot asked him if he wanted to return to the U.S. for palliative treatment. After reflecting on the meaning of his life, he declined, and then wrote his family a letter explaining why he had done so.

He felt that the life of a monk was more than just one of outward simplicity. It is instead one of inner detachment, not only from the niceties of the world but also from the needs we all have within us. Bill had reached that state of complete detachment. He no longer needed to cling to anything, including his own material existence. He knew why he had lived and he knew that he had accomplished what he set out to do. It was a letter of letting go, of acceptance, and of the serenity that comes with that.

He died on Holy Saturday, forty days later, in a state of great peace.

I believe that Bill is still with me. I have told you his story in order to express that belief in a way that I hope you will find comforting at such a dark time for you and your family.

Bill is with me because of the example he set. He led an authentic life. His outer life fully manifested an inner truth that in turn animated everything he did. 'Anima' is the Latin word for soul. When we saw his life, we saw his soul shining through it; we saw who he truly was.

Bill is still with me because he gave me something that remains alive inside of me. In him, I saw something of myself reflected back to me, as if, by looking in a mirror, I saw my own face for the first time. My face has always been part of me and yet, if I never saw a mirror, I would never know what that part of me looked like. In the same sense, I learned from my uncle what a deeper part of me looked like, a part I might never have known otherwise. His life showed me my own inner life.

Once I saw my face in a mirror, I knew what it looked like. Once I saw my inner life reflected back to me, I knew who I was, and I will always know it. Even though I can give it no name more specific than an inner life, I know it is very real indeed. It is perhaps the most real part of me.

It is in that sense that I believe Bill is with me. He is more than a faded photo or a memory in one frame of my life. Part of his life is alive within my life. When I meditate, I feel something of him connected to something deep within me. It did not die, and I believe it will not die.

It is in a similar sense that I believe Mark is with me.

Like my uncle, Mark has mirrored something back to me. He is my teacher, a guide on my journey. Through the example of his life, I am better able to accept and let go. Because he has already been where I am trying to go, he will always be with me as I travel the path. It is in that sense that I will never lose him.

I'm not sure where Mark is just now. But I believe his soul is listening. And I am deeply grateful that he once had a chance to read my letters.

Peace be with you,

Bill

On February 20 Zita called with cautious good news. Almost four weeks after his admission, Mark appeared to have turned a corner. Prednisone had stabilized his vasculitis enough that the doctors cut his dose by two-thirds. His chest x-ray improved sufficiently that they decreased his ventilator support from eighteen to ten breaths per minute. Dialysis improved his kidney function. The bleeding in his bowel stopped after an administration of clotting factors. He started to wake up, and although the tube in his trachea prevented him from speaking, he could understand words spoken to him. He still couldn't move his arms or legs, but Zita said that the doctors were more hopeful. To her, I tried to be encouraging. To myself I thought, "Take this one day at a time."

Mark's miraculous progress continued. When I called Zita a week later, he was out of the ICU, off the ventilator, and breathing on his own through the tracheostomy tube. His kidney function had improved enough that the doctors discontinued dialysis.

Zita became caught between cautious hope that Mark might improve, worry that he might re-aspirate, and an impossible task of detaching if he did. She worried that outside of the ICU he wouldn't get the care he needed. She was anxious about leaving him. She felt guilty taking a break, and reluctant about going to a concert with Paul.

2/27/01

Dear Bill,

Thank you for talking to me over the phone. You help me so very much. A simple "thank you" seems so inadequate.

Paul and Diana think I spend too many hours at the hospital, but I know it helps Mark. I read and listen to the music he loves. Several doctors told me that being there and letting Mark hear the beautiful music was perfect medicine for him.

Besides, how can I help it? Deep down Mark is always in my thoughts. He lies in his bed completely helpless. When I tell him how much he means to everyone, a smile slowly forms on his lips. There is nothing more beautiful to me than to see that. I give him the messages from you. The nurse tacked your message about being with him on the wall when they moved him to the new room. After I told him that you are holding his hand, his lovely smile spread to his eyes. So you see, Bill, you are very much a part of Mark's life now. He knows you are with him.

I take each day as it comes. What happens will happen. I am very realistic about Mark's condition. I ask God to take Mark if He wants him now, but please, do not let him suffer any more. This is my prayer. I just feel sad that all this is happening to my child.

Thank you again for your caring and connection with us. It is very important.

Zita

Although she was often frustrated, anxious, and upset, after months of turmoil it was remarkable that Zita handled so many stresses so well. I reflected often about how remarkable her whole family was. As I did so, I thought about my own family.

My brother Don had osteoarthritis in several joints from sports injuries. A worn-out hip eventually hurt so much when he walked that on January 24 he had hip replacement surgery in Cincinnati. A week later we convened in Hilton Head, where I could help him convalesce in warmer weather.

Don's recovery was uneventful, but he had difficulty dealing with its physical constraints. He had lived an energetic life and hated the thought that someday arthritic joints would limit his lifestyle. He abhorred even more the thought that "someday" had arrived earlier than he had anticipated. He asked me, "Bill, how can I get back to doing what I want to do?" It was a thought-provoking question.

For years I taught patients to replace painful activities with substitutes that still gave them satisfaction. "You don't have to give up all your activities," I'd tell them. "Think about why you enjoy a favorite activity, and then substitute something else that meets that need but doesn't hurt your joints." By satisfying patients' inner needs, substitution often solved both their pain and their frustration.

This, however, was no ordinary patient. I knew Don down where his demons lived. To the Greeks, hell was "pan-demonium", the place where all the demons were on the loose. Confinement let loose all of Don's demons. When I mentioned that he might have to switch to less vigorous activity, he protested, "I want to stay active! That's why I had this operation! If I can't be active...I'd rather die."

I had heard those words from Mark as he fought to keep driving trains. I heard them within myself as I fought to remain a doctor. Now I heard the same words from my brother as he fought to do what he had always done. I thought, "We all keep clinging and fighting to hang on. Why? The world promised us that if only we fought hard enough, we'd win. If only we were competitive or cool enough, funny or flirtatious enough, we'd be safe. We'd be accepted, admired, and perhaps even loved."

The promise was false. None of the prizes gave lasting satisfaction. I remembered my father's words at Mepkin. As old age overtook him his accomplishments faded and his achievements felt empty. In the end, even winners felt alone.

My Uncle Bill let go of that struggle. So did Mark. That's what they taught me. "Stop clinging. Don't just substitute the next activity and then the next, one after another after another, until you finally crumble into an exhausted heap. Let go of what was. Remain open to what might be."

While I was with Don in Hilton Head, an earthquake shook Seattle. Images of its broken buildings reminded me of how much I had changed. When I gave the substitution talk to Don, I looked and sounded like the old Dr. Gruber, the man in the white coat who once solved patients' frustrations by substituting one activity for another just so they could keep on doing. I wasn't that man anymore. Like the buildings on TV, the foundation of my convictions had crumbled, the façade was cracked, and the tectonic bedrock of my beliefs had irrevocably shifted. In this encounter with Don I saw the impact on me of the lesson in Mark's life. We all tried desperately to avoid, to run, to hide, but ultimately to no avail. It wasn't enough to solve the physical problems that caused our pain, if by doing so we avoided the fear that caused our suffering.

Letting go felt terrifying, almost like dying. Maybe it was a kind of dying. Or maybe I was letting go of something lifeless to begin with—the abandoned cocoon of a butterfly that was finally ready to shed its shell and fly away. I could hear Mark's words, *"If we can open to it, a new life will be there."* He showed me that it was true. He found what he had been seeking for so many years: a caterpillar who finally found that the butterfly was inside all along.

In the Smetko family, unceasing tension was pushing everyone to the edge of their endurance. When I called Zita on March 6 she was despondent. Even though he appeared to be improving, Mark had pleaded, "I want…to go home."

The sadness in his request overwhelmed her. She felt caught in the closing vise of an impossible situation. She worried that if Mark came home and then aspirated again it would kill him. Medically, that was probably true, but her worry came more from fear than fact. Perhaps it was fear of walking into his room one morning and seeing what she saw that dreadful day in January. Perhaps it was fear that the moment of ultimate loss loomed directly in front of her. She was a mother tired to the marrow of her bones. For months she had cared for Mark without respite. Now, unable to avoid the inevitable, she could only plead silently, *No…Please…I'm not ready yet. Not now…Not yet.*

Paul was caught as well in the same sadness and exhaustion. Crisis after crisis had emptied him emotionally. He grew up with his brother, bore similar scars, and carried the same worrisome diagnosis. He knew that Mark faced chronic dialysis. He said later, "I didn't want Mark to keep suffering. There was no point to it, no meaning anymore!" When Zita called, she said that a hospital terminal care committee requested a conference with them the following day. It wasn't my place to suggest alternatives. I couldn't escape the sadness either.

When she called two days later, Zita sounded better. Mark had announced during the conference that he wanted to live. The St. Vincent staff agreed that, under those circumstances, he should stay in the hospital. Paul was okay with that. Zita was relieved. Mark said he'd like to try physical therapy. His doctors, caught between disbelief and amazement said, "That sounds like a good idea."

A month before, in early February, I debated about flying to New York because I doubted that Mark would make it to April 1. Now I was beginning to believe that, once again, Lazarus was going to prove me wrong.

The following morning as I meditated, I focused on his words, "I want to go home."

3/15/01

Hi Zita!

In this letter, I'd like to share some reflections that have occurred to me recently. I've mentioned the image of my hand resting on top of Mark's at the side of his bed. From time to time it seems that I can feel my hand touching his. I know that doesn't make any sense at all, nevertheless it is so. Last week, after Mark said he wanted to come home, while this image was in my mind, I heard the words "Come home, Mark. Come home to everyone who loves you."

To me that gave a different meaning to his words, "I want to come home." Perhaps his words weren't about giving up or about coming back to a specific place. Perhaps instead he wanted to come home to what your house stands for. To me his words came from a lonely place inside where he is drained, empty, and terribly tired of a barren hospital room. Perhaps all he wanted was to return to a place of caring, to the warmth and love that your home symbolizes. Knowing how much your family has cared, I'd want to come home too.

The second impression I wanted to share arose after our recent phone conversation. You spoke to me about joining you and your family for dinner at your house on the Sunday evening of my visit. The morning after we talked, I saw all of us gathered at your table. Then I saw Mark's chair next to me, unoccupied, and a place setting at the table that was untouched.

Sometimes that image can be associated with loss—"He's no longer here." But in this case, my impression was exactly the opposite. The place setting said that he was there, that although he couldn't be physically present, he was nevertheless very much part of our gathering. Then in my thoughts, words from scripture appeared—"Where two or more of you are gathered in my name, there I will be in the midst of you."

To me the empty place setting said that, in some way, Mark would be there when we gather. He may or may not be physically present. It is impossible to say anything about that yet. But I sense that even if he can't be physically present, he will be there with us. In that sense, he will be home.

I look forward to being there.

Warmest regards,

Bill

By mid-March Mark was stable enough that the hospital suggested a rehab center. His long-term needs made the family's search difficult. He was still at risk to regurgitate food and aspirate it into his lungs. He still needed the tracheostomy tube to protect his airway. His nutrition came through a stomach tube. His debilitation predisposed him to bedsores. His risk for infection required isolation precautions in a private room. He had difficulty communicating basic needs to the nurses. At night he dreaded the darkness and the loneliness that came with it. During the day, with waning energy, he fought depression and the hopelessness of his future. It was not easy to find a facility that could handle all of this.

Infection precautions isolated Mark from more than microbes. A private room cut him off from human contact. He was a man sustained by reaching out to others. As his awareness improved, his quarantine became oppressive. The family was present as much as they could be. The nurses were kind, but tight schedules left them little time to keep him company. Loneliness began to grind him down in a way that his physical afflictions couldn't. The staff spoke of it as a variant of ICU psychosis and suggested a psychiatrist. That saddened me. I remembered my hospital rounds with him. He didn't need a psychiatrist; he needed a friend.

3/19/01

Dear Bill,

First I want to say I hope all is well with you. Please let me know. You must know that you have become a very dear and treasured friend.

Mark is, to use your words, lonely, empty and drained, and he feels the isolation of his room constantly. We cannot wheel him out of the room because of fear of infection. We spend hours with him, but he becomes very sad when any of us leaves.

I asked him today if he was looking forward to your visit and he smiled with a broad smile, which we don't see very often. He shook his head up and down and said "Yes" very emphatically. I tell him that you are with him and that your hand is holding fast to his. I firmly believe that your hand resting on his really happens every day. I attribute much of his recovery to your closeness, not in person, but because your soul has been in the room with him. I believe he felt your presence even though he was in a coma and unconscious for so long. Each day, when I tell him this, he nods his head in agreement and then smiles and closes his eyes in peace.

We, too, are looking forward to your visit. Your image of Mark sitting at the table is very real. You will sit at a table on a chair that has been part of his life for over fifty years. Even though his physical body lies on a hospital bed, he will be with us in a spiritual way. I firmly believe where love is, there is a connection. It transcends every barrier. Your reflections are very clear to me. I find a healing meaning in everything you expressed in your letter.

Thank you and please stay well.

Zita

Mark was as helpless as a turtle on its back. He could do nothing to change his position in bed. He could barely shift his head. He couldn't use his fractured right arm, his left arm was motionless and his left leg nearly so. The neurologist initially thought the weakness was due to a stroke. The word panicked Mark. The image of permanent paralysis terrified him. Paul said "He hated this state more than anything." At the rehab center a different doctor changed the diagnosis to peripheral nerve injury. That meant that the weakness might, with time and therapy, improve. It was only a glimmer of hope, but it was all Mark had to ward off his fear.

He hated confinement indoors as much as he hated being helpless. His isolation and immobility fueled intense claustrophobia. He desperately needed to feel free again.

"Zita," I said during a call, "Mark needs a train."

"Yes, I know he does, Bill."

"Remember when he was like this before, when I asked you to put up a picture of a train in his room at Northwest Hospital?" I thought, "That was four miserable years ago—four years stuck in this devouring quicksand, fighting to get free."

Zita replied "Yes, I do. I brought another picture into this room, a big one of a steam locomotive. I hung it on the wall right across from his bed."

"Good. He gave me the picture from Northwest. Tell him I still look at it. Tell him the locomotives in it are still pulling."

"I will, Bill."

Loneliness was sucking Mark downward. A year ago his letters had lifted me out of that pit like an outstretched hand. Now I wanted to do the same for him. He needed more than trains. He needed a friend. The next morning, for the first time in months, I wrote, via Zita, directly to him.

3/25/01
Subj: The First Letter to Mark

Hi Mark!

I've been in touch with your mom for many weeks by e-mail and phone. I wanted to be in touch with you as well, but since January that hasn't been possible. I couldn't talk to you, but every morning as I meditated, I visualized my hand resting on yours. It isn't much, as practical communication goes, but I hope it helped.

I don't feel my connection with you was ever broken, but I do miss talking with you. I'm going to try to resume our conversations by writing directly to you. I recognize that it is hard for you to communicate back to me. Don't worry about it. I'll solve that by showing up in person in a week!

I know our visit will be for a limited time. It will have a beginning and an end. To soften those limits I would like to start our conversation now, so that when I do show up we won't feel like we have to cram a lot into too little time. And after I leave, we can keep right on talking like this.

Between now and Friday's flight to New York I will try to send an e-mail every day. I'm going to make each one brief, so it won't fatigue you. In each note, I will try to give you just one thought to keep with you.

The main message of this note is that I am out here, and I have missed you.

To be continued…

Warmest regards,

Bill

3/26/01

Dear Bill,

I read your first letter to Mark. He listened carefully and nodded his head several times. He was especially touched when I read the last sentence, "I am out here, and I have missed you."

In his difficult way of communicating he replied, "Tell Bill I am happy he is coming to visit me. Please tell him I won't be able to talk much because I am almost mute, but I will try my best to tell him that I did know he was with me all through my illness. Tell him that I never had the chance to write the letter I wanted to write to him. Now I am trapped, but I know he will understand."

"Tell Bill that I have felt his hand on mine and it will hardly be more real when he is actually doing this, because I've always had that image with me throughout the conscious part of my illness."

Mark's reply took a long time because he can only say a few words around the tube with each breath, but I wrote down everything. He also said, "I am looking forward to his visit and the letters. This letter today means a lot to me." With that he broke down.

I wish I knew what I could do for you to let you know how much all of your caring for Mark means to me. It is so inadequate to say only "Thank you," but it comes from my heart and soul. I shall never forget what you have done to help me through this difficult time.

Zita

3/26/01
Subj: The Second Letter to Mark

Hi Mark!

This morning, as I reflected about coming to visit you, a thought crossed my mind that made me smile—"I'm coming to visit a locomotive." I love that image. I love to think about you, not in a locomotive, but as a locomotive.

I often look at the picture of the Great Northern diesels that you gave me just before you left Seattle. This December, you sent me more pictures by e-mail. This time they were huge 4-8-8-4 steam locomotives, the biggest ones you knew. They are images of incredible power. I began to get the real message.

Your photos are much more than just pictures from your past. I believe they are also images of something inside you.

Over the past eight weeks, I think we've seen how much power, how much strength you actually have. None of the images of your locomotives do justice to that power. They don't even come close.

I realize that part of you feels exhausted, weak and alone. I know that sometimes those feelings have been overwhelming. That is understandable. More than once in the last eight weeks, I thought that a person less resolute than you would be dead by now.

Instead, your inner strength has awed your doctors and amazed your family. I'm not saying that lightly. Several times, when things looked especially grim, the hospital staff shook their heads in hopeless resignation. Your family hung in there and gritted through it, knowing that you had survived stuff that bad before and could do it again. And you did.

Inner strength is hard to talk about. It's not that it isn't real; it's just that it's hard to imagine. So to visualize it better I use an image we both understand. I use your image of a huge locomotive. The thought I want to leave with you today is that I am coming to visit a locomotive. I will hold your hand. It doesn't matter that the hand itself is weak and frail. What matters is that I will touch the strength inside it.

More later,

Bill

3/28/01

Dear Bill,

Here are the words Mark said to me after I read your wonderful second letter to him.

"Tell Bill that I understand what he is talking about regarding the locomotive and its power. I used to marvel at what they were capable of doing. Yes, my hands did control that powerful machinery. I used to look at Dr. Gruber's hands and ponder what a marvelous gift God gave him for his work in surgery."

We're looking forward to Sunday! Paul plans to pick you up. Will let you know more later.

Zita

Mark needed every image of strength he could muster. His afflictions were imploding in on him from all sides. At night his anxiety erupted into full-blown panic attacks. He awoke alone in the darkness with his heart pounding inside his chest, gasping for air and groping helplessly for a call button he couldn't find. Drenched in sweat, he was unable to shift his head or shout for help and was terrified that if he vomited no one could reach him in time.

One morning, as I meditated, a verse from a performance of Handel's *Messiah* came into my thoughts: "He was cut off from the land of the living. He was despised, rejected...a man of sorrows and acquainted with grief." "For our transgressions was he wounded." As I slowly repeated the phrases, their meaning began to deepen. I heard Mark's cries in the night. Questions floated in front of me.

What is the verse about?

"Someone rejected. Someone cut off...from the land of the living."

What cuts someone off?

"Fear. Defensiveness...Something we want to hide."

Who is Mark?

"He is someone isolated, cut off. That's how I know him. I know that isolation. I lived there for years, separated from everyone. When I reach out to Mark, there's a connection present. I can feel it. It's like my hand resting on his."

What does your hand touch?

"That image keeps appearing. I saw it when I wrote him about the ceiling of the Sistine Chapel. It's an image about the act of touching. Maybe I'm touching...the part of me that was cut off from others for so long. Maybe connecting to that...is what makes us alive."

I felt drained, confused, almost scared. I sensed that the meaning of the journey was in this dialogue, but I couldn't grasp the meaning with my mind. Instead of thoughts that I could express in words, there was only a frustratingly vague awareness that I couldn't force into cognitive form. I struggled against that, struggled to bring what I sensed into conscious definition. "If only I could write clearly enough, then I would understand what all of this meant."

Have you learned nothing? Let go of struggle. Let go of "if only..." Rest in stillness and listen.

The words of the poet Rumi appeared. "Stay bewildered in God, and only that."

3/27/03
Subj: The Third Letter to Mark

Hi Mark!

I just finished talking with Zita. She told me you enjoyed the letters. I want you to know that I cherish her account of your words in reply.

Our conversation means a lot to me. Even though I always felt an unbroken connection, it feels good to hear your words again. I know you speak slowly and that much of our connecting will still be eye to eye and touch to touch. But words are like music. They are good to hear.

Zita told me about your sense of isolation, your sense of claustrophobia and your sense of wanting to go home. When I heard about how hard it has been for you, I wanted to reach out and help you.

This morning as I thought of you, music began to form in my head. My thoughts of you are often associated with music. I think it is a symbol for the beauty inside you, just as the locomotives show me the power that is there. The music was from a performance of *Messiah* that I heard recently. The words were: "He was cut off from the land of the living, a man of sorrows and acquainted with grief." In those words, I imagined the loneliness of a soul cut off from the love of others. That is an empty place, a place of feeling forsaken and abandoned.

There is so little I can do to help your physical conditions, but I want at least to help you with your feelings of being cut off and isolated. The message I want you to keep from this letter is that you are not alone, not now, not at night, not ever. Hundreds of hands are reaching out to you. The walls of that room are not thick enough to stop them.

Rest now, knowing you are not alone. Rest knowing that you are loved.

More later,

Bill

3/28/01

Dear Bill,

Thank you for your kind and gentle third letter. I shall read it to Mark tomorrow. It will be a wonderful help to him because it addresses something he said to me today: "I want to see Bill. But you know what I am afraid of? I'm afraid I might be all freaked out and not be at my best." I told him that you would understand because you love him and would be holding his hand to let him know that you are aware of all that is troubling him.

"All freaked out and not be at my best" sounded like it was from a man mortified that he might not measure up. I didn't care if he was at his best. I just wanted to see him again. I sensed that something important was burdening him. Zita went on:

Mark said to me, "Mom, I am so disturbed about my sickness. I am going to die."

Mark knew this would be our last visit. His kidneys were failing. In the anxiety of each night's darkness, he saw face-to-face his own mortality. Like a man on the last day of death row, he knew that for him time was running out.

I thought, "He's not ready yet." From her letter, I saw that Zita sensed it too. Perhaps we were all at the brink, but none of us was ready for the next step. There was still more to learn, but I didn't know what it was.

I couldn't keep writing with the intensity of the first three letters. Something inside me needed to back off. On Thursday I wrote Mark a fourth letter filled with light descriptions of family members and wedding plans. On Friday morning, March 30, Bev and I left Seattle for New York.

Being Together

Four generations of my family gathered in Brooklyn that weekend to celebrate my nephew's wedding. We started with a relaxed rehearsal dinner Friday evening, during which two convivial clans met and enjoyed each other with toasts and roasts. The Saturday afternoon ceremony brought everyone together in a beautiful church setting to honor the bride and groom. During the formal reception that evening there was a genuine feeling of happiness. The whirl of it all ended Sunday with a casual buffet brunch at the home of the bride's parents.

After the brunch I took my time walking back to our hotel. I needed to let the feeling of festivity subside before visiting Mark.

As I walked, I reflected on how these two experiences, so intense and yet so different, were being compressed into one weekend. I truly enjoyed the wedding, but I was a guest there, not a participant. Attending it paled in priority compared to visiting my friend. The juxtaposition of the two events became a metaphor for the two different worlds in which I found myself. In the outer one I was a bit player wearing a black-tie costume for a brief moment upon the stage. In the inner world I was intensely aware that I had already discarded my actor's mask.

At noon, Paul picked me up in front of the hotel. The family resemblance helped me recognize him at once. It felt good to see him again. As I got into the car and we began to talk I had an instant sense of being at ease.

It was short-lived. After pulling out into traffic, he began twisting through the narrow back streets of Brooklyn as only a native driver could. Neither oncoming traffic nor double-parked cars were a deterrent. I looked over at him as he threaded his way through them. He noticed me checking my seatbelt. "Not to worry, Bill," he grinned at me. "This is nothing. When I was young I used to work summers driving cabs in Chicago."

"Paul, uh…I think I might have guessed that!"

As we headed from Brooklyn toward the Narrows Bridge, he talked about his life in the city. I often felt alienated in large cities. Paul was the polar opposite. He thrived in New York. He had always wanted to live there. He drank in all that the city had to offer, especially its cultural life. His work, his passions, and his driving blended perfectly into my outsider's image of New York.

Winding into a quiet residential area on the north end of Staten Island, he told me more about their life there, about the courses he taught and the caseload of his practice, about Diana's work with foster children and their own new family. His energy and ambitions gave no hint of the limits imposed by his afflicted joints.

Zita stood waiting at the front door of the house. The stress of the past two years hadn't changed her appearance from the person I remembered. At last I could deliver in person the greeting I used on my e-mails to her. "Hi, Zita!" I shouted, bounding up the walk toward her. "I've been looking forward to this hug for a long time!"

We went in to a dining room table piled high with bagels and spreads, fruit and sausages, pastries and delicacies of every kind, as only New York can produce them. As I attempted to finish my second brunch of the day, Zita talked about Mark's room, a bedroom and sitting area next to the kitchen in the back of the house. She was impatient to point out his possessions.

The walls of his room were lined from floor to ceiling with books. They were more than just a random collection; like his locomotives they were instead a projection of his personality. His books on the Civil War reflected his commitment to social justice, the books on the cosmos his sense of wonder, the books on history his appreciation of time, and the countless CD's his love of musical beauty. As Zita talked and pointed out one special title after another, his personal space filled me with impressions of his depth. Later, I joked that she tried to show me 4000 things, but all I could absorb was 2,500 of them.

I drove Zita to the rehabilitation center, but we had to park several hundred yards away. She walked briskly in front of me to the entrance, talking as we went, without missing a breath. In March she had turned eighty-six. She was disappointed, she said, about having to slow down recently when walking uphill.

As we entered the lobby I paused for a moment while she checked in at the nursing station. I wanted to be as aware as I could of what was happening. As we walked down the hall toward Mark's room, I felt the confinement of the hospital close in around me. A familiar, antiseptic smell made the air noticeable.

I first saw him resting in a propped-up position in bed. His hair, completely gray now, was wispy and thin. His skin was pale and his muscles were wasted. Breath escaped around the tube in his trachea as he tried to speak. None of that mattered to me. As he turned his head weakly and smiled a greeting, I felt joy just at being able to see my friend again. "Hi, Mark," I said softly. Despite the pallor of his face, his eyes lit up. We grinned at each other like schoolboys, and then I bent down and hugged him.

Even though it seemed that we had so much to talk about, conversation with Mark couldn't be hurried. He expended enormous effort merely attempting to talk. It took him several breaths to say one sentence, and he needed to rest often to catch his breath. If he turned to look at me he was too weak to straighten his head up on the pillow. The water he sipped had to have a thickener added so he could feel the fluid in the back of his throat and not aspirate it into his airway. In a hesitating voice he said, "What I wouldn't give...for just a drink of plain, clear water."

During his pauses I became aware of the minutes passing by. There wasn't going to be enough time to say everything I wanted to say.

There is only this moment. Be fully conscious of everything that is happening in it.

I sat by his bed, listened quietly while he spoke, and rested my hand on his. For weeks I had visualized that touch. Now it alone was enough.

He was frustrated because he couldn't think clearly enough to say what he wanted to say. He was embarrassed because the Xanax he took for his panic attacks caused him to nod off. He was scared that he might have an attack while I was there. Beyond all of these burdens, however, was an awareness neither of us could escape. He knew that he was dying.

He was characteristically forthright in not wanting to hide the subject during our visit. He wanted to be open about it, and trusted that our relationship could tolerate talking about the pain of that passage. In a halting voice, he spoke about his diagnosis of Barrett's esophagitis, the probable cause of his repeated aspirations and pneumonias. "They told me...five years ago that...it was precancerous and that...it would probably kill me...long before the arthritis would. They told me then that...I might reach a point where I...couldn't swallow, and...that's where I am now. There's really...no way out of all of this...except to die."

He knew he would keep aspirating. He knew that his kidneys would fail, and had probably known that for at least a year. As he talked about dying, I realized how long he had labored to move from hopelessness to acceptance of that one central realization.

I didn't have the courage to look over at Zita. I thought silently, "I'm just a friend and I'm struggling with the feelings of this moment. She's his mother! She bore him, raised him, and stayed with him through years of hospitalizations. She's been sitting here since January, experiencing this day after day. What does it take to do that?"

Mark spoke until he was too tired to go on. Both the turmoil of the topic and the effort of talking had exhausted him. He had to rest.

From where I sat I could see a set of photographs on the wall directly across from him. Zita followed my gaze and changed the subject by telling me about them. Several photos showed Mark clowning around with his brothers. "Getting into mischief," Zita said, rolling her eyes and smiling. She pointed to a photo of her and the boys hiking in Switzerland and said with nostalgia, "This is one of our favorite memories." In the picture they were all standing together on a mountain path, looking off to other peaks that were waiting to be climbed. The picture captured the camaraderie that bonded them all.

There was a touching picture of Mark with his girlfriend. I asked about it. He replied with a sigh, "Yeah…She was…really special but…I never quite got…to the point of…settling down." His answer barely concealed his lasting regret.

I noticed that there was no picture of Mark's father.

Above and to the left of the photos was a large hand-lettered sign that said, "Bill is here with you, Mark." Zita saw me look at it and said, "We make sure it's in every hospital room he stays in, Bill."

"Well," I smiled, "I finally got here in person."

At Zita's suggestion, I had brought along two of Mark's model locomotives from the house. As soon as I got them out, he started to talk about them. One was painted Burlington Northern colors. He said, "They had…a couple of…different color schemes…as the railroad companies…went through mergers. I liked…that one." The tube in his airway may have slowed his voice, but it didn't dampen his enthusiasm.

The other locomotive was unpainted—a gleaming brass replica of a large freight hauler. It had exquisite detail, down to the controls in the cab interior. I admired its realism and told him how amazed I was at its workmanship. He smiled proudly. In fact, the more we talked trains the more he smiled, and the more the mood in the room lifted.

On the wall opposite Mark, just below the family photos and directly in his line of sight, Zita had put a two-foot long black and white picture of a steam locomotive pulling out of an old-time station. I looked at the engine closely and then asked, "That's a 4-6-4 Hudson, isn't it?" Mark looked at me and nodded. I went on, "You told me about seeing steam engines like that when you were a little boy back in Chicago, right?"

"Yes," he whispered. He sounded pleased.

"I bet you thought I'd forgotten all that stuff. No way! I remember those conversations." He said nothing, but his smile spread to his eyes.

I looked at the picture for a minute and then turned to him and said, "You know, I think that picture's missing something. There's too much machine in it and not enough of you." I spotted a roll of adhesive tape nearby, tore off a small piece, folded it into a circle, drew a smiley face on the circle of tape and then stuck the face on the window of the engine's cab.

"There!" I said. "Now it has a soul. It has you driving it."

The little face was Mark, the soul of the machine, smiling out the window of the cab. It was also something Mark could gaze at as he drifted off into dreams. Now, in the twilight of his life, even if he couldn't be in that locomotive physically he could still be there in his dreams, and as the light started to fade, that was what mattered.

Zita handed me a photograph she had brought with her. "Here, Bill. We wanted to give you this. It was taken quite a while ago, when Mark was making freight runs down to Portland." It was a picture of Mark at the controls in the cab of a Burlington Northern diesel.

I had had an immediate connection to it. I thought, "This is the photo he wrote me about in December! This is the one he wanted me to have that was so important to him!" This wasn't just a taped-on smiley face. This was Mark, the inner Mark, young and vigorous. In the photo his face was bathed in light from the windows of the cab and he smiled with the joy of being exactly where he wanted to be in life, highballing on the high iron with seven thousand tons of train behind him. As Zita handed it to me, I knew that this photo was the only keepsake I would ever want.

Suddenly a nurse popped into the room. She said she would have medications there in just a moment, and then left just as quickly. Her abruptness broke the spell. Zita sighed. The dearth of nursing staff stirred a raw, maternal anxiety in her. There was no physical therapist available on Sunday, either. Watching her worried look, I offered to do Mark's PT for him.

Zita described the exercises Mark had been getting, and I began. As I moved one leg and then the other through repetitive motions, I felt both of his knees and smiled. There was no warmth or effusion in either one. I looked at the long, thickened scars that ran down the front of them and thought of all the surgeries it had taken to save the joints I was gently moving.

When I cautiously started to move his left arm, Mark's shoulder joint popped in and out with an ease that told me it happened all the time. There was no stability left. His disease had destroyed all of the joint ligaments. As Zita loosened the pajama top from around his right arm, we both saw a large effusion in his right shoulder. I said nothing, but both of us thought immediately about infection. Out of the corner of my eye, I saw Mark grimace and briefly close his eyes.

As we worked through the exercises, I noted that he had regained a flicker of finger motion in his left hand. I talked of hopeful expectations and told him that peripheral nerve injuries often recover. The small voice reminded me, *Yes, they do, but does it matter? He loved to hop up into his train and drive it eighty miles an hour. You love to ski. What if you couldn't do that anymore, Bill? What if it took everything you had just to wiggle one little finger? Could you write about God being good to you? That's what he did. Where did he find that inside? Could you find it?*

Mark talked about his dread of being trapped. "I...I told my mom that...I want to be...cremated rather than...buried. I just...can't stand the...thought of...being enclosed. I want to be...out there." He had reached the point where anything was better than being walled off inside.

I asked how I might help his isolation. He was too weak to write letters. I wondered if he could at least dictate thoughts into a tape recorder or even to Zita. It wasn't a realistic solution. I had no realistic solutions. I had no solutions at all. It was just me again, trying to solve a problem out of thin air. It was only a talk of wishes, a dream of anything that might overcome his imprisonment.

The exercises exhausted him. I felt caught between wishing we could keep talking and wanting him to save his energy—caught between wanting him to rest, but not wanting minutes of our visit to slip silently away. I suggested that he rest for a moment, and I would talk to him.

There's no time left now, no time. Whatever you're going to say, tell him now.

"Mark, it gives me great joy just to be here." We looked at each other.

"I wrote you about Dr. Gruber as the mask I once had, the white coat I once wore. Dr. Gruber used to care by doing. He diagnosed things, fixed things, and tried to make everything better. Even now, you bring him back. As I stand here, moving your legs, I want to do that all over again. But you helped me to let him go.

"I don't think I could have gotten past that without the example you gave me. You taught me how to do it. There was a time in my life when I could never have seen what I see now. I could never have known what I know now if you hadn't shown me. I owe you more than I can ever tell you. I wanted you to know that." He looked at me and nodded. Tears formed at the corners of his eyes.

He was fighting to stay awake, but the effort was beyond him. The watchful light in his eyes waned. As his eyelids slowly closed, I sat quietly next to him, holding his hand. It was a hand that had once guided a locomotive; now it rested motionless, swollen, and deformed. None of those changes mattered. Touching him mattered. Connecting mattered, more than any words I could find to express it.

The room became quiet except for the sound of Mark's breathing. I focused on his closed eyes. Objects at the edges of my vision began to blur. I sat there silently, moment after moment, until time itself seemed to disappear. In the stillness, the voice within me spoke to him.

Hands from everywhere are reaching out to you. Mark...know in the core of your soul...that you are loved. You are loved without reason and without reservation. You are loved without cause and without limit.

It was always there. It was there in the very beginning. It is there now, and it will always be there. It is there in a world that has no end....

Everything within me, everything in the visit, perhaps everything in the past ten years seemed contained within that message.

Mark slept. For a while it was a peaceful sleep, but then his muscles began to twitch and quiver until in a moment or two his whole body began to shake and his face clenched into a tightening grimace. Zita stood up, alarmed. She glanced, first at him and then at me, and then whispered, "It's a panic attack."

The tremors worsened. He didn't wake up or cry out, but we could see the fear contorting his face. I leaned over him to rub his chest gently with my left hand and cradle the back of his neck with my right. Dumb with futility, all I could say was, "It'll be okay Mark. It'll be okay."

As the shaking subsided he woke up, looked at me standing over him, and tried to focus on what had happened. I said, "You had a panic attack. You're okay now. There wasn't much I could do...but I want you to try to remember the feeling of my hand rubbing your chest. Remember this moment. Remember my voice and my hand. Perhaps you can call upon that memory when another time comes." It wasn't much to give, but it was all I had.

He smiled faintly and said, "I'll...try to...do that." Then he closed his eyes, exhausted. I sat there a while longer, with my hand resting on his. Zita watched us both.

Inevitably, the time arrived when Zita and I had to go. Silent sadness crept in around us until it filled the room. Zita said her goodbyes. I stood up to go, paused, and then slowly bent over and kissed Mark's forehead. I looked at him, only inches away from me, and said softly, "You are loved, my friend. You are deeply loved, and you always will be."

As I drove Zita back to the house, she talked about living with her losses. She described the violin lessons she taught in Wenatchee. "Eventually the stiffness in my hands prevented me from fingering the strings or playing tremolo notes. When I couldn't do that anymore I had to give it up." I knew how much her music meant to her. She had given up more than just a livelihood. Part of her brimmed with an ageless energy, but another part realized that she was eighty-six. She said, "I just can't do it all anymore." She said it not with bitterness or regret, but rather with a tone of realistic acceptance.

As we walked in the front door, savory smells came from the kitchen. Paul and Diana were pressing every pot and pan into full production. The kitchen soon became crowded with two cooks, two kids, two dogs and two spectators. Zita and I kept talking; Paul and Diana kept cooking. Soon the table groaned under wienerschnitzel, chicken and dumplings, sweet and sour cabbage, spätzle, cheeses, vegetables and breads.

When dinner was served, Zita asked me to sit in Mark's place. I paused, knowing how much that meant. In a toast to the family, I tried to express what I had written to Zita about the meaning of an empty place at the table: "In many ways Mark is here." We said the blessing slowly.

After dinner everyone sat around the table and told stories, first about our own lives and then about Mark's. As we did so, for the first time Zita mentioned details I never heard in the medical histories I had once recorded. "Mark's house in Seattle was small and messy." "He never married." "He was always on the railroad." They formed a picture of a fragmented life. As the stories drew me into the Smetko family, Mark's depression and isolation took on deeper meaning.

Paul described what happened when disability had forced Mark to live with his parents. I knew about his loss of independence. Now I learned there was more to it than that—a lot more. "He couldn't run anymore," Paul said. "He was cornered." Zita listened quietly.

I asked about the remarkable degree of acceptance in Mark's letter of early December. Paul felt that it was real. "Mark changed a lot after moving here and settling in." Paul used words like "actualized" and "centered," the words of a psychologist. Diana had a different perspective. She saw the changes when Mark interacted with the children, especially Stefan. "They loved him."

As if in response to that, Stefan climbed up onto my lap. He spread a long row of his favorite toy dinosaurs across the table in front of me, and in his small voice asked which ones were my favorites. I told him I always liked triceratops and stegosaurus best. Stefan moved those to the front of the line and laughed. He didn't leave my lap until his bedtime. As I held him and played with his dinosaurs I thought, "Someday, Mark...someday Stefan will play with your trains, just as you wrote me. Later on, perhaps he will hear the stories about those trains. And much later on, I hope he realizes what they meant."

While Paul and Diana attended to the children, Zita and I cleaned up the dishes. Afterwards, I sat briefly in the living room recliner, reflecting on the flood of impressions that were forming. I thought about the photos on the wall in Mark's hospital room, and the revealing comments Paul and Zita made. Behind the medical image of Mark I had formed as a doctor, I now saw shadows that he had never shared. Where was Mark's father in all of this? At the end of a long day I couldn't find the energy to sort through the questions, much less find their answers.

Diana called out that it was time for dessert. Our table conversations resumed over deep-dish apple pie, until the time was nearly up. With only a gentle suggestion from Zita, Paul walked over to the piano that stood in the corner of the living room. He flexed his fingers briefly to rid them of their stiffness and then sat still at the keyboard for a moment, concentrating. He looked at me and then softly began to play a Chopin nocturne. Sitting next to him, I watched his hands until I became completely immersed in the experience. Under the practiced touch of his fingers, music poured like poetry from the piano—beautiful music, clear and exquisite as only Chopin could write it. It was also the music pouring out from Paul. It was his gift.

The evening ended. At the front door, it was time for goodbyes and come-agains with Diana. Zita joined Paul and me for the trip back to my hotel in Brooklyn. There we parted with one last hug.

The next morning my family and I took a shuttle van from our Brooklyn hotel to the Newark airport. As we crossed Staten Island on the freeway, the rehabilitation center came briefly into view. From the back seat I quickly pointed it out to Ken. He got in only a quick glimpse. To him, it was only one brick building among many that flashed by at sixty miles an hour. Then the buildings disappeared behind us.

No one else in the van knew what that moment meant to me. My visit with my friend, like the fleeting view of the hospital, had flashed by all too quickly and slipped away into my past.

Pieces of the Puzzle

I spent the next ten days in Hilton Head with my parents. It was hard for me to describe my visit with Mark to them. I described the events of the afternoon, but those alone sounded shallow and inadequate. Describing the depth of the visit proved impossible. I couldn't clearly communicate what had happened to me, because I didn't understand it myself.

I wrote Zita a thank-you note. The task of writing to Mark was far harder. I remembered his look when I left his room—a look frozen in infinite sadness that still stared at me. How could he watch his mother and his friend leave, and then helplessly face four bare walls again? What was it like to fight, all alone, against panic attacks that haunted him every night? As I sat down to write him I wanted to console the sorrow I saw in his eyes.

4/3/01
Subj: The fifth letter to Mark

Hi Mark!

This, like the other letters, will be a short note. It is my effort to continue our conversation. The theme of this letter is that we didn't really say goodbye.

I knew for weeks that my visit with you would pass too quickly. I knew that we would linger for as long as we could, that we would talk about a next time, and that it would be hard when I had to leave. I knew you would feel down afterward. I did too.

That's why I'm writing this letter. In fact, that is why I wrote the first four letters last week. I'm writing to tell you that the real connection will go on.

When I visited you I was physically present, and then I physically had to leave. In one sense that is sad, because it means I can't talk with you, rest my hand on yours, exercise your legs or look into your eyes. Those things have to be done in the physical world. I cherished the chance to do them with you then. Now I can't.

But in a different sense, none of that matters.

It doesn't matter if I could have done those things with you for another day or another week or another month. It doesn't matter if we could have gone out on the town or off to a concert or even away to Cold Harbor. It doesn't matter because, even if all of those things could have happened, they too would have eventually come to an end. Sooner or later, any time together, in the conventional sense of time, would have ended.

In the physical world, all things are finite. In that world, our "if only..." wishes, "If only I were well," "If only Bill could stay longer," "If only we can get together again," are all illusions. None of them can promise lasting contentment. All of them eventually pass away. It is incredibly hard to let go of them. But letting go is one of the things you are teaching me.

As a physical person, I will die. My daughter will die. Her children and her children's children will die. That is the nature of the world. Wishing it otherwise changes nothing.

The only thing that doesn't pass away is the inner reality. Call it the soul, awareness, the Presence Within or whatever you wish. Words become inadequate here. Whatever you choose to call it, I believe that it will not die. I believe it is part of a seamless Whole. I believe that with everything I am. And I believe it is through that seamless Whole that you and I connect. It didn't end when I left your room. It is still going on, and I believe it always will.

It is in that sense that we didn't really say goodbye.

Peace be with you.
More later,

Bill

Zita soon wrote me back.

4/3/01

Dear Bill,

I am glad you arrived safely at Hilton Head. I am sorry that our visit came and went so fast. I was very sad when I said goodbye to you.

Your visit was a great blessing to Mark. He told me today that when he felt a terror attack beginning, he remembered what you had told him and he said, "I felt Bill's hand on my heart. I know he was close to me and it helped. Please tell him that I fell asleep and was at peace."

I believe he felt very comfortable with you on Sunday and felt sad when it was all over. I will read the wonderful thoughts and words in your fifth letter tomorrow, and I know he will ask me to wipe the tears from his face. You mean very much to him.

Zita

4/6/01

Dear Bill,

Mark was in good shape today. He asked me to read your last letter again. He said he couldn't absorb it when I first read it to him, because he was in such turmoil with claustrophobia. I will write exactly what he said at different times during the reading.

"Tell Bill he is in my thoughts and prayers. I missed him when he left and I felt a real void."

"Bill, your visit did more than all the therapy I've received. I am sorry I had a few rough moments, but your being there with me was invaluable. I know we are spiritually connected, so your presence still goes on in that sense. Distance makes no difference, because friendship transcends time and space."

"Tell Bill he is still an integral part of my team. I couldn't do without him. I want to thank him for all the letters, which I want Mom to read to me often. Tell him that the letter she read today touched me deeply, because it said all the things I want to think about and say.

"Right now I can only say so much to respond to you and then my mind gets fuzzy. I want to write a real letter to you when I am able. I want you to know we're friends for life and after life, too. There is no goodbye."

He went on to say, "I worry about your health, Bill. Please let me know how you are. I'm sorry I didn't ask you about that. I wasn't thinking straight."

"I'm sorry I didn't ask you about your health." This was a man who craved a simple drink of water, who spoke a sentence only with gasping effort, and who shook with panic in the night, yet he worried about my health and apologized for not asking about it. Was it any wonder that I felt such appreciation for the example he set, and such gratitude for the chance to see him again?

Zita and I spoke often, but our calls were conversations in a comfort zone. On the phone I stayed event-oriented and stuck to conventional questions and surface solutions. I had learned long ago that to go deeper I needed to pause, to slow down in a way that doesn't fit the cadence of normal conversation. To find depth I had to write rather than talk.

Writing the fifth letter to Mark took time, but the process helped me to sort out my jumbled feelings about our parting. As I wrote in my journal about our visit, the same slow introspection began to assemble the pieces of a puzzle about Mark's fears. As a picture of his past emerged from the pieces, I decided to take a chance and share some of my notes with Zita.

4/7/01

Hi Zita!

Thanks for your note with Mark's comments. As always, his words meant a lot to me.

After you called Tuesday, I spent time writing in my journal. I hope it is okay to share some of my notes about Mark with you. These thoughts are only speculation, random reflections after our visit. I have no real evidence for any of them. Perhaps they have a grain of truth to them, and if so, perhaps they may be helpful to you. It is in that hope that I have included them.

From the Journal…

"After I left, Mark became very depressed. Zita said that he wanted to die. I was afraid of this. At one level, his depression is like postpartum depression. He has a huge post-visit void, an emptiness I tried to address in my fifth letter to him. But unlike postpartum depression, Mark knows he will never recover. He knows he is trapped in a body that is relentlessly falling apart and he wants to leave it. That's not depression. That's appropriate. "Why do I have to do this? I don't want to do this! I want out!" Zita knows all of this. Paul knows it. I know it.

It seems to me that the only way I can truly help is by letting Mark know that he is not alone, that although he is dying, he is not abandoned, that in a profound sense he is known, he is understood, and that it all means something important.

The other thing I can do, rather than talking about hanging onto or letting go of life, is to talk instead about letting go inside. To me, that is what matters. That is what is truly unburdening. I wrote Zita about resting in peace. To me, letting go of fear, of the burden inside, is the only real path to peace. If a person can realize that, then death doesn't matter. That is how Uncle Bill died, detached from all fear, resting in peace with his life, surrounded by those who loved him.

It's hard to pull this into thoughts. It's hard to imagine any of it. But when my letter connected with Mark, his fear went away. All of his physical afflictions were still there, but he found peace. He said so. What explains that?"

Zita, as I wrote in my journal about our visit, some comments you and Paul made after dinner came to mind. They puzzled me. I hope this is not too sensitive a subject to bring up.

"Zita has alluded to Steve several times, as if she was trying to tell me something. I got the impression of a father walled off, someone who could never reach out to Mark, and someone with whom Mark could never connect.

Zita told me that in some respects Mark still sees me as Dr. Gruber, that is, as an authority figure. She wrote about how Mark was "freaked out" that he might not function at his best during our visit, worried stiff that somehow, he might not measure up. That made no sense at all to me, but to him it was a deep-seated anxiety.

Am I just a stand-in for Steve? Is the real authority figure the ghost of Mark's father? Is Mark still worried about not performing adequately for him, about not measuring up for him? Is that what is still terrifying him, still freaking him out?

After all these years, could it be that in his dying months, Mark finally found in me a male authority figure who didn't ask him to measure up? Could it be that, for once in his life, a man appeared who had no obligation to care about him, but who cared and worried anyway, simply because Mark is a good person? Could he finally have found the father figure he always craved, a man who reached out to him and rubbed his heart and told him that he is loved without reservation, without reason, and without limit?"

Zita, I really don't know much about Steve. I don't know if any of this is likely or even possible. But if it is, I hope I have given Mark something he has been seeking for a long, long time. I hope I have helped him to let go of his fear that he is alone. I hope it helps him be free now, free like the picture of him in the cab of his locomotive, roaring along with the wind and the power, free with a smile on his face.

Who knows if this is so? But the thought of that possibility left me deeply moved, so I wanted to share it with you. Zita, I'm not sure of any of this. Please let me know.

Bill

These weren't lightweight questions. Somewhere within them rested the key to the puzzle. I was apprehensive about sending my notes. This was a sensitive area of Zita's life. If my speculations were off, they might exhume feelings best left buried. If I were accurate, however, sharing the notes might open a world of help for Mark at a critical time. I took the chance.

4/9/01

Dear Bill,

Your journey of the heart arrived at its destination for Mark on April 1 and will reside there forever. Mark will never forget your visit. I have read your letters to him repeatedly. Your letter from Saturday has been read and reread, and it is so poignant that I need to have more time to answer you. You have touched on many of my concerns and I feel that you know much about me without ever having been told.

Mark is aware that his life is fragile and that his body is indeed falling apart. He understands the way you use the words "letting go" very clearly. He knows that peace will come to him if he truly lets go of his inner fears and concerns. I believe it is happening.

Mark is very sensitive to the feelings others have for him. Bill, he knows you are with him and that you would never abandon him. He knows you understand his fears and possible failures and therefore he doesn't mind admitting them to you. He treasures every word you have written. Your visit opened the door to a place in which he entered and found you. You gave him the outward signs of caring—the gentle hugs and loving hands which forever he had sought in vain from his father.

It is all right for you to discuss Steve with me. I can talk about it now and would like to do so.

Deep down all four of my boys still hurt inside and talk about it on occasion. Steve did not know how to be a father. He kept his distance. He talked little to them, and seldom took them anywhere. He was proud of their achievements, but never told them. He knew how hurtful all of this was for them but he never tried to change.

My three other boys went to counseling for many years trying to come to terms with themselves, trying to realize that they were worthwhile human beings and to free themselves from the insecurity of their childhood. Mark never sought any help and consequently never achieved any security about his own worth. He went white in the face when Steve spoke harshly to him or when Steve didn't agree with something Mark had said. This happened even when Mark stayed with us after his illness in 1997. It was not an easy situation, and lasted until Steve's death.

Before his death, Steve finally found the words to apologize for the unhappiness he knew he caused. It was a blessing that Mark was there. When we were leaving the hospital room where Steve died, Mark turned back, bent over and kissed his father. It was a beautiful gesture that I have never forgotten.

The other three boys talk about that when they see Mark's present condition. They remember how hard he tried to win his father's approval, but never succeeded. You found the real Mark as his father never did. Yes, Mark did see you as an authority figure at one time, but since you have been so kind to him, he is like a child seeing a man who respects him, understands him, and gives him the hugs and words his father never could. Yes, Bill, you have given him a "male authority figure" that he loves and trusts without the fears and terrors of his childhood. It is not authority anymore. It is the kind of love a person has for someone who cares. It has been a healing for Mark's soul and for this, I am forever grateful.

There is much more in your letter which I want to write about, but this is long enough, so I shall spare you anymore. I hope you had a good trip home.

Zita

The pieces all fit together. The words of the prophet had resonated for a reason; they were true. *"He was despised…rejected…a man of sorrows and acquainted with grief."* Mark was indeed wounded, cut off from the land of the living for years. The real source of his suffering was not his disease. It was his relationship with his father. His anxiety about being dependent and his fear that he would never measure up came from there. So did his sorrow when I left.

How little I knew about all of this when I visited my friend, and yet in retrospect how deeply we connected. Was he afraid that he would be forever alone? All through the visit, my hand rested on his. Was he afraid he would die without anyone knowing who he truly was? I put the smiley face in the cab of the locomotive, as if to say, "I know what the locomotive means. I know about the power. I have your letters." Was he afraid that he would never measure up? The man sitting at his bedside told him openly, "I owe you more than I can ever tell you." Was he afraid that he would die rejected? "Mark, hundreds of hands are reaching out to you. The walls of your room are not thick enough to stop them." Did he finally feel loved unconditionally? From deep within I whispered, "Know, in the core of your soul, that you are." I hoped Mark knew that now. I hoped he finally possessed what he had always craved: the knowledge that he was lovable.

How little I knew during our visit, and how little that mattered.

Zita wrote to me to share the burden she had carried for so long. At first I was the doctor who treated her son, knew his diseases and could answer her questions. In time I became a friend who cared deeply about him as well. In recent months she found in me someone with whom she could share her many sorrows.

Why, I sometimes wondered, did I write back the way I did? My letters to her were not from the surface of life. The thoughts in them came from somewhere deep, as deep as I could reach, from the inner life I learned about long ago.

So often in the shadows of my past there had been no one with whom I could connect at this level, the level at which I was most alive. So often I felt that there was no place to go with the words that welled up from within and spilled out faster than I could write them. In time I grew apprehensive that anyone would ever understand. This fear from long ago was the wellspring of the "quiet apprehension" I felt when I first wrote to her.

Zita shared memories she might have kept buried with her husband and wrote repeatedly of her gratitude. In my next letter I wrote about what she had given to me, and why I felt as grateful in return.

4/10/01

Hi Zita,

I have written about all that Mark has taught me. Now I would like to tell you how much you have taught me as well.

Each of us has our own fears. To others they may seem as nothing, but within each person they feel very real. Each of us has to confront our own shadows in our own way and let go of them at the edge of darkness.

Just as I had a chance to rub Mark's chest, in a similar way you have comforted me when I needed it, in a way you could not have known. In what follows, I will tell you how this is so. It is my way of saying thank you.

As you know from my writings, I live in a world of vivid feelings. I seem to sense at a level that is intensely real for me, but has always been hard to communicate adequately to others. It seems to be different from the conventional perceptions of seeing, hearing and touching. I call it sensing only because I have no other name for it. For a long time I had no name for it at all, only the awareness that around others it often made me feel odd and alone.

Unlike many men, I have no difficulty being in touch with these feelings. Indeed, I am often flooded by them. Instead, my problem is to communicate them—to have others understand them. There often seemed to be no reflecting mirror for the self whose words you have read in our correspondence. My fear was a fear of the Silence, a fear of having a remarkable world inside and of trying to share it, but having no one answer. The Silence is a state of forever being cut off, alone, unconnected. In retrospect, you can see that much of my correspondence reflects this theme.

Like all fears, this isn't rational, but it is nevertheless very real to me. At a critical time in my life, when the protective shell of Dr. Gruber disintegrated in front of me and I began what I have come to call the journey of the heart, I shared this world with you. That inner world was where the letter of November came from.

You and Mark answered at a deeply connecting level. By doing so you have helped me in that journey, beyond anything you might have guessed. Your subsequent correspondence freed me from an abiding apprehension that what I wrote wouldn't mean anything. Your letters allowed me to detach from that fear, just as I hope my visit with Mark helped him to detach from the fear that he was forever unlovable. It was for that reason that, in December, I wrote you the words, "You have given much, and know not that you give at all."

In our correspondence, I hope I have met Mark's needs and yours. But you have also met mine. You have met mine in a transformational way. You have allowed me to see, to recognize by its very presence what has been missing, and to let go of my fear of forever hearing only the Silence.

And so now you know why, every once in a while, I close my letters with the phrase, "Thanks for listening."

More later,

Bill

4/11/01

Dear Bill,

We all seem to have shadows that are part of life. I believe that your journey has erased many of yours.

I have been aware of your intense feelings since our correspondence began, but I believe I knew something of this in 1997 when Mark was so ill. I saw you work with him. I heard your concern when you talked to his brothers and me outside that ICU room. I knew that you were very caring about him, as I am sure you were with all your patients. I felt your hand on my shoulder when you told us the seriousness of Mark's condition. You recognized my pain.

I believe that you once fulfilled your place in the world by caring and "fixing" people as you expressed it. I am glad that you now have found the inner part of you that wants to write deeply. This is something so special and I hope that you are finding quiet times to do just that. I appreciate that you share your thoughts with me. I read and reread your letters and I know that I have found a true friend.

You certainly must know how important your connection and friendship have been to Mark and me. We have both tried to let you know how dear you are to us. I hope and pray that all is well.

Zita

I had entered a different dimension. Zita's reply took us over a threshold, into a land I had lived in alone for a long time but now shared with her.

Two days later I sent her another letter for Mark.

4/13/44
Subj: The sixth letter to Mark

Hi Mark!

I've had a chance to reflect a bit about how I wanted to spend today. I decided that one of the best ways was to write to you. The thought of you reading these letters and conversing with me always brings a smile to my eyes. It is one of the best presents I can give myself.

You see, the date up there is no accident. Today is my birthday. When I thought how I wanted to spend it, writing to you came first.

Birthdays bring to mind the passage of time. Today the nature of time itself seems different.

In my past life, time was something I fought to control. My appointment book told me where I needed to be months in advance. Time was something I coveted. There was never enough of it. "Can we squeeze in one more patient tomorrow?" I was welded to memories of the past or worries about the future. "When will we be able to pay off the mortgage?" Time was finite, something that slipped inexorably away. How fast it seemed to fly by.

Now, that has changed. I have no schedule; indeed, I have no appointment book. All of my prior efforts to control time seem to be an illusion, and a sad one at that. Instead, there is now a remarkable spontaneity to life, an increasing awareness of this moment, the experience that is happening to me right now. As a result, time seems much less finite. I can't describe any of this well, but something about this process is slowly awakening within me an awareness of the infinite.

Fifty-seven years ago today, I first saw the light. In a different sense, I think I'm still looking for it.

Sunday is Easter, a time of rebirth. You will be in my prayers.

More later,

Bill

Awakening

While I was piecing together the puzzle of Mark's past, Zita had a new worry. Her sister was sick. Josepha, known as Fafa, had lived in Wenatchee near Zita for years. Recently Fafa had moved to a nursing home near Tacoma to be close to one of her sons. She was eighty-nine years old and now faced a failing heart.

4/9/01

Dear Bill,

This will be a short note. My sister has been ill. I had planned to go to Wenatchee to visit her. Now she is in a nursing home in Gig Harbor and is failing fast. I need to say goodbye to her. I fly out of here on Easter Sunday and will return the Sunday after.

My son Johnny is coming to spend the week after Easter here. He will take my place at Mark's bedside while I am in Washington. It was a hard decision for me to make but hopefully Mark will stay stable. I know he will be happy to have John here.

Zita

I called Zita to discuss the details of her trip. The news was not good. That morning Fafa had been hospitalized in Tacoma with congestive heart failure.

4/12/01

Dear Bill,

My sister is critically ill. A valve is closing up and her lungs are filling with fluid. They treated the lungs this past week, but her heart will fail. Because of her age, there is nothing they can do for her. I am simply grateful that she survived the attack Monday night when they expected her to die, and that she is now somewhat conscious. The first thing she recently asked her daughter was, "Did I miss Zita's visit?"

I am very torn about what to do. Mark isn't eating much, his color is gray and he is very lethargic. The doctor said yesterday that he remains seriously ill. At the same time my sister is unconscious and on life support. I'm mentally and emotionally in two places, and they are a continent apart.

I will stay in Gig Harbor with my nephew and then probably stay several nights with my niece, Monica, who lives in Edmonds. It's all a scrambled mess, but I do want to see you. I shall call you on Monday and we can set up a time and place to meet. I believe Edmonds is probably closest to you.

Zita

Zita arrived on Easter Sunday, went directly to the hospital and was able to say goodbye to her sister. Four hours later, Fafa died.

Monday, Zita—by now completely drained—called me to discuss what would happen next. She planned to visit her niece in Edmonds, near where I lived, on Tuesday. I asked if I could help by driving her up from Gig Harbor and invited her to join us that evening for dinner if her time allowed. She accepted.

During the ninety-minute drive north she decompressed by telling me all about Fafa. The fatigue of the last several days showed in her voice. Despite her remarkable resilience, I suspected that Zita was running on empty. All I could offer her was a brief respite, a pause between her rushed trip to the hospital Sunday and Thursday's funeral in Wenatchee. I turned to her and said, "I would like this to be a moment of tranquility for you. In the time we have, we can do whatever you want."

She replied, "What I want to do is just unwind."

At the house, I introduced her to Beverly. As they became acquainted, I recalled the time Zita introduced me to everything in Mark's room, opening a window into all that was meaningful there. Now the reverse was happening. Beverly, the house, and the garden were a window into my world, a context into which Zita could place all of my letters.

It was a pleasant April afternoon. Out in the garden the beauty of camellias and early rhododendron blossoms beckoned to a tired lady. We walked slowly along the paths, and then for a time just sat on a bench and rested. As the peace of the setting slowed the pace of her life, Zita began to see what surrounded her. In her perceptive way, she asked how the garden came to be.

In twenty minutes, I tried to explain a landscape that had taken me twenty years to create. Just as trains expressed something about Mark and violin music expressed something about Zita, the garden in springtime expressed something within me. Like Zita's too-brief description of Mark's books, my explanation of how I built the garden felt like a barely adequate beginning.

Soon it was time for dinner. Paul and Diana had welcomed me in New York with wienerschnitzel and spätzle. Beverly served fresh salmon accompanied by an arrangement of red rhododendron blossoms. The three of us chatted after dinner until a phone call took Bev downstairs to her office. In the living room, Zita curled up in a recliner and kicked off her shoes. Sinking into relaxation, she began to reminisce. Her stories started with Fafa.

"There were just the two of us. She was only a few years older than I was. Growing up, I was a young girl who always had an older sister to be with. We did a lot together. It was a special relationship."

As a child, Zita knew hard times. "My father was a mathematician and a chief engineer at Cadillac until he was fired because of anti-German sentiment during WW I. Then he tried to make it as a farmer in Maryland, but he went bust during the Depression."

Zita's mother gave her a lasting love of music. The nuns at school provided the violin lessons that gave that love its lifelong voice. As an adolescent, Zita had to work to help support the family and put herself through school. Despite that load, she found scholarships that let her continue her violin lessons.

As her life story unfolded, I began to see the origins of her endurance. Her early hardships produced remarkable resiliency that she had in turn passed on to her sons. She was a survivor, not in the hardened sense, but rather in the sense of someone who could continue to give after years of adversity. I sensed that the caregiving I had witnessed revealed only a fraction of her inner strength.

"Were you able to stay close to your sister after you grew up?"

"Oh, yes. We lived near Chicago most of our married life, but the boys often spent the summers in Wenatchee with Fafa. It was a great escape for Mark to go out there each summer and get away. His summer experiences were part of the reason he settled in the Northwest."

"How did you wind up there?"

"We moved to Wenatchee after Steve retired."

"You mentioned Steve in your e-mail…"

"Yes. It's a long story…"

Then everything started to spill out. A woman who had walked endless miles with a painful stone in her shoe finally had the chance to sit down, take off the shoe and shake out the stone. Without any prompting, Zita recounted story after story. "If he came in and saw something wrong…he'd just slap the first one he saw, and a lot of times…that was Mark." I winced at the scenes she described. She continued, "I tried to protect them, cover for them but…it wasn't enough."

During my visit at Staten Island, I had glimpsed only a few pieces of the puzzle. Now Zita turned face up a hundred more, until the whole picture emerged in terrible clarity. For his entire life, Mark had craved recognition of his basic worth as a human being, only to find it forever withheld by a father he couldn't reach. "Steve just stayed walled off."

"How was school for Mark?"

"He was bright and sensitive, but he couldn't perform. I remember one time at St. Leonard's. One of the nuns kept pushing him to give an answer, and he just froze with fear in the front of the room." I knew that scene from my own early schooling. "Steve flew into such a rage about poor grades that I had to hide the report cards. Finally, around sixth grade," she said, "it got so bad they kept Mark back a year."

"Kept back" labeled a boy. I could hear the names and the snickered ridicule on the playground during recess. School had provided no refuge for Mark. Instead, I saw a sensitive soul standing petrified and stuttering as his teachers ingrained still more shame. I shook my head. "I bet that was bad."

"It was awful," Zita replied. "I should have taken him out of that school. I always regret that I didn't, but…we didn't realize at the time what was happening to him. From then on," she said, "he thought he was dumb."

I didn't want to believe what I was hearing. I knew a different man. I read his letters and heard his dreams. I saw the books in his room and the breadth of his interests. I saw his boundless enthusiasm and a curiosity that carried him to the edge of the cosmos. Incredulous, I asked, "Did it ever change?"

"Not really. The other boys found ways to hide…but not Mark. All he could do was run."

"How did you take care of yourself?"

"My music. I supported my own interests by giving violin lessons. I joined a string quartet in Wenatchee. I had lots of friends…"

As she reminisced, sometimes from bright memories, sometimes from dark ones, I saw that Zita had been supporting, defending, and caring all of her life. Now she could unload both her stories and her worries to someone from Seattle who wouldn't judge any of it.

We could have talked well into the night. Her age, the three-hour time difference from the East Coast, and everything she went through with Fafa didn't seem to matter at all. Unwinding mattered. By the time we quit it was after midnight, her time. We chatted lightly as I drove her to her niece's house in Edmonds and dropped her off.

Monica didn't bring Zita back to the house until noon the next day. A chance to sleep in had done her a world of good. She appeared refreshed, or perhaps unburdened. The two of us sat in the den for a while and talked. From the prior night's conversation, I guessed that it was okay to ask more about Mark's past.

I knew that he lived alone, loved being on the railroad and had never settled down. In the context of Zita's stories, his life looked fragmented, a long series of loose ends. "Zita, did he spend his entire life running?" She nodded in agreement.

"He told me he never married. Did he ever come close to settling down? Was he ever in love?"

A look of enormous sadness crept into her eyes. "Do you remember the girl in the picture in Mark's hospital room?"

"Yes," I replied, "I asked him about her."

"Her name was Abby."

Zita had learned the story from Mark's lifelong friend, Karl Sundstrom. Abby was the love of Mark's life. They met in the lobby of the Seattle Opera House. She had come by herself, and so had he. They looked at each other across the crowded lobby, he approached her, asked if she wanted to watch the opera with him and she said "Yes." She was pretty, and she was good to him. She helped him exercise and saw that he ate right. "Karl said it was the most intense relationship Mark ever had."

Abby loved Mark, but he couldn't love her in return. After months of seemingly wonderful times together, he broke it off. "Mark told Karl it was because 'she was getting too close.' He was afraid to be that open." He couldn't trust her enough to be truly intimate, "so he drove her away." Later, wracked with regret, he tried to see her again, only to find out that she had quit her job and left Seattle. "She left no forwarding address."

I remembered the remorse in Mark's memories: *"Yeah…she was…really special. But I never quite got…to the point of…settling down."* The walls around his wounds had been insurmountable. He couldn't get out, and she couldn't get in. What began as a fortress to protect his heart became a prison from which it couldn't escape. I thought, "So much wreckage…and so much hurt." I couldn't ask Zita any more questions.

Paul arrived at 1:00 that afternoon. He had been up at 4:30 a.m. for a flight from JFK that served only a meager airline breakfast, and he hadn't eaten since. It didn't take us long to get to the topic that mattered most. "Paul, where would you like to go for lunch?"

"Someplace close."

We went to a waterfront restaurant in Edmonds. Zita gazed out over the quiet waters of Puget Sound to the Olympic Mountains, still glistening with winter snow in the afternoon sunshine. "I'm glad I had the chance to say goodbye to Fafa," she mused. "It was a gentle passing. And I've had time to rest now. It's been a good visit." There were no regrets. Even so, the coming week would not be easy. When we dropped her off at Monica's, I told Zita I would remember her each day. She smiled and gave me a hug.

I drove Paul back to the house. His flight and our lunch had kept him sitting all day. As he got out of the car I noticed that his joints didn't tolerate that very well. I suggested a walk. A mile wasn't his daily workout, but it was all his schedule allowed. Afterward we sat at the kitchen table and talked for the rest of the afternoon.

Like Zita, there was a lot on his mind, a lot he wanted to share. I mentioned that I was puzzled about why a man who seemed so bright and inquisitive was held back in school. Zita's stories came from a mother's heart. Paul delivered his in the terms of a trained psychologist. His perspectives were different, but the story was the same.

"I don't know why he got held back. There was no formal diagnosis, like ADD, but somehow Mark processed differently."

The unending abuse and belittlement multiplied his alienation and anxiety. "He wanted to be recognized for who he was. The rest of us left in one way or another, but Mark couldn't. He kept coming back to his family of origin, looking for that recognition, trying to make everything right and he kept getting beaten up in the process. He could never get out of that dynamic. He couldn't become autonomous, make his own life.

"He was powerless to confront the source of his pain because he projected all of the power onto his father. He couldn't break through the walls. He would get anxious and it fed on Steve's tendency to shut him out. Mark couldn't accept therapy because in a shame-loaded relationship he saw any suggestion of therapy as just one more criticism.

"He couldn't be intimate, so he never had a partner to help him out of the mess. His chronic depression sapped his attempts to build a life. And then, on top everything came all of the wreckage of his rheumatoid disease. And that, Bill, is where you walked in."

I sat silently and shook my head. I had no idea, no idea at all. How could anyone climb out of a pit like that? How could someone so burdened stay so positive, surgery after surgery? How did he do it? I said, "Paul, Mark wrote me. He's been writing to me for a year. They're incredible letters. They're kind. They're gentle. They're filled with trust and faith. Where did they come from?"

Paul looked at me for a long time. "I don't know. But it's real. It was just in this last year or so, but everybody sees it. He's very different."

Bewildered, I asked, "What's going to happen?"

Now it was Paul's turn to shake his head. "Nobody knows. They told us at the hospital conference in March that Mark was in renal failure and that pretty soon they would only be able to keep him alive with dialysis. We stayed hopeful, because every time Mark would be dialyzed he'd perk up. He'd look a lot better. Mom would be hopeful that he'd turned a corner. Then, three or four days later, the toxins would build back up and he'd look awful again. He was getting a little better. The time between dialyses stretched out to the point where he could leave the hospital and go to the rehab center. But nobody knows what's going to happen next."

When I asked him more about Mark's change, Paul began to talk about the path out of prison. "I think we learn to hide parts of ourselves to protect them from the threats we see around us. What's sad is that the parts we hide are often our most sensitive or unique traits. The irony is that to keep them hidden we build a shell that looks like the people we tried to hide from."

I was amazed. He was describing what had happened to me.

"When we reconnect to those disowned parts, we finally see that the personality we wear on the outside is false. Once that happens, things that used to be important don't matter anymore. I think that's what happened to Mark."

He went on, "Let me tell you a story. The word 'personality' comes from a Latin phrase, 'per sona' that meant 'to sound through'. I discovered that it was the name given to the mask that medieval actors wore. They sounded their part through the mask. Sometimes the mask had a smile, sometimes a frown, but because of it the audience recognized the actor's role in the play. Nothing has changed. That definition is still true. Our personality is only a mask for the role we play in the world, while the real person stays hidden inside."

I had read a bit about this, but Paul's stories explained what I had experienced. He agreed. "Reading books about it isn't enough. All I can give my students is book knowledge of psychology, but you can't just read about this. You have to experience it. Books just give us the words for the wisdom we have to learn from life. There is no other way. I tell them, 'Once you experience it, then you'll know.'"

I nodded. "Books tell us what's 'out there.'" I told him some of my story. "In the last two years I think I've learned more about what's 'in here.'"

He smiled. "I think a lot these days about what's 'in here.'" He paused reflectively, and then went on. "It's interesting. The word 'religion' comes from 're ligare,' meaning 'to tie something back together.' I'd translate it as reconnecting with what was lost inside. Maybe that's what I'm trying to do."

"You know a lot of Latin."

"I was in the seminary for six years."

"And then you went into psychology and therapy?"

"I was trying to find my way out, but therapy can take us just so far. Gurus by the side of the road of life aren't the real answer. I think that ultimately, the real answer is inside."

He mentioned seminars in therapy and spirituality. I asked him his impression of them. He talked about the nature of the journey, the price of choices not made, and the way meditation helps us listen to the whispers within. He said, "I guess that's what the seminars are really about. I guess I'm still looking."

I replied, "You're not alone."

Fafa's funeral was Friday. I sent Zita an e-mail card. She wrote as soon as she got home.

4/23/01

Dear Bill,

Thank you so much for your card. You selected a piece of music I love very much, *Pavane for a Dead Princess* by Fauré. It was very special to hear it and to read your note.

The time with you was very helpful, Bill. Thank you for making everything more bearable. I also was happy to meet Bev. She is a lovely lady and it was a privilege to spend some time with her too. I thank you both for the delicious dinner.

I shall miss Fafa's phone calls. Our phone conversations were comical. She was almost deaf, but would never wear hearing aids. I would have to repeat a word over and over, then spell it slowly, and then say it in German. In the end, she would laugh and say, "Never mind, it probably wasn't important anyway." She was a good lady, and we had a long, good life together.

After I got home, I fell asleep for four hours! I feel much better for this. I hope I find Mark in better condition tomorrow. He had a bout with pneumonia while I was gone. He is very unhappy because of this. But all in all, he is still a trooper.

Please give my regards to Bev.

Zita

4/25/01

Hi Zita,

It was good to hear from you. I'm glad that you were finally able to get some rest. You can exhaust yourself caring for Mark. I've seen it happen. Prevention is easier than cure. Take care of yourself.

I'm also glad you had a chance to see the garden. I hope you can carry its image as a place of rest with you.

Say hi to Mark and Paul for me.

More later,

Bill

Because of the press of events, there were more phone calls than letters. In her letters Zita tried to remain positive, but over the phone she sounded drained. She admitted that "I'm becoming more resigned to the fact that Mark won't live long."

4/28/01

Dear Bill,

Thank you for your letter titled "Gardens." I have a vivid memory of the lovely garden that you created. It was a most peaceful place and if there had been time, I'd have sat down on your meditation bench and cleared my mind of many unhappy thoughts. But then I would have missed the opportunity to talk to you about the unhappy things that have bothered me for years about Mark.

The picture of your paradise is very clear. Since seeing it, I have imagined myself on that bench and I have had more peace within myself. Your garden with its silence is part of me now. That you know about Mark's past and his problems is part of me as well. Thank you.

At present my thoughts are very much taken up with Mark. I saw quite an improvement in his finger movements and he can press his fingers more solidly over my hand. On the other hand, I am very concerned because Tuesday he vomited five times. I cancelled my bus back to the house so that I could be there to sit him up quickly and call the nurse. When I arrived yesterday, he had vomited again and was shaking with panic.

I told Mark I am writing a letter to you and he asked me to say hi from him. He was happy that I had visited you in Seattle.

Zita

Mark was back to the pattern of November. He vomited repeatedly, aspirated again, and suffered another round of pneumonia. By May 1, too sick to stay in the rehab center, he was sent back to St. Vincent for another attempt at treatment.

For ten years I had watched Mark struggle against his sickness. Everyone asked, "Why does he go on? What is he fighting for?" Now I knew a different dimension of his life, and with it, the answer to those questions.

What if he had died that desperate day in September 1997? What if all our efforts had failed, the anesthesia alarms had fallen silent, and we had wheeled a white-sheeted corpse out of the OR? Mark would have died hidden behind his walls, his inner life forever unrevealed. He would have died depressed, cut off from those who cared about him and filled with rage. Had he died that day, his life would have been lived on the run, a meaningless life, fragmented, full of pain and without redemption. Had he died that day, knowing what I knew now, I would have felt only grief, recrimination, futility and regret.

In the two remarkable years since I last saw him in my office, all of that had changed. In his letters, and with his family, he had found his true voice and awakened to a new abundance of life. He found love within himself, and with it he found at last, openness and joy. As a doctor, I was amazed that time after time he transcended his physical afflictions. Now, having learned the hidden story of his life, I was awed that he had transcended the sufferings of his soul as well. He taught me what life was about in a way no book ever could. He was whole, and he was free. If he died now, I would not feel grief. I would feel only gratitude for having had the chance to know him as I did.

Letting Go

Mark's evaluation at St. Vincent confirmed the cause of his recurrent vomiting. His lab values were severely elevated. The tests showed terminal loss of kidney function.

As kidneys fail, they no longer filter from the blood the metabolic wastes that the body produces. Levels of urea and creatinine, toxic end-products of protein breakdown, begin to rise. The blood becomes increasingly acidic. The delicate balance of sodium and potassium deteriorates beyond the tolerance of the tiny signals within the heart and brain. A toxic sea surrounds cells everywhere, a condition called uremia.

Despite these derangements, kidney failure is not a death sentence. Dialysis returns the blood to nearly normal values. Repeated dialysis can keep patients alive indefinitely. In a temporary truce with death, Mark had been tethered to this treatment for months.

On Friday, May 4, he underwent four hours of dialysis. His vomiting stopped, and because he felt nearly normal he no longer needed to be in the hospital. Despite his frailty, the doctors suggested that aggressive treatments could help his lung condition, and vigorous PT might restore more limb function. The price would be chronic dialysis and an indefinite stay in the rehab center.

Mark hated the thought of going back there. He hated its loneliness and claustrophobia, its terrors and its despair. He no longer needed to cling to his collapsing existence. He saw more treatment in rehab as only a miserable prelude to inevitable mortality and concluded that the benefit wasn't worth the price. Saturday morning, fully alert and aware of its consequences, he made his decision. He would have no further dialysis. He wanted to go home, and he made Paul promise that once he went home, no matter what happened, nobody would call an ambulance to bring him back.

Sunday, Zita wrote me.

5/6/01

Dear Bill,

Mark is smiling and happy at the thought of coming home. He is completely at peace about doing this. He is hopeful, but also accepting of what will come in the future. Please pray for us that we make all the correct decisions.

I would like to refer back to your letter written on February 9. Each paragraph had so much to say to me. At that time, Mark could not comprehend any of it but I have kept it close to me to read as a source of strength. It has become a kind of prayer. I read your words, "I see a soul free to experience unbelievable power….I see a soul free to be at peace….This is the place of letting go of all that matters in this world…the place of acceptance. I have learned so much from him, and am so deeply grateful." So much of what you wrote has come to pass. Mark is at peace.

I believe your connection, both spiritually and physically, has been the most powerful help of all. He felt your hand and knew you were always with him. I will read this letter to him today, and I know it will give him even greater peace and strength. His mind is clear, and he will understand just what your connection with him has been all about.

Zita

Even though the family knew that Mark's situation was terminal, they didn't know how long he would last. Monday, Zita busied herself recruiting a nurse's aide for continuous care and an RN to do daily checks.

Mark came home Tuesday. Zita sounded relieved when she called me with the news. "Bill, when we brought him in, he had a huge smile on his face." He wanted to talk to me. He was tired from the trip home, had difficulty talking clearly, and could say only a few words, but I was glad to hear his voice. He said, "Bill, I want you to know…how happy I am…to have finally…made it home."

I knew how happy he was. I knew how far he had come. No one ever thought he would reach this place, but he did. He was no longer alone. He had at last come home.

Despite his happiness, the rising tide of toxins rapidly eroded Mark's energy. That afternoon he vomited and grew more lethargic. That evening a hospice nurse came to evaluate the situation. After her assessment, she gently explained to the family that in several days Mark would get very sick and would probably die from uremia within a week. They were stunned that it would be so soon. Paul said, "We had no idea..." Zita's nursing arrangements faded into irrelevance.

Thursday morning Zita called me. Her voice sounded softer and slower, as if she were farther away.

"Bill, a lot's been happening..." As the story unfolded, I sensed that she needed to do more than inform me of events. By telling me what was going on, Zita was also telling herself aloud: Mark was dying.

She paused, unable to bear the sound of that word. "Here, I'll let you talk with the hospice nurse. She'll be able to tell you."

I phrased my questions so the nurse could answer succinctly.

"My impression is that he is rapidly becoming uremic. Is that correct?"

"Yes."

"There are no plans to take him back to St. Vincent?"

"True."

"Everybody's okay with that?"

"Yes."

"He is on comfort medication now?"

"Yes."

"Will IV's be used?"

"No."

"So it's a matter of a day or so then?"

"Yes."

That was all the information I needed. I thanked her and asked to speak to Zita.

"How are you doing, Zita?"

"I'm doing okay." There was resignation in her voice, but I didn't hear the fear I had heard in March. It was time now. It wouldn't be easy, but it was okay. After several brief questions she asked, "Bill, could you talk to Mark? He's weak and may not be able to answer, but he can still understand. I think it would help."

"Certainly."

His bed was in the room I had visited. She cradled the phone next to his ear. I could hear his labored breathing.

"Bill?"

"Hi, Mark. How are you doing?"

"I'm doing...good. I feel...a little sad. It's hard going...but...I'm okay."

"Mark, it was good for you to come home. There are many people reaching out to you just now, all of the people who love you. We are gathering all around you."

"Thanks. I...know that." He was fighting to stay focused, fighting just to speak one or two words.

"Mark, you won't be alone. I'll try to follow the path you showed me. Light the way for me, will you? Someday...someday I'm going to try to catch up with you."

"Good. I'll look...forward to that."

It's time now. It's time to stop fighting. It's time to say goodbye. You have to let him go now. That's what he taught you.

"I love you, Mark."

"Thanks, Bill. I feel...the same way."

"You're a wonderful person, my friend. Rest now. Be at peace."

"Thanks...I will...That helps. Goodbye, Bill."

"Goodbye, Mark."

All the feelings I had heard in Zita's voice now belonged to me. My voice had the same slower sound; my thoughts were edged with tears. I sat quietly, looking at the picture of Mark in the cab of his locomotive. "There's joy present there," I thought. "He's facing the light. That's where he's going now. All of the energy in the locomotive is taking him there." I reflected on all that he had taught me. I asked that he might have grace at this moment, strength for what he faced, and peace when it was over. I put on Mozart's *Requiem*. As the beauty of immortal music swept over me, I meditated on the person in that cab and the journey he was on.

Friday afternoon Zita called. Her voice was drained and hollow. "Bill, the hospice nurse said that Mark's kidneys have shut down. He isn't putting out anything. He looks to me like he has pneumonia again. His breathing is slow and shallow. At times it doesn't look like he's breathing at all. He isn't responding to our voices anymore."

As resigned as she was, Zita was running out of reserves. Paul worried about her. She had briefly become short of breath. He wanted her to rest, but she called anyway. She couldn't hold back what she had to say.

"Mark had seizures last night. It was horrible to watch. For a while he just kept convulsing. They started him on morphine and that quieted him down, but I felt so helpless.

"Bill, I know that if we took him to the hospital they might be able to treat his pneumonia with antibiotics...but I also know that...treatment isn't the right thing now. This isn't like where we were in January. It's different this time. His kidneys are gone. I know that. Nothing's ever going to make them better. Mark wanted to be here, at home. You heard him say so.

"He can't tell us anything now, but...we don't think he should go back to the hospital. We think he should stay here. I know this is the right decision. It's just that...it's horribly hard to face it."

It was a plea for help to let the inevitable happen.

"Zita, this is the right thing to do. There's no place for medical treatment now. He's where he wants to be. He's in his own room, surrounded by the people who love him. Your decisions have made that possible. When my time comes, I hope I have a family as caring as you all have been."

"Thank you, Bill." There was a long pause. My reassurance wasn't enough.

"Bill, there's something else that's bothering me. Yesterday Mark said to me, 'I don't think I'll live much longer, Mom. I don't really want to...but I don't want to die either, because...I don't want you to be sad about me leaving you.'" Zita's voice wilted. "I put my head down next to his and said, 'How could I not be?' As I pressed my child to me, I felt my heart would break."

It became hard for her to continue. "Bill, it still troubles me. He needed something from me, something important. Today he tried to tell me again, as if he hadn't gotten it across the day before. He said, 'I need you to acknowledge...' but he couldn't finish the sentence. Then he said, 'Help me!' I didn't know what he wanted. I tried to reassure him. I begged him to let go of all his fears and just rest. I told him he was the best human being I knew. I felt helpless. There wasn't anything I could do for him."

Something critical was happening between son and mother, but Zita couldn't tell me what it was, and I couldn't guess. I tried to reassure her, just as she had tried to reassure Mark, but when our call ended, I felt as helpless as she did.

Zita's sorrow surrounded me. I went outside and gazed at the garden. Subdued sunlight filtered through it. The flowers were at their peak. Azalea and rhododendron blossoms covered the hillside. I wanted to share their beauty with her, as if by doing so I could lift her burden. As I sat quietly in the garden's tranquility, silent questions appeared.

Why are you here?

"I'm sad. I feel empty. I want to experience this beauty as fully as I can."

Why?

"In a few weeks the flowers will be gone."

Will you be sad when they are gone?

"No."

Why not?

"Because…I'm not attached to any of them. It is the nature of flowers that they fade and fall away and are gone tomorrow."

Where does suffering come from?

"It comes from…clinging, from desire for more. It arises from attachment to things that will pass away. At least I've learned that much."

What is Mark asking of you?

"It's like the flowers. He wants us to accept his passing, just as he has."

Can you acknowledge that to him?

"Mark…it's all…okay now."

It's all okay?

"Yes. Yes, it is. It's all okay. Everything that needed to be finished…is finished. Everything is as it should be. If I believe that, will it will help him?"

What were his words to Zita?

"He said, 'I want you to acknowledge…Help me.' What did he want from her?"

Who is Zita?

"Zita is his mother. No…that isn't enough. That isn't nearly enough. I see now. Zita is so much more than just that word. She's…the center-point, the embodiment of all the love he ever knew. That love sustained him through his whole life, through all of his suffering. When his shell finally shattered, that's what was inside, shining. She's more than his mother. She's his mirror, the reflection of what was within him from the very beginning, the love he finally found within himself."

What is the task?

"It's time to leave. He's asking for her help. He's asking her to let go of him. Is that possible?"

The task that is the hardest holds the key.

Everything became clear. This was the last attachment, the one Mark had struggled with all his life. Day after day he fought to transcend pain and turmoil and be known as the person he truly was. Year after year he fought to find a way out of his shell. When he finally did it, he found indescribable freedom, the freedom from all his suffering. I saw this. We all did.

Mark wanted to give that freedom to his mother. In his dying request, he wanted to release her from her suffering and her grief. He knew that for her to accept his death was the hardest task of all. This was the loss she feared the most, the one she had resisted so long. He knew that only by accepting his passing would she gain the peace and freedom he had finally found. Acceptance was the greatest gift he could give her.

"I want you to acknowledge..." he said, "Mom, that it's all okay. Everything is completed. Everything is as it should be. If you can acknowledge that, then at last we can both let go. If you can accept what is, then you will reach the freedom where I am. Help me...," he asked her, "with this."

The insight overwhelmed me, as if I finally understood his teaching. The garden that surrounded me reappeared.

What do you see?

"All around me are flowers."

Are you attached to the flowers?

"No."

Why are you drawn to them?

"Each one is exquisitely beautiful."

They are only the illusion of beauty. Each one is only a brief reflection of the beauty that is within. True beauty lies there. It is within you, always. Seek it there.

"What will happen now?" I asked, into emptiness.

The beauty of the flower will fade. The petals will fall. The seed at the center of the flower will become one with the ground. Then the life that is within the seed will return a hundred-fold.

I sat quietly in the warm spring afternoon, in a place where time disappeared, and flooded intensely.

In the middle of the night Zita called. "Bill, I just wanted to let you know that...Mark died." It was a peaceful passing. As the light within him faded and his breath ended in a sigh, she told me that he seemed to smile softly.

We talked briefly. I thanked her for calling. After the call I stayed awake a long time, staring out over the lake as the light from a waning moon stretched in a shining path across quiet water.

At mid-morning, Zita called again. I listened without interruption as she described the night's events in detail. She had kept vigil at Mark's bedside until two in the morning, but finally drifted into a fitful sleep. Shortly after four a.m. the nurse gently awakened her. Mark's breathing had stopped. Zita sat quietly at his side for a while and then told the nurse that she wanted to bathe him. As she spoke to me of how she did so, gently washing him from his head to his feet, her voice filled with tenderness. It was her last act of mothering.

"Zita," I replied softly, "There's nothing left to do now. You've done everything you can. I'd like to be there with you. I'd like to come for the service."

"Thank you, Bill. That would be a blessing for me."

After we talked, I sent her a note and a short poem. The following day I received her reply.

Dear Bill,

This morning I awoke and heard the birds singing outside my window. Yesterday, as Mark left his home at 4:10 a.m., the birds were just awakening and their songs accompanied him on his last leaving from home. I stood by the door and waved him farewell as I had always done throughout his life. This time it was so different. I stood there and relived so much of Mark's life.

I felt him close to me, Bill. I know he doesn't want me to grieve, but I find myself weeping with pain. I need to write to you, but I can hardly see the keyboard, so if I make mistakes, please understand.

Thank you for the beautiful letter you sent yesterday. My boys, with whom I include you, are so wonderfully helpful but I am having a hard time coping right now. I know it will get better, but please keep sending your thoughts and love to me during your meditations. I know it will help me. Mark will bless you for it.

I thank you for coming. That seems so simple to say, but for you to do so is very meaningful. Bill, I want you to be part of my family, for always and particularly on Tuesday. Please walk with me then. I want you beside me. I will never forget this generosity of yours.

I really can't write anymore right now but I feel your hand on my shoulder all the time. Thank you.

Zita

Zita's e-mail was dated Sunday, May 13, 2001. It was Mother's Day.

Return to the Circle

Monday I flew to New York, checked into a hotel near the house, and obtained directions to the funeral home. Before entering the visitation parlor I paused for a moment, took a deep breath and tried to focus on what I would experience. I didn't want this to be just an emotional blur.

At the doorway, Paul welcomed the guests. His face wore the fatigue of sleepless nights, and his eyes were empty. I gave him a long hug. Zita, together with Carl and John, came over to greet me. At times tearful, she was nevertheless as gracious as ever. After a moment of conversation she guided me to a poster board and proudly began telling me about the photos of Mark growing up with his brothers. In the center of the display was the picture of him in the cab of his locomotive.

As she talked, Paul played a tape, recorded years ago, of Zita performing Schubert's *Ave Maria*. Soon its soft refrain enveloped us all. Paul was playing this music for a reason. In the photos of long ago, Zita was a young mother, holding close her beloved infant. Now a grieving widow stood next to me, but the violin was still her voice, and with it she was still whispering this melody to her departed son.

The parish priest read several passages, spoke briefly, and then he and the other visitors paid their respects and left. Zita asked to have the casket opened briefly. I felt the family's graciousness for including me in such a private moment. She turned to me and said that she had placed my letters to Mark in the casket with him. The evening ended in a moment of silent reflection.

Tuesday morning I returned from my hotel to the house. The family was busy attending to last-minute details. Paul, alone in the living room, seemed subdued. I learned that he had been up nearly all night writing a eulogy for Mark, struggling to fit a lifetime of feelings into a few brief words. Now he wanted to commemorate the bond with his brother in a way beyond words. In the midst of multiple distractions, he focused on recording Mark's favorite Mozart for the funeral service. I recalled the nocturne Paul had played for me. The recordings had to be perfect. This music was his gift to Mark.

247

I followed the family to the funeral home. In the parlor, Zita wanted one last moment for her memories. As I stood behind her near the open casket, I was near tears, but strangely enough, mine were not from sadness. Instead, even though an ocean of grief surrounded me, when I looked at my friend for the last time I was overwhelmed with gratitude.

To me, the gray fragile shell resting there was as nothing now—a burnt-out bulb whose time was past. What mattered was the light that had once glowed within it. The light was gone, but in its time it had shown me the lessons of my life. Mark taught me how to reach out and connect to the source of that light—a source that still surrounded us, like the electricity that lit the lamps. The gratitude I felt was for a teacher and his gift, the same gift I saw on the ceiling of the Sistine Chapel.

A slow cortege carried the casket to the parish church for the funeral Mass. Zita wanted me to walk down the aisle next to her and to sit with the family. From the choir loft behind us came the gentleness of *Jesu, Joy of Man's Desiring*.

The gospel and the sermon were about Lazarus. Long ago, I knew that story from a book; this time I had witnessed it in person. I watched a man come back to life, back from a death of a different kind, back from the darkness inside. What was the power that made him alive again? I knew how the original Lazarus story went. How did it happen this time? I had no answers. I only knew that I was looking at the questions very differently.

After the Mass Paul gave his eulogy, his daughter Cecille read a poem she had written, and then Paul played Mozart's music. For a moment afterward the church became very still. In that silence I heard music of my own inside, music that danced with a living promise. I had written to Mark about the song in December. Since then, its message resonated in the writings I had sent:

> *"They cut me down but I leapt up high*
> *For I am the life that will never, never die.*
> *I'll live in you if you live in me*
> *For I am the Lord of the Dance said he."*

We walked out of the dim church into clear sunlight. Zita stood there, surrounded by her family, her head unbent as the black hearse took away the body of her son. *"They buried my body and they thought I'd gone, but I am the dance and I still go on."* Through my tears I could see Mark smiling.

After a reception we returned to the house. I stood for a moment in my friend's room, in the place where he had breathed his last. I wanted to fix the moment and the place in my mind. Zita asked me if I wanted some of his books. I replied, "You have already given me the picture of Mark in his locomotive. It said everything about him that I want to remember."

One by one the guests left. Zita sank into a recliner in the living room, exhausted. Family members had flights to catch. The tide of the day was ebbing. We said our goodbyes. There was a last hug, and then it was time to go.

I spent the next day on a flight back to Seattle, pondering countless impressions. Thick clouds obscured the land below me. The sky above appeared endless. The setting prompted me to sort through the meaning of Mark's passing.

It was time for Mark's suffering to end. Medically, there were no meaningful measures left. Chronic dialysis could have kept him alive, but that was not life; it was existence without meaning. He realized that, accepted it, and acted on it.

His life was authentic. His decision to drive trains wasn't just a job change; it was a dream that expressed his inner life. When we saw his work, we saw him. When I looked at his picture in the locomotive I never felt grief. Instead, it always made me smile. He did what he loved to do for as long as he was able to do it, and died happy about the days he spent driving trains.

His life was transcendent. He overcame what fate handed him in a way I could scarcely imagine. He wrote that his disease was a gift that had helped him to detach from his job, his possessions, his needfulness, and in the end even his physical existence. Compared to the world he found within, everything else became insignificant. His was an indelible lesson about what is of lasting worth.

His life was complete. I believe he finally achieved the wholeness that had eluded him for so many years. His letters speak for him. Everyone who saw him in the last year of his life knew he had changed. Once he reached the place of peace he had no reason to trudge onward. There was nothing left to cling to, no unmet need that held him here. Knowing full well what it meant, Mark told me he was happy to be home. He chose a conscious death in the best sense of the word: a death of awareness and completion.

It is a privilege to be present during that kind of dying. It is more than acquiescence at the end of a struggle. In a conscious death there is no struggle at all, no resigned defeat, no trace of resented capitulation. When a person has truly let go, even of their own body, their freedom is complete and their victory unmistakable. A pervading feeling of peace is present. There is a tranquility that everyone at the bedside can sense, an inner smile, as if death was a friend being welcomed into the room. I believe Mark's smile came from that place. I believe he knew that everything was at last truly okay. I could feel no grief about his departure.

Indeed, as I said to Zita, when my time comes, I would feel fortunate to leave as he did.

As I looked out the window at the miles passing below me, I sensed that central to many of these impressions was the nature of time itself. I once thought I knew what time was. Now it seemed very different. My changing perception had evolved over more than a year, but it became clearer when I visited Mark in April. That afternoon we had neither past nor future. When I was present with him, time stood still. Only the present moment mattered. In my subsequent letters I tried to write about it, but my insights seemed inadequate. If time is the stage on which the events of the world play out, my encounter with Mark changed the stage, and from then on everything in the play changed as well.

After I returned to Seattle, Zita went to Chicago with her family. On a misty day, the kind that Mark loved, they interred his ashes on the grounds of a monastery near John's house. A mile or so away was a railroad, and during the service the family heard the distant, drawn-out sound of a diesel locomotive passing by.

After she returned home, all of Zita's caregiving echoed in Mark's empty room. There was no one there to nurture now, no son to comfort or embrace. Each day she opened Mark's door and instead found stillness. She wrote, "I am desperately looking for help inside myself, but often I just find utter emptiness, a complete void. Your connection is very important to me." I knew that place. I knew how empty it was. Mark helped me when I was there, and I tried to help him when darkness filled his heart. Now I wrote to Zita, hoping to find words that would help her.

5/24/01

Dear Zita,

Shortly after I returned home, a friend of mine asked me, "How are you going to find peace in this loss?" In this letter, I'll try to answer that question. In doing so, I hope I can help you find peace as well.

Last week I tried to find peace by reflecting that, for Mark, it was time. That statement was true, and my reflections about it were consoling, but they were only reflections from the surface of an ocean. As I sat quietly, the words took on a much deeper meaning, about the nature of time itself.

In my last letter to Mark, I described how time has changed for me. A world plagued by the past or obsessed with the future is gone, replaced by its opposite, an increasing awareness of just this moment. That awareness has changed how I look at life.

Our culture perceives time as the interval between events, a line along which all events have a beginning, a duration, and then an end.

Our culture perceives life along the same line. Life appears to have a beginning, it moves through a series of events and then it ends, "a poor player who struts and frets his hour upon the stage and then is heard no more."

When life is seen as a line, there are only two ways to get more of it. One is to stretch out the life line as far as we can, forever fighting to live a little longer. The other is to do more, achieve more and acquire more, forever fighting to cram more into what little life we have.

Neither of these choices seems very satisfying. All lines, no matter how long, eventually end. There can never be enough. When life ends like that, it leaves behind loss, grief, and emptiness. It is "a tale told by an idiot, full of sound and fury, signifying nothing."

I have learned that our culture's perception is not the only way of looking at time, or at life.

Other cultures didn't experience time as a line. Without clocks or schedules, they instead experienced time in terms of the great cycles of the world around them. Events were not a sequence that began and ended, but the continuous flow of a tide that always returned. Time was when the flowers appeared again, when the snow fell, when the moon would be full once more. Living within these cycles, the people of these cultures experienced time as a circle.

Within those cycles, life was a circle as well. When the salmon lived out its life in the open waters and returned home, as do all living things, to the place from which it came, the circle of life began again.

In these cultures, a solitary and difficult journey often marked passage into adulthood. It was a journey to find the inner self, and to find the gift that the self was meant to manifest in the world. When people lived out that inner life and bestowed that gift, the circle of their life was complete.

For the remainder of their life, their task was to expand their circle, making it larger and larger by reaching outward. Completed people, open to everything, drew more and more into the circle of their life until, at the moment of death, their circle embraced the cosmos, and "I", the individual, became one with all that is.

My friend had asked me, "How are you going to find peace in this?" In the culture of linear time, I found no peace. There was only loss. I needed to return to the wisdom of the circle.

Zita, every time I look at the picture of Mark smiling in the cab of his locomotive, I have a feeling that he lived a completed life. I find peace there and a never-ending sense of gratitude because, as the circle of Mark's life grew larger and larger, he drew me into it. Unlike a line, within a circle there is no end. I am within that circle, and I always will be.

When I left Mark on April 1, I knew that, as the world measures it, our time together was over. That was saddening for both of us, so I searched for a deeper sense of what had happened during that visit. I wrote to him that despite my departure, I believed we remained connected.

I believe we still are. The circle remains unbroken. Within it, we are all with him.

I hope this helps.

Bill

5/25/03

Dear Bill,

It was so good when I opened my e-mail this morning and found your letter. As always, it means more than you can ever know.

Mark has made an impact on many lives. You have been dear to him since you opened up to him, and he to you. I know that Mark's circle of life was complete, as you so beautifully say. I cherish the thought that you are within his circle. His life didn't just end in his room downstairs. You are right, Bill, within a circle there is no end.

Please take care of yourself,

Zita

In the Northwest, the long summer days had returned. One evening I went to Edmonds to walk the beach and watch the sun set over the Olympics. Nearby was the restaurant where I had taken Zita and Paul to lunch. A hundred yards beyond it was a railroad crossing.

As I walked along the waterline and watched the ebbing tide, flashing red lights and a shrill clang-clang-clang signaled that the crossing gate was coming down. Soon the deep resonating rumble of a Burlington Northern Santa Fe freight locomotive filled the air. As the train thundered through the crossing, the engineer sounded a series of wailing blasts on the warning horn.

It took only a short time for the train to pass the spot where I was standing. I smiled to myself as the sound faded away. Then I resumed walking along the beach, watching little waves lap along the sand. The pastels of the evening sky deepened to twilight behind the distant mountains.

Some people enter our lives and leave without a trace. Others enter and remain indelibly present. I don't believe I will listen to the sound of a passing train in quite the same way ever again.

"In my afterlife, I know exactly where I want to be—in an engine cab, high-balling down the high iron."

Mark Smetko

1944–2001

Epilogue

Life must be lived by going forward, but it can only be understood by looking back.

—*Søren Kierkegaard*

In June Zita sent me copies of eulogies that friends had written about Mark. Most of them wistfully commemorated good times together. A few described encounters with Mark that were remarkably similar to mine. A doctor at St. Vincent who had known Mark for only three weeks wrote one of them.

Dear Mrs. Smetko,

I was saddened by the news of Mark's death, despite knowing that he would succumb to his disease sooner rather than later.

The three weeks that we interacted were nothing less than profound. He was very sick and required my full attention. Yet it was not the intellectual aspects of his case that were so engaging. The greatest gratification, both professionally and personally, came from interaction with Mark himself. That interaction was a life-changing event for me.

My profession is couched in myths of omniscience, infallibility and paternalism, all of which necessitate interpersonal distance. I had none of those to offer your son, only my friendship and attention. Little did I know that in caring for Mark, I would learn what true healing entails and that in turn, he would heal me in unanticipated ways.

I saw in Mark a body whose maimed internal organs were being destroyed before my eyes, but the person I interacted with was heroic. He was realistic about the prospects, or the lack thereof, for the future, yet he remained optimistic, hopeful, joyful and selfless. We shared many anecdotes about baseball and railroads. Not a day passed without mention of you and his brothers. We spoke of death and, more importantly, about life. His unassuming, matter-of-fact view of the world, in light of the Job-like suffering he endured, was nothing less than inspiring. We spoke about religion. His life in many ways provided insight into a spiritual experience that no book or sermon could ever provide.

As trite as it sounds, I have thought of Mark often and will think of him often in the future. In a world that is full of falsehood and pretext, I felt I had the privilege to interact with one of the representatives of truth on earth. Your son revealed to me the difference between doctors and being a Doctor. He revealed that the latter requires being quite human, complete with all of the joy and pain that it entails.

Yes, I will think of Mark often.

Warmly,

Richard Sidlow M.D.

I looked at that letter for a long time and reread it often. It told me that my encounter with Mark wasn't unique to me. Far from it. It didn't matter if it was Gruber in Seattle or Sidlow on Staten Island. Each of us walked in as a doctor to see a patient, and each of us walked away changed. In his ever-widening circle, Mark embraced anyone who opened to him. In turn, everyone who encountered him felt grateful for having known the man. How is it that each of us responded in such a similar way? My friend had no fame, no possessions, no wealth as the world measures it to give to anyone. Instead, I believe his life revealed to each of us the best of what resides within us all.

In late-June Zita began the painful task of sorting through Mark's possessions and sent me some of his books. I in return planned to collect Mark's correspondence from my e-mail files and send her copies as a keepsake. As if reading my mind, she wrote me,

7/1/02

Dear Bill,

Would you mind if we retrieve your letters to Mark from his e-mail? I don't want to intrude on your correspondence with him unless it's okay with you, but your letters to him were an important part of the journey for both of you. Mark would tell me "Mom, I had a wonderful letter from Bill. He helps me so much." I would like to put all of them together and have them bound. What more inspiring book could I possibly find?

Thank you again for your letters, which always seem to come just at the right time. Give my best to Beverly and tell her I hope I will see her again someday.

Zita

Assembling the letters in sequence allowed me to look backward through my life. Our collected correspondence put the events of the past ten years into new perspective; I saw meanings that I didn't realize at the time the letters were written. Zita suggested gathering the letters into a book. In July 2001 I sat down and started to do so, searching for the words that could tell this story.

Acknowledgements

I am deeply indebted to the Smetko family, whose openness, encouragement and generous support made this book possible.

Foremost in my gratitude is Zita Smetko, one of the most remarkable people I have ever had the privilege to meet. Her correspondence in the story speaks for itself.

In addition to suggesting the initial idea for the book, over the past two years she encouraged its progress in many practical ways. During my preliminary research, from July through September 2001, she supplied countless details of Mark's early years, many of which were undoubtedly painful to reveal. She read the book's first draft in the months approaching the first anniversary of Mark's death, a task that required fortitude and resilience. After reviewing the second draft in November 2002, she gave me many suggestions for revision and the names of other people to interview. In June 2003, while recovering from a broken hip, she read the third draft twice in an effort to catch the typographic errors that slipped past the computer's spell-checker. One of my most cherished videotapes is of a trip we took together. In September 2002 I met Zita in Chicago, and together we rode the rails that Mark once did on The Empire Builder, westward to Seattle.

In addition to the three visits mentioned in the book, several more visits with Paul and Diana Smetko have deepened my appreciation for their support of my efforts and their kind hospitality. Both of them agreed to interviews about difficult material. Paul reviewed the second draft, supported the psychological profile of Mark in the book, and offered further details of the dynamic at work. Despite a busy professional schedule, he was generous enough to come to Seattle twice to discuss the progress of my writing.

I interviewed John Smetko at his home in Chicago—actually, it was in a nearby Irish pub one evening with his wife Nell—and extensively by phone. He provided wonderful details about his brother's boyhood, including the trip out west in the boxcars. He was also kind enough to review the third draft in June 2003, during a very busy time of the year for him professionally, and confirm the details of the family narrative.

I visited Carl and Beverly Smetko in their home near Los Angeles. I am deeply appreciative of their hospitality, the many details they supplied during a long interview, and the head-snapping ride Carl gave me in his 580 hp red Mustang Cobra. I could write about Mark's euphoric smile in that car because I sat in the same seat myself.

Mike Harle is Zita's nephew and Mark's cousin. He lives in Gig Harbor, and during a lunch interview filled in details of Mark's life during the late seventies and early eighties when Mark first moved to Seattle and his RA slowly worsened.

Dr. Jeff Carlin is a former racquetball partner, a close friend, and the person who sent Mark into my life. He provided constant help during Mark's orthopaedic care and subsequently provided many clinical and research details about the intricate disease known as rheumatoid arthritis.

Dr. Lee Barnes, anesthesiologist and friend through many outdoor activities, provided more clinical details of Mark's resuscitation on September 15, 1997 than I remembered on my own. I have no doubt, and am deeply grateful for the fact that on that day, within the space of a crucial half hour, Lee saved Mark's life.

Dr. Dale Peterson, a physician in Wenatchee and close friend of the Smetkos for many years, was kind enough to research and confirm many of the medical details of Steve Smetko's final month.

Karl Sundstrom, probably Mark's closest friend from childhood on, was very generous with his time and encouragement throughout a lengthy phone interview and e-mail follow-ups. He provided numerous details about Mark's childhood love of trains and their work together in the Clyde freight yard. He provided invaluable details about Mark's symptoms early in the course of his disease (1975–1985) and sensitive insights into Mark's family and personal life.

Rich Zaper was a railroad electrician who met Mark in 1972 at the Corwith freight yard on Chicago's south side and remained a close friend, going with Mark and Karl to Gettysburg in the summer of 2000. He rode in a locomotive with Mark in 1982 when Mark was doing long freight runs. Rich provided fascinating details of life on the rails, the freight yards, the interior of locomotives and the details of operating one. His enthusiasm was infectious. If I hadn't liked trains before I started this project, Rich would have had me loving them by the time I finished.

Mark McLean is the yardmaster at the Balmer yards of the Burlington Northern Santa Fe RR at Interbay in Seattle. He was kind enough to give me an impromptu interview when I took Zita to visit where Mark had worked. He remembered Mark well and confirmed details about his job and the locomotives he ran.

Special hugs go to those who nurture beginners.

I have a student's gratitude for Martha Brockenbrough, an accomplished author, editor, and my foremost mentor when I first began to write. She supported me with general advice about the craft of writing and specific encouragement when I didn't have the foggiest idea how to begin a book. She helped me execute the cover graphics. She also reviewed the first draft, which I look back on as unreadable, but she felt had promise. Her faith in the story helped bring this book to completion.

Anne Shumway-Cooke was my associate during years of research on fall prevention in the gait lab. She is an exacting writer who has given me books about the passion and craft of writing, gifts my readers will probably appreciate as much as I did. She was kind enough to read the second draft and suggest the direction I needed to take with it: radical cuts in wordiness. Beyond that, she is a dear friend who has trod her own spiritual path through a difficult disease and who, through many conversations, helped me to recognize the path I was taking.

Emily Russin is a professional writer, editor and "book doctor" who lived up to her recommendation by Martha. Her extensive suggestions for the second draft helped change a story I wanted to tell into a book others might want to read.

Sincere appreciation goes to Ann Brockenbrough, a technical editor for Microsoft Word who spent many hours combing through the third draft and offered both helpful comments and encouragement as I headed into the final round.

Words of gratitude are not enough for two special people. Teachers are all around us. One of them is my daughter, Cathy, who has meditated daily for the past nine years. By her example and encouragement, she helped me rediscover an inner life I had left behind a long time ago.

Finally, I would like to express tender appreciation to my wife, Beverly. At the practical level, she read and offered many helpful suggestions for the third draft. Far more appreciated than that, however, has been her support, encouragement and forbearance as together we lived through the years of *Letting Go*.

Appendix

The front cover is an interpretation of the Buddhist concept of letting go. In the world of form and shape, the object identifies itself through its exterior form. It believes that it is a drop. Its surface is a reflection of other forms that surround it. It attempts to preserve this form, to remain attached and to be secure. Surface tension relentlessly distorts the drop, however, until eventually it is forced to let go, and hurtles downward into the darkness. This detachment happens to everyone, either during life or at the moment of death.

The back cover interprets what happens next. The drop emerges from the darkness and returns to the ocean from which it came. As it does so, it loses its separate identity as a drop, but discovers that this identity was false anyway, an illusion, a construct. It discovers that all along its true essence—its inner reality—was water. Within the ocean, it reunites with that essence. It is no longer fearful, constrained, or separate, but instead becomes one with all that is. The ripples of its passage spread outward.

Everything in this book actually happened. I changed the names of prior patients of mine to protect their privacy, but otherwise have made every effort to establish the accuracy of the book's contents. The following were the primary source materials:

1. My correspondence with Mark and Zita Smetko

2. Mark's inpatient record from Northwest Hospital

3. Mark's outpatient record from Northwest Orthopaedic Clinic

4. Consultation and clinic notes from Central Hospital, Wenatchee, WA

5. Medical records from St. Vincent Medical Center, Staten Island, NY

6. Extensive personal journal notes written contemporaneously to the events

7. Meeting notes from my tenure as Chief of Staff

8. Extensive interviews with the Smetko family and Mark's friends

9. A videotape I made at Mepkin Abbey that preserved many of the visual details of my retreat there

I began this book by assembling the records, notes and correspondence in chronological sequence. The medical records were the starting point for Part I. The operative notes were too technical to include verbatim in the body of the book, but I have appended one of them here, the operative note of Mark's right knee revision surgery in June 1998. I have done so because, for those who are interested, the style of the note, more so than its content, provides a unique literary lens through which to see the way surgeons process information and events. Just as his letters to me were a window into the world of Mark Smetko, the style of the operative note is a window into the mindset of Dr. Gruber.

Unlike a book, operative notes are composed without creativity or revision. Surgeons dictate an operative note immediately after the case, often when fatigued and rushed. Unlike authors, they seldom have time to ruminate or reflect on their choice of words. After dictation, transcription is verbatim. We have no chance to clean up with a second or third draft either the grammar or the syntax of the spoken word. What is said is what is read.

I was trained to dictate entirely in the passive voice. In the note you will see that the surgeon is completely depersonalized; there is no "I" in it. It was a habit of expression I found difficult to overcome when describing my professional activities to lay readers. It is long leap from "An incision was made down through the subcutaneous layer," to "I surgically invaded his knee."

Operative notes depersonalize the patient as well. Like the aperture in the OR drapes, this op-note reveals nothing of the human being beneath the knife. Unlike the book, the note is not about Mark or me. The subject of the note is a problem that has to be solved. Problem solving permeates a surgeon's thoughts, words and deeds as water permeates a sponge. Letting go of this mindset was extraordinarily difficult for me on many levels.

The format of an operative note is highly patterned. In both the procedure and the dictation that describes it, specific content is compressed into a generic sequence: "Pre-operative diagnosis, Post-operative diagnosis, Procedure performed..." To a reader looking for creative writing, the note's ritualized format is rote and meaningless. To surgeons, however, operating room rituals are an almost religious part of their life.

The technical terms in the note are precise, specific, and reflect years of mastering this specialty. Another orthopaedist can follow exactly what happened during this case. To the lay reader, however, technical terms are mind-numbing idioms that rapidly kill any interest in Mark's surgical ordeals. My task when editing the op-notes of Part I into readable text was to find a middle ground between jargon and accuracy.

The note contains concise and complete information about what was performed, but there isn't a shred of emotion in it. Tension, anxiety, frustration, elation, despair—all of these are present every day in the OR; not one of them is present in the dictation. You will never read in an operative note, "I really worried that this might not work," but it was very much present that June day. The dry style of this note is a window into the way surgeons repress these feelings while they operate.

As dry as this note may seem, however, the lay reader should keep in mind that to the surgeon, this is a memoir of mortal combat. Our opponents are injury, disease, deformity, and death. In the note are discipline, aggression, and blood, but few illusions. We usually win the battles. Death wins the war.

Op-notes are permanent evidence. We dictate what happened and then can't hide from the written word. Our peers review these notes, and if something goes wrong, so do attorneys. If you wish to be one of the reviewers, you may judge for yourself. Here is what happened to Mark's right knee on that June day, told in the manner in which I was trained.

DATE OF SURGERY: 6/15/98

PREOPERATIVE DIAGNOSIS:

1. S/P Bilateral removal of infected total knee arthroplasty components with insertion of spacers.

2. Longstanding Rheumatoid Arthritis

3. S/P Generalized sepsis

POST-OPERATIVE DIAGNOSIS: same

PROCEDURE PERFORMED:

1. Removal of previously placed polymethylmethacrylate spacers, right knee.

2. Revision total knee arthroplasty, right knee, using NexGen cemented tibial and femoral components:

   a. Size G femoral component with 5-mm posterior femoral augmentation blocks and 16 mm stem extension

b.   Size 7 NexGen tibial component with 16 mm stem

c.   Constrained 23-mm polyethylene tibial insert

d.   No patellar component

3.   2 gm of Tobramycin powder were added to the methacrylate.

SURGEON: William A. Gruber M.D. ASSISTANT: John Gullage P. A.

ANESTHESIA: femoral block plus general anesthesia

DESCRIPTION OF PROCEDURE: Following the induction of satisfactory anesthesia the patient was prepped and draped in the usual sterile fashion. The prior midline scar was utilized and the incision carried down through subcutaneous tissue to the bursal layer. A bursal flap was developed medially using electrocautery. This was developed to the edge of the patella. The joint was entered and cultures taken. A median parapatellar incision was then utilized and developed.

The patient had had a prior partial tear of the medial aspect of the patellar tendon. This had healed, but was thin. A double flap was fashioned for subsequent reinforcement. The patella was able to be reflected without undo strain on the attachment of the patellar tendon. The patella itself was covered with smooth, gristle-like material with only minimal membrane. The remainder of the joint appeared clean. Fluid was clear. There was moderate pseudomembrane but very little in the way of angry-appearing reactive synovium.

The previously inserted antibiotic-impregnated polymethylmethacrylate spacers were then removed. The bone deep to them was satisfactory without significant erosion. It had formed some degree of sclerotic margin over approximately 50%. The fibrous membrane deep to the spacers was then removed using a combination of curets and rongeurs. The prior stem holes were re-developed. Excess synovium and scar tissue was cleared away. The tibia could then be easily subluxed forward from the femur.

Beginning on the tibial side a series of trays were trialed and ultimately a #7 selected. No actual reaming was carried out. The bone was sufficiently osteoporotic that reamers were simply pushed in by hand until a 16-mm stem could be easily accepted. The appropriate cutting jigs were used to create the tibial stem hole. A 7-mm trial tibial component was then inserted with its stem. Satisfactory tibial coverage and alignment was achieved.

The femoral side was then shaped. A similar amount of hand reaming was utilized. A size G trial was then utilized and an offset stem was utilized to achieve satisfactory position. The femoral component rotation was verified and the degree to which augments were needed was assessed. A series of trials of trials was carried out, culminating in 5-mm posterior augment blocks. This gave satisfactory contact on all bone cuts.

There was a striking discrepancy between the flexion and extension gaps and so a small amount of the distal portion of the femur was removed and a 23-mm trial constrained insert was then positioned. This was found to give satisfactory medial-lateral stability and satisfactory correction of the discrepancy between the flexion and extension gaps. There was good preservation of the collateral ligaments without significant erosion and good stability in both 0° and 90° of flexion.

With the trial components in place, attention was then turned to the patella. It was felt that the patella was too thin to implant a button without jeopardizing fracture. It would also thicken the extensor mechanism and make closure difficult. For this reason, the existing wafer was left in place. An extensive lateral release was carried out and tracking found to be satisfactory.

The trial components were removed. All of the components were assembled. Two grams of Tobramycin powder were then mixed into the powder of the polymethylmethacrylate thoroughly. Following this, the monomer was added. Concurrently the cancellous bone was thoroughly irrigated with a liter of pulsatile lavage, followed by pressurized antibiotic irrigant. It was dried thoroughly. A double batch of cement was inserted at low viscosity using a plug syringe. The femoral and tibial components were cemented into place without difficulty. Following removal of all excess cement debris, range of motion, stability and tracking were again verified and found to be satisfactory. The area was thoroughly irrigated with antibiotic solution. A ConstaVac drain was inserted. The patellar tendon flap was then folded back on itself and sutured with 0-Vicryl to reinforce the area of previous rupture. The tendon was reinforced at its attachment to the tibial tubercle with #2 Ethibond through bone holes. Capsule was closed with 0 interrupted figure-of-eight Vicryl and bursal tissue was closed with 2-0 Vicryl. The skin was closed with wide skin staples. A sterile dressing was applied, anesthesia was terminated and the patient returned to the recovery room in satisfactory condition.

Tourniquet was inflated at the time of femoral trials and deflated at the time of capsular closure. The tourniquet time was 1 hour 38 minutes. Estimated blood loss was approximately 150 cc's. The patient received 1 gm of Kefzol preoperatively. Sponge and instrument count were correct x2. There were no complications.

cc: W. Ehni, M.D./J. Carlin, M.D./P. Nutter, M.D./R.M. Tucker, M.D. (Wenatchee)

The op-note describes a linear sequence of events: "This happened, then this happened, then this, and then we finished." Bing, bing, bing. When I began this book, I assembled all the medical and operative notes into a similar sequence, smiled and said, "Well, here's what happened." Reading such a sequence is as exciting as counting sheep. The first draft of Part I was precise, accurate and unreadable. The stylistic journey from these notes to the book you have just read was a lengthy one.

The American Academy of Orthopaedic Surgeons, the Northwest Orthopaedic Clinic, and most of the profession use the etymologically correct spelling for our specialty. The word "orthopaedic" is derived from the Greek word *orthopaideia*, which means "straight child-rearing." It came from the days when the focus of the specialty was bracing children crippled from deformities or polio.

The public usually spells it "orthopedic," which is the way Mark spelled it in his letters. The professional spelling is part of my heritage and so I have chosen to use it in the remainder of the text. I hope the reader will put up with the conflict.

Most memoirs are written retrospectively. The heart of this book, our correspondence, was written in real time. Mark, Zita and I wrote our letters as the events and transformations were unfolding, before any of us knew how the story would turn out, and before I recognized how I was changing.

After the events, I read or reread many of the books in the following bibliography. I was amazed to find how many books—in fields as diverse as physics, psychology, neurobiology, sociology, marriage counseling, mythology, and spirituality—described events, stories and meanings that were remarkably similar to what I had experienced. From 2001 to 2003, while writing the text, I used these books to help me better understand what had happened.

I personally picked out very few of the titles in the bibliography. Most were given to me, as if family and friends were trying to tell me I needed to learn more about subjects that are normally not on a surgeon's reading list.

Mark told me about *A Brief History of Time* by Stephen Hawking and *The Tao of Physics* by Fritjof Capra, both of which explore realms in the natural sciences beyond the reality that is apparent to us. To a physicist, neither time nor the material world is what we think it is. The theories of quantum physics echo in the quote I used from Shakespeare's *Hamlet*.

After Mark died, Zita gave me all of his books about railroads in the Pacific Northwest. It was both an act of kindness and an open door that allowed me to explore further my friend's heritage.

Years ago my brother Don gave me *The Seasons of a Man's Life* by Daniel J. Levinson. Its sociological research introduced me to the idea that specific stages of adulthood have specific tasks, and that if one doesn't accomplish the task at hand it is not possible to move on to the next stage. That idea paved the way for my interpretation of Bardo.

He also gave me *Man's Search for Meaning* by Viktor E. Frankl, an extraordinary account of a psychiatrist's survival in a concentration camp, which I reference in my discussion of Mark's crisis of choice.

Along with many other timely and helpful books, my daughter Cathy suggested Joseph Campbell's *The Hero with a Thousand Faces*. It planted the seed that much of Mark's story, indeed, everyone's story, has a universal theme within it.

Beverly McDevitt, a counselor and guide through the turmoil of transition, gave me *Keeping the Love You Find* by Harville Hendrix. It introduced the idea that we are only able to love openly when we rid ourselves of the walls that keep us needful.

After his April 2001 visit, Paul Smetko gave me Herman Hesse's *Siddhartha*. I read it in one night. It seemed to speak directly to me. Guides and mentors may help, but the real work of detachment and acceptance has to come from within.

Many years ago I began to explore, through Thomas Merton's writings, the similarities between Eastern and Western contemplative wisdom. Anne Shumway-Cook gave me Sogyal Rinpoche's *The Tibetan Book of Living and Dying* and The Dali Lama's *The Good Heart, A Buddhist Perspective on the Teachings of Jesus*. She also introduced me to the writings of Basil Pennington, O.C.S.O, a Trappist abbot who, together with Thomas Keating, O.C.S.O, extended what Merton wrote and has integrated Eastern meditative techniques into contemplative Christianity. Anne's gifts became a pivot point in my life.

John Gullage gave me *Full Catastrophe Living* by Jon Kabat-Zinn, which develops a similar East-West integration from a different approach. Derived from the author's extensive research at The Stress Reduction Clinic at the University of Massachusetts Medical Center, it documents the degree to which meditation, yoga and relaxation techniques can relieve chronic pain and emotional distress. In 2000, John probably thought I should read something about emotional distress.

Bev gave me the book *Death of a Hero, Birth of the Soul: Answering the Call of Mid-life* as a Christmas present in 1998. She said she was wandering through a bookstore and bought it on a whim. I read it over that holiday vacation and thought it was interesting. Then I put it back on the shelf and went back to work, anticipating that 1999 would be the same as any other year. The book didn't come back into my awareness until October 1999 when I was packing for the trip to Mepkin Abbey, saw the book sitting on the shelf and impulsively tossed it into my suitcase. At the Abbey, sitting by the riverside, I coincidentally opened the book to the poem by Jelaluddun Rumi.

It took me a discouragingly long time to wake up to what these books and the people who gave them to me were trying to teach me. Typical is Stephen Levine's *Who Dies? An Investigation of Conscious Living and Conscious Dying,* which I bought on a whim while browsing through a small bookstore during my three-week vacation in September 1997, the weeks when Mark became septic. At that time the book was difficult for me to read. The author's ideas seemed foreign and hard to grasp. My notes and underlining stopped after the first several chapters, indicating where I gave up and put it down. In 1997 I probably had no interest in what the book was trying to tell me.

In May 2001, as I packed for the trip to Mark's funeral, I saw the same book sitting on my bookshelf, brought it along and devoured it on my flight to New York. In the four-year interval, the book hadn't changed, but my perceptions had. Its message matched the silent conversation I had experienced in my garden about the importance of detachment and the difficulty of achieving it. The book also gave me several of the ideas that I subsequently developed in my e-mail to Zita about cultures that look on life as a circle.

As Paul Smetko said, "Books just give us the words for the wisdom we have to learn from life."

My altered appreciation of that book strikes me as a metaphor of the last ten years. Meanings in my life that had once been obscure became clear, as if during the years of *Letting Go* I slowly took off a set of dark glasses.

August 2003

Bibliography

Campbell, Joseph. *The Hero with a Thousand Faces*, Second Edition, Princeton NJ, Princeton University Press, 1968

Capra, Fritjof. *The Tao of Physics, An Exploration of the Parallels between Modern Physics and Eastern Mysticism*, Fourth Edition, Boston, Shambala, 2000

Downey, Michael. *Trappist; Living in the Land of Desire*, New Jersey, Paulist Press, 1997

The Dali Lama. *The Good Heart, A Buddhist Perspective on the Teachings of Jesus*, Boston, Wisdom Publications, 1996

Frankl, Viktor E. *Man's Search for Meaning*, New York, Simon & Schuster, 1984

Goleman, Daniel. *Emotional Intelligence*, New York, Bantam Books, 1995

Hawking, Stephen. *A Brief History of Time*, New York, Bantam Books, 1996

Hendrix, Harville, *Keeping the Love You Find*, New York, Pocket Books, 1992

Henry, Patrick. editor, *Benedict's Dharma, Buddhists Reflect on the Rule of Saint Benedict*, New York, Riverhead Books, 2001

Hesse, Herman. *Siddhartha*, Boston, Shambala, 2000

Kabat-Zinn, Jon. *Full Catastrophe Living*, New York, Delta Books, 1990

Leachman, Rob. *Northwest Passage, Twenty-Five Years of the Burlington Northern in the Pacific Northwest*, Mulkiteo, Washington, Hundman Publishing, 1998

Levine, Stephen. *Who Dies? An Investigation of Conscious Living and Conscious Dying*, New York, Anchor Books, 1982

Levinson, Daniel J. *The Seasons of a Man's Life*, New York, Ballantine Books, 1978

Levoy, Gregg. *Callings: Finding and Following an Authentic Life*, New York, Three Rivers Press, 1997

Merton, Thomas. *The Seven Storey Mountain*, New York, Harcourt Brace & Co, 1976

Merton, Thomas. *Entering the Silence*, New York, HarperCollins, 1996

Merton, Thomas. *Mystics and Zen Masters*, New York, The Noonday Press, 1967

Morgan, David P. editor, *Steam's Finest Hour*, Milwaukee, Kalmbach Publishing Co., 1959

Pennington, M. Basil. *Centered Living, The Way of Centering Prayer*, New York, Doubleday & Company Inc., 1986

Pennington, M. Basil. *True Self/False Self, Unmasking the Spirit Within*, New York, The Crossroad Publishing Company, 2000

Rinpoche, Sogyal. *The Tibetan Book of Living and Dying*, San Francisco, HarperCollins, 1993

Robinson, John C. *Death of a Hero, Birth of the Soul, Answering the Call of Midlife*, Sacramento, Tzedakah Publications, 1995

Schrenk, Lorenz P. and Frey, Robert L. *Northern Pacific Classic Steam Era*, Mulkiteo, WA, Hundman Publishing, Inc., 1997

Williams, Donna. *Like Color to the Blind*, New York, Random House, 1996

Williams, Donna. *Autism and Sensing, The Unlost Instinct*, London, Jessica Kingsley Publishers, 1998

Wood, Charles R. and Wood, Dorothy. *The Great Northern Railway, A Pictorial Study*, Edmonds, WA, Pacific Fast Mail, 1979

About the Author

Bill Gruber is a retired orthopaedic surgeon living in Seattle.

0-595-29207-0

Printed in the United States
18569LVS00004B/52-135